Cultivating Democracy

MODERN SOUTH ASIA

Cultivating Democracy

Politics and Citizenship in Agrarian India

MUKULIKA BANERJEE

OXFORD

UNIVERSITY PRESS

Oxford University Press is a department of the University of Oxford. It furthers
the University's objective of excellence in research, scholarship, and education
by publishing worldwide. Oxford is a registered trade mark of Oxford University
Press in the UK and certain other countries.

Published in the United States of America by Oxford University Press
198 Madison Avenue, New York, NY 10016, United States of America.

CIP data is on file at the Library of Congress
ISBN 978–0–19–760187–7 (pbk.)
ISBN 978–0–19–760186–0 (hbk.)

DOI: 10.1093/oso/9780197601860.001.0001

1 3 5 7 9 8 6 4 2

Paperback printed by LSC communications, United States of America
Hardback printed by Bridgeport National Bindery, Inc., United States of America

For
Julian

Like the sailor, the citizen is a member of a community. Now, sailors have different functions, for one of them is a rower, another a pilot, and a third a lookout man, a fourth is described by some similar term; and while the precise definition of each individual's virtue applies exclusively to him, there is, at the same time, a common definition applicable to them all. For they have, all of them, a common object which is safety in navigation. Similarly, one citizen differs from another, but the salvation of the community is the common business of them all. This community is the Constitution; the virtue of the citizen must therefore be relative to the constitution of which he is a member.

—Aristotle on the "General Notion of the Virtue of Citizen" in *Politics*

Constitutional morality is not a natural sentiment. It has to be cultivated. We must realize that our people have yet to learn it. Democracy in India is only a top-dressing on an Indian soil which is essentially undemocratic.

—B. R. Ambedkar, *Constituent Assembly Debates* (1948)

There is no single word in the entire history of human speech to and through which more has happened than the word democracy, not even word God, though over an even lengthier time the words for God or gods have proved still harder to translate between the languages of the world. At least in the countries of the West, and probably now across the world as a whole, one salient prerequisite for improving political judgement is to recognize just what has recently happened to and through the still sometimes-charismatic but almost never clarificatory term democracy.

—John Dunn, *Breaking Democracy's Spell* (2014: 5–6)

Democracy is, in fact, part of the political enchantment of modernity. It introduces a new principle of the political construction of society which leads to exhilarating moment – by making some unprecedented changes possible. But it also leads to despair by making people expect too much, often by turning the conception of democracy – in some forms of naïve thinking – into a secular equivalent of paradise. . . . Indian democracy is in fact a historical scandal because it defies all the postulated prior conditions . . . . India provides one example of the expansion of democracy in a world within which Europe does not constitute the whole of the continent of democracy, but a province.

—Sudipta Kaviraj, *The Enchantment of Democracy and India* (2011: 1, 13–14, 22)

We produce knowledge in a mode of intimacy with our subjects. Hence ethnography as a genre seems to be a form of knowledge in which I come to acknowledge my own experience within a scene of alterity. After all, it is the nature of everyday life that the significance of events is not given at the moment of their occurrence and it is in the nature of experience that its meaning eludes us . . . In being attentive to the life of others we also give meaning to our lives.

—Veena Das, *Between Words and Lives* (2015: 404)

Contents

Preface

This book was completed in the middle of a pandemic that revealed the fragility of held certainties. An invisible virus about which science knew little, took lives across the world forcing a halt in activities that we had come to take for granted such as travel, classroom teaching, and hugging friends. In a few weeks it also became clear that the degree of devastation in each national context depended on its quality of political leadership. Some countries did better than others and discernable patterns emerged. Democracies did not do better, as they had done in the previous century, in managing famines for instance. In fact, the worst-performing countries were all democracies, India among them. This has focused our attention on reexamining whether the twentieth-century certainty that democracy was the best-among-worst solutions of political arrangements still held true. Research and writings produced through the pandemic drew attention to the democratic cultures in a variety of national contexts and showed that formal democratic procedures did not necessarily create what was required in such times, namely a democracy of spirit of civic commitment and trust in government. These had to be cultivated and nurtured alongside the formal structures. The recent turn in formal democracies to polarized opinions and trust in strong men who wasted no time striving for consensus and relied instead on inflammatory and partisan utterances, did not facilitate forging a collective response to such a challenge.[1] The democratic spirit was thus constantly under threat and needed to be continually regenerated.

Meanwhile, medical experts pointed out that greater civic engagement was pivotal to a successful public health campaign to manage the virus. The political lesson of the pandemic therefore was that democracies could only succeed in tackling a crisis when its citizens were active and engaged, which is the theme of this book.

As the world's largest institutional democracy, India requires critical attention especially as it was among the world's top three countries adversely affected by Covid-19. As the initial panic of the disease ebbed, the lack of investment in public health infrastructure that could be expected from an accountable and responsive elected government was revealed. Instead, what was introduced were a slew of laws and surveillance techniques designed to curb democratic freedoms in the guise of epidemiological measures. The pandemic has been disastrous for democratic freedoms.

The Indian government's mismanagement of the crisis, also led to an outcome that highlights the need for one of the contributions that I hope this book will make. This outcome was the emergence of the rural as an important place in the public imagination. A sudden lockdown, at four hours' notice without any safeguards for those who had migrated to cities in search of work, created the largest forced migration in independent India, as workers traveled back to their rural homes from cities. In this mass exodus to the rural, the village emerged as a place of refuge and of humanity, in contrast to their stereotype in the popular imagination as the source of inequity and discrimination—themes that are germane to the pages that follow.

This book covers the period from 1988 to 2013, and in hindsight it seems be a privilege to have studied democracy while it still existed in India, in defensible form at least. During this period, democracy in India functioned in its unique form, continuing to thwart the reservations expressed by many in 1947 when it chose to adopt the democratic form of government. But in recent years there have been three major changes to procedural democracy in India that have shaken the integrity of its democracy. First, the Election Commission of India, a constitutionally mandated independent body that conducts elections in India and had a hard-won reputation as the most respected public institution, has now become much less non-partisan. It no longer enjoys the electorate's confidence in conducting free and fair elections. Second, campaign finance, which has always defied a proper regulatory framework, has now been made officially opaque. Electoral bonds were introduced in February 2015 without any parliamentary discussion, having been appended to a non-debatable "Finance Bill," and these new instruments allowed donations to political parties to be made completely anonymously, except to the government and the state-controlled State Bank of India, which managed the transaction. In November 2019, it was revealed (unsurprisingly) that 95 percent of the money from electoral bonds had been donated to the ruling party. Third, Indians no longer vote in an altogether "secret ballot." With the introduction of electronic voting machines, the tally for each machine per polling booth for about a thousand voters was publicly available. Parties are therefore able to intimidate and victimize areas that did not vote for them in the last election. The Election Commission did commission a machine to electronically mix votes before counting (as used to be done with paper ballot in large drums in the past), but the ruling party and others blocked its introduction. The integrity of elections and procedural democracy in India thus stand thoroughly compromised and it can be defensibly argued that elections in India have become a game to be won at any cost, and may result in the death of democracy through its own institutional forms, conforming to a script outlined by the authors of *How Democracies Die* (Levitsky and Ziblatt 2018).

These particular changes in procedural democracy have inevitably led to a larger transformation, recently termed the 'degenerations of democracy' (Calhoun, Gaonkar, and Taylor 2021). Analyzing this transformation in India, political scientists Christophe Jaffrelot and Gilles Verniers propose that the national elections of 2019 and the comprehensive win by the Bharatiya Janata Party (BJP) brought about not just a new phase in Indian electoral politics but a whole "new political system." In a special issue of the journal *Contemporary South Asia* the authors

> analyse electoral data and go beyond them to show that over and above changes in the party system, India is experiencing changes in its political system. Merely analysing the results of the last General Election as an outcome of a recent transformation of the party system or as a re-enactment of the previous election, is both insufficient and, to an extent, misleading. Such analysis obfuscates the changes in the BJP's mobilization strategies and, more importantly, the transformation of India's political institutions under BJP rule between the two elections but even more so since the May 2019 verdict. Indeed, the 2019 elections may appear retrospectively as the moment when history accelerated. (Jaffrelot and Verniers 2020: 2)

This accelerated history delivered three key changes—and each of these redefined, and threatened, the Indian republic. And each of these was met with protests from citizen groups who wished to re-claim the republic, organizing under the banner of "We, the people of India." On August 5, 2019, the state of Jammu and Kashmir (the only Muslim majority state in the country) was divided into three parts and turned into Union Territories controlled directly by the central government. Past and current elected representatives of the state assembly were placed under house arrest, and the human rights of the entire population in Kashmir were taken away. Second, in November, the Supreme Court passed a judgement allowing the construction of a temple to Ram on the site where a sixteenth-century mosque used to stand. The mosque had been razed to the ground by thousands of young men on December 6, 1992. These two moves confirmed the Hindu majoritarian agenda of the new government and a political system that was committed to keeping India's 200-million-strong Muslim population as second-class citizens. This was confirmed by a further comprehensive move in December 2019, when the Indian parliament passed an amendment to the Citizenship Act that gave state functionaries discretionary powers to exclude Muslims from citizenship of India. In the weeks following each of these moves, the country witnessed widespread protests as they violated the basic structure of the Indian constitution which was secular in spirit. The scale and nature of the protests varied across India and overseas but everywhere, remarkably, there were mass recitations of the Preamble to the Indian constitution, that began with the words "We the People of India, solemnly resolve to give ourselves. . . ." These were the words all Indians dimly remembered from the frontispiece of their government-issue school textbooks and in wishing to give voice to their collective protest against the actions of a democratically elected government, they recalled those foundational words of the Indian constitution.

These seemed especially poignant during my most recent visit to my research site, the villages of Madanpur and Chishti that are the setting for this study, in September 2019 to attend the Islamic festival of Muharram.[2] This time, the famous stick-fighting contest of the last day, while robust as ever, was heartbreaking. As always, teams of young men from the neighboring villages gathered in a small clearing in Madanpur to show off their skills in wielding long bamboo poles (*lathi khela*), and for their team "uniforms" they had chosen imitations of the Indian cricket team's strip and they sang the song "*Sarey jahaan sey achcha Hindustan hamara*" (Our country is the best in the world) as their final anthem. The sight of young Muslim men and boys celebrating the nation and their attachment to it at a time when each of them was hopelessly vulnerable to random acts of public lynching and to laws that reduced them to second-class citizenship, was deeply desolate.

And yet, while India's credibility as a democracy is in jeopardy in the middle of a pandemic, the protests against the Citizenship Amendment Act (CAA) and their afterlife provide small glimmers of hope. For when the anti-CAA protests were abruptly halted by the pandemic, in a display of civic virtue the same citizen groups that had protested to preserve India's republic seamlessly transformed themselves into groups that untiringly provided food and care for the most vulnerable citizens and migrant workers whom the government appeared to have utterly forgotten while announcing the abrupt lockdown. As Yogendra Yadav has observed 'mass mobilization and popular resistance outside the electoral arena are going to be prerequisites for any effective reversal of the hegemonic power' (Yadav 2020: xxxi). These gestures by ordinary Indians serve as a reminder that it is this sense of civic duty performed by citizens and their commitment to the collective good that are essential to the cultivation of democracy. In the pages to follow, we will explore the vital necessity of these republican values in creating a democratic culture in the sovereign, democratic Republic of India.

*

1

The Event and Democracy

In April 2019, ahead of the fourteenth national elections in India, a visit to the villages I call Madanpur and Chishti revealed new developments. The Comrade, who had dominated all politics in these villages for decades, had passed away, key actors of the rival Trinamool Congress were missing, and young men rode through the village on motorcycles on which fluttered little red flags that said "Jai Shri Ram" (Victory to Lord Ram). Lord Hanuman was being enthusiastically worshipped after clay idols of this deity had mysteriously appeared under trees and on highways from where they had been retrieved and small shrines had been built for them. The Hindu majoritarian Bhartiya Janata Party (BJP) which, despite its national dominance, had yet to make a significant electoral presence in West Bengal, mobilized support around the fairs and feasts held at these shrines. Traveling across the state of West Bengal, this trend seemed widespread as it became evident that new fissures were opening up, primary among them being the one between generations. Restless and impatient young men, desperate for a new politics that they could call their own, and one that was different from the rivalry of Trinamool and the Left Front that had consumed their parents' lives, had turned to the masculinized politics of the BJP in the hope that it would fill that void. Many of them were educated but emasculated by the dearth of employment opportunities and in the run up to the elections filled their free time by mobilizing crowds to worship Hanuman and disseminated messages from WhatsApp forwards received on their smartphones. Hanuman was a lesser-known deity in Bengal, but his muscular frame and devotion to the god Rama was familiar and his worship presented the perfect pretext to rally support for "their" party. The BJP had itself first come to dominate national politics through its mobilization of public support for a temple to Lord Ram to be built on the very site where a sixteenth-century mosque had stood. In December 1992, thousands of restless young men, not dissimilar to the ones roaming the Bengal countryside now, had torn down the mosque, aided with not much more than the most basic tools of hammers and ropes. In the tense and febrile atmosphere of the 2019 elections and the dominance of the workers of Trinamool Congress, the slogan "Jai Shri Ram" and Hanuman worship became secret codes for a nascent support base to express their admiration for the Prime Minister Narendra Modi and his Hindu majoritarian agenda. The strategy seemed to work, and in May 2019 the BJP, which had previously won just two out of forty-two national seats in West Bengal, now won eighteen and captured 40 percent of the vote share to emerge as a top contender for the first time. The state elections for the government in West Bengal in 2021 were only two years away, and victory seemed within reach. Time would reveal that despite their confidence ahead of the elections in April 2021, the BJP did not win and was instead routed by Trinamool Congress and retained power with an overwhelming victory.

The state of West Bengal has always presented something of a conundrum to analysts of Indian electoral politics. It holds the record for the longest elected communist government from 1977 to 2011, which ended after a successful challenge from the new Trinamool Congress party, led by the maverick female politician Mamata Banerjee. Mamata herself defied wider South Asian trends of female political leadership by forging an entirely self-made political career without any male relatives or mentors, unlike all her female peers across the region. But after two terms as chief minister, her own political survival was at stake in 2021 as she faced the challenge of the BJP after its phenomenal performance in the 2019 national elections. The new conundrum is to explain the rise of BJP (which lost the 2021 election but gained seats) and whether its success can be explained by its ability to tap into a nascent Hindu majoritarian opinion as well as lower caste mobilization in the West Bengal electorate—both of which had been held in abeyance by prior political parties.

The analysis presented in this book suggests that big electoral stories such as the kind West Bengal has seen can be truly understood through the study of minute changes on the ground. The period covered in this book is the fifteen years between 1998 and 2013 that saw the routing of the seemingly invincible Left Front by a new political party a decade into the new century. As we will see, understanding a dramatic electoral story comes from a textured study of not simply elections but also the non-electoral temporalities that interleave it. An ordinary village serves as the perfect setting for such a microscopic examination, for it reveals the actions of individuals, the changing alliances of partisanship, the ethical resources that nourish social action, and the ways in which democracy and citizenship are constituted in the everyday.

*

In May 2011, as I alighted at the familiar bus stop by the villages of Madanpur and Chishti ahead of the West Bengal State Assembly elections, a surprise greeted me. Strung across the main village lanes were green and orange posters of the political party Trinamool Congress, unimaginable even a few years ago. The very first time I had visited these two villages in March 1998, and in the years that followed, the dominance of the communist parties had been so overwhelming that even the name of any rival party could only be mentioned in terrified whispers, if at all. To see the flags of the rivals occupying the landscape now made for an unimaginable sight. Looking at the familiar lands surrounding the villages, I noted how little paddy had been planted that year. The shoots of the swarna paddy should have covered everything in green by now, but instead, brown fields stood empty. A truck laden with bricks rumbled by me and a motorcycle overtook it sharply, nearly knocking me off the narrow lane (although I did receive a cheeky grin and wave of apology from the bearded young man riding it, a face familiar from school homework clubs I used to run some years ago). As I walked into Chishti, I continued past the high walls of the Comrade's house and stopped at the first house, which belonged to the schoolmaster, Mustafa. His daughter-in-law, with eyes the color of emeralds, opened the door, but unlike the customary printed sari she was now draped in a black hijab that highlighted her unusual Persian eyes even more. It had been just over a year since my last visit, but the imperceptible changes from year to year now felt pronounced. I noted the growing number of pucca houses replacing the old thatched huts that were the norm when I first visited and how the few double-storied houses of the Syeds now stood out less. A significant number of people seemed to be involved in the trade of pilfered coal, poppy, and sand—each an illegal commodity—as agriculture had become less sustainable. People looked more stressed and exhausted despite the additional profits of these new ventures. Some sons had been sent for education to faraway madrasas as local schooling opportunities stagnated, and they returned sporting long beards, white clothes, and hitched-up trousers, the young man who had nearly run me over among them. Living on a different continent, I had missed out on the daily incremental changes, making them stark during annual visits. What had not changed much over the fifteen years, however, were the voter turnout figures, which had held steady for every election at over 85 percent. It was this enthusiasm for elections, despite low adult literacy and a general state of impoverishment, that had first drawn me to these villages. Their enthusiasm for voting, far from being an exception, was representative of India's vast rural population, which made up two-thirds of India's electorate at the turn of the century. My project was to understand what people like those who lived in Indian villages like Madanpur and Chishti, with high rates of adult illiteracy and pernicious poverty, thought about democracy and its processes. As an anthropologist, it seemed obvious to me that in order to do this, it was necessary to study not just elections but also the time in between them, to explore a wider habitus within which electoral participation was situated. This book presents the results of this study.

Cultivating Democracy is a study of Indian democracy that pays equal attention to its credentials as a republic. In 1950, India constituted itself not just as an independent nation, but as a sovereign democratic republic. While the choice of democracy indicated the character of the vertical relationship between citizen and state that would exist in the new nation, the term republic outlined the texture of the horizontal relationship between citizen and citizen. Together, they defined India's new political identity, in which Indians who had been hitherto subjects of a colonial government would become sovereign citizens with the right to elect their representatives in government, and live in a society in which they would be tied together through bonds of social citizenship and mutuality. The constitution adopted in January 1950 held a promise to create a political democracy of institutions and procedures, alongside a democracy in social life. This was an aspirational vision given the grim reality of caste and inequality in Indian political and social life at the time of independence, but a constitutional commitment to the need for a profound transformation was made. Thus, seventy years later, any assessment of Indian democracy needs to attend to its record both as a political and an institutional democracy, as well as its capacity for creating democracy in society for a republic of fraternity.

A republic is not merely the absence of monarchy but the presence of an active citizen body that through vigorous participation in public affairs safeguards the freedom and security of the individual and also, crucially, of the republic as a whole. Aristotle's definition of a citizen, presented as an epigraph to this book, states: "One citizen differs from another, but the salvation of the community is the common business of them all." Such a notion is premised on the idea that citizenship is a collective activity that requires effective and continual engagement by each rights-bearing individual. The term had a long history of usage associated broadly under the concept of "republicanism" and the intellectual trajectory of the term in Europe intertwined with that in India through Ambedkar's thought and culminated in his proposal as Chair of the constitution drafting committee, on the adoption of the word "republic" to describe independent India. His insistence on including both the words—"democratic" and "republic"—drew attention to the distinction within the role of the citizen across the two concepts. The term *democracy* indicated the relationship of the citizen to the state and by the middle of the twentieth century had come to represent a procedural form of liberalism which established a legal framework of rules of just and equal treatment of citizens. Within a political democracy, therefore, citizens had rights and could make claims on the state. But such a procedural form of democracy did not emphasize the horizontal relationship a citizen had with other citizens, and it was to this aspect of citizenship that Ambedkar wished to draw attention and institutionalize with the use of the word "republic."

In the case of India, this was an important delineation because here, procedural democracy had to bear "the burden" of counteracting the everyday order of the caste system and its social inequalities (Mehta 2009). The formal proclamations of political equality in a democracy—"one person, one vote"—would remain meaningless, according to Ambedkar, if they were passively left to the law of procedure. Instead, such a goal of equality could only be achieved when active and vigilant citizens sought to ensure that "each vote also had equal value." Without this, there could be no "social democracy" as Ambedkar defined it—that is, a democracy in society too that was based on genuine fraternity within the citizenry. The republican idea of active citizenship that would actively strive toward its creation was therefore essential for a wholesome and genuine democracy in India.

This book examines the relationship of formal political democracy and the cultivation of active citizenship in one particular setting: the villages of Madanpur and Chishti in the state of West Bengal.

On the face of it, the setting chosen here presented some of the worst conditions for its cultivation—it was rural, communist, and mostly Muslim. The village as a site of social action was, from the very start, characterized as a "den of vice" by Ambedkar, and Marx's view of French peasants as potatoes in a sack—that is, a mere aggregate of isolated entities unsuitable for any solidary action—has remained remarkably persistent.[1] In addition, formal communist ideology self-avowedly rejected any form of democratically elected governments as "bourgeois democracy" that concealed the vested interests of the capitalist classes, rather than voters. Beyond that, the concept of the international Muslim community of *ummah* had always existed in tension with the imagination of a national democracy. Thus, to explore the culture of democracy in a location where these three elements determined the social and political context may seem incongruous.

But as this book will show, a deep anthropological engagement with the people in these villages and a "receptivity to the events in the world," as Veena Das puts it, to the nature of the village, communism as it existed in reality, and the practices rather than theology of Islam in a South Asian context challenges any pre-existing biases, as each of these elements offered unexpected possibilities (Das 2015: 217). *Cultivating Democracy* thereby presents an anthropological analysis of the social imaginaries of an agrarian village society and its relationship to democratic values. Forms of life and ideas about how to live together compose the agrarian setting of a village, creating affective solidarities across different regimes of labor, caste, and religious affiliations to sustain and reproduce a community over time. Given intractable social differences, these forms require cultivation as ways of living together have to be continuously created, assessed, revised, and re-created to make social life possible. This process of cultivation, as we shall see, occurs in all aspects of life, whether in work arrangements, religious rituals, neighborliness, and marriage rules and generates the social imaginaries that orient people's action, creating desirable values for an ethical and meaningful life. The term *social imaginaries* is borrowed from Charles Taylor as "the ways in which people imagine their social existence—how they fit together with others and how things go on between them and their fellows, the expectations that are normally met and the deeper normative notions and images that underlie these expectations" (Taylor 2007: 119). These social imaginaries are distinct from formal social theory because they are not the preserve of a small elite but are widely shared by the majority of the people in any society and, unlike social theory, social imaginaries are not always clearly articulated but are nevertheless understood and reproduced by most members in a society.[2] They refer to "the ways of understanding of how the world works that orient people in their action" (Calhoun 2012: 161). The term thereby evokes two key ideas—the foundational nature of the social and the role of imagination—and both of these are central to the analysis presented here. The use of "imagination" as foundational to apprehending the texture of ordinary life owes its debt to Arjun Appadurai's seminal book published in 1996 in which he made the case that new technology in a "postelectronic world" required us to pay much greater attention to the role of imagination. His argument rested on three principal points—first, that imagination was no longer the property of only artists but had "entered the logic of ordinary life"; second, that it was distinct from fantasy as it anticipated action in a "projective sense"; and third, that it could be constituted as a collective form and not just in an individual sense (Appadurai 1996: 5–8). While Appadurai's theory of imagination is tied to his broader work on the role of a new culture of globalization, it is his re-conceptualization of imagination as a collective, agentive, and everyday aspect of people's lives that I draw on. In the pages to follow, I show how non-explicit sources of the political, such as agricultural work or religious rituals, fire the imagination to create the values of moral obligations and collective life that are essential for citizenship. Similarly, scandal and gossip have the potential to generate ideas of attentiveness and mutuality that equip individual citizens to become able participants in demos. Calhoun makes an argument for the role of nationalism in providing "an area for public debate and culture making" and for providing "cultural support for structures of social integration" (2007: 157, 172) that are required for democracy; I do something similar with regard to particular social institutions. The argument of this book therefore turns on the idea that the social imaginaries of agrarian life generate values that share an affinity with, and provide a resource for, republican democratic practice in India.

The settings for the book are the adjacent villages of Madanpur and Chishti in Birbhum district in the state of West Bengal from 1998 to 2013. Such an agrarian setting was typical of large parts of India in its basic characteristics. The people of the villages were mostly Muslim and low-caste Hindus, most adults had very little formal education, and they were involved in paddy cultivation and daily wage labor; they also voted assiduously in each election. Three key stories of change—in Islam, in paddy cultivation, and in politics—dominate the period between 1998 and 2013. In 1998 people were devout Muslims yet were relaxed in their religious practices, but by 2013 everyone was more aware of the more austere and exacting practice of Deobandi Islam that contrasted with their older syncretic forms. In 1998, the state of West Bengal was the highest producer of paddy cultivation, but fifteen years later, relying on agricultural income was no longer economically viable through a combination of market dynamics and environmental change. Finally, the backdrop to these changes in Islam and in paddy cultivation was also one of the most remarkable political stories of contemporary India. In 1998, the Left Front, a coalition of communist parties, had been in power for over twenty years, a feat not achieved by another political party in any other state in India. But by 2013, the Left Front had lost the local panchayat elections in a dramatic defeat to the opposition led by Mamata Banerjee's newly formed Trinamool Congress, having already lost power in the State Legislative Assembly two years before, in July 2011. The intersections of these three arcs of change in Islam, paddy, and politics form the backdrop to this study. In *The Rise of Islam and the Bengal Frontier, 1204–1760*, the historian Richard Eaton notes that "the interaction between the delta's Sanskritic, political, agrarian and Islamic frontiers form one of the great themes of Bengal's history" (Eaton 1993: xxv). As we will see, this complex interweaving of the evolving nature of Islam, paddy, and politics has remained the theme right up until the present day.

Event: The Manchester School and Beyond

Over the fifteen years of ethnographic investigation, a few key events stand out—a scandal, a harvest, the Islamic ritual of animal sacrifice, and elections. Of these four events, one is explicitly religious and the others not, but as events they share a family resemblance: they occurred periodically, lasted for a finite period of time, they brought people together in unprecedented ways, and they created a realm of experience that stood out from the quotidian. Each of them occurred in the present, containing past inheritances of thought and conduct, and held future possibilities. As a category of time, each held past, present, and future together in its duration and thereby presented a temporal complexity in the moment. And each of these events created a transcendental experience of radical possibilities. An exploration of such "events" or key moments has been a well-established tradition in anthropological writings. In the 1950s and 1960s, the Manchester School, led by Max Gluckman, drew our attention to the value of studying a single event in its complexity to uncover dynamics of history and society normally hidden from view. Gluckman's essay *The Bridge: A Situational Analysis* provides an account of the inauguration of a bridge built by the colonial government in South Africa and lays bare the subtleties of race, power, hierarchy, and religion in the colonial context. By unpacking the minutiae of that one single event, Gluckman was able to communicate the intricacy of the colonial project, race and color hierarchies, and the exercise of power. Gluckman characterized his subject matter as "a series of events as I recorded them in a single day" (Englund 2008). Such a situational analysis—"the *in situ* examination of social processes and locating those processes within their broader economic, geographical and historical contexts"—has been an especially helpful mechanism to capture the complexities some of the events presented here. A small example of such a situation, when there was a sort of "pause in the general flow of life, when there is a standing back from things" (Keane 2010: 69) was presented in the lighting of a kiln in the villages.

When a brick kiln was ready to be baked, a little ceremony was held to mark the moment. The entire workforce involved in the making of the kiln gathered together in somber silence and a modest offering of fruit, flowers, incense sticks, and some sweets—each of which were rare objects in a poor village—was made to the kiln before lighting it. Everyone watched as an outsider who had been hired, at considerable expense, struck the match and started the fire, and once the fire began to spread across the kiln, the group dispersed and the ceremony ended. This small event can be read as the sort of pause in the everyday when people stood back from the flow of their lives and in the few moments of silence as the match was struck, a few ideas were recognized by those present.

First, building the kiln provided a common purpose for members otherwise divided by social schisms. A kiln relied on a division of resources between capital and labor and these followed caste, class, and gender hierarchies; elite Syed men owned and provided the capital while the lower caste Shekh and Pathan men and women supplied their labor. Most of the daily wage laborers spent eight hours a day on back-breaking work of carrying, molding, baking, and layering bricks under the hot sun while the owner of the kiln and the supervisors kept an eye on the pace of work, coordinated groups, set the schedule, arranged trucks, and kept accounts. But the increases in daily wages and costs of transporting the bricks meant that the kiln owner had smaller profit margins than before and existed with real vulnerabilities of not being able to recover his costs; these conditions allowed a sense of solidarity and mutual dependence to develop between groups. For those providing the labor, work in the brick kilns was an important supplement to agricultural income and enabled people to stay in the village rather than migrate to urban areas for work. In the small ritual just described, when all of them came together physically to mark the firing of the kiln, the varied nature and interdependence of those present was made manifest to all. It was not mandatory to attend the ritual, but I was told that no one missed attending this moment.

Second was the recognition of cooperation and collective action. Building a brick kiln required a variety of skills and the labor of a large number of people, as it was impossible to achieve by a single individual. It took about a month of everyone's inputs to complete the process during which sand was mined from the riverbed, carried on tin pans by women and children on their heads, molded into bricks and baked in the sun by men, before being carried to the kiln and arranged into an edifice rising from the ground. Specialists created the flues into which they sprinkled small pieces of pilfered coal supplied by young men trading them from sacks on their cycles. It took constant and noisy activity of nearly a hundred people over a period of several days to construct a large kiln. The kiln was thus a material manifestation of the result of cooperative labor and collective action through which the final product exceeded the aggregate of individual actions.

Third, the ritual was marked by silence and solemnity, which was highly un-usual within a village where life was loud and noisy. The silence created an affec-tive state that allowed the group to take a moment to acknowledge that while the village community was marked by hierarchically placed castes, gender divisions, and varying access to capital, there was a need and possibility of collective labor and also to share the collective guilt of setting fire to earth. While the availability of sand and earth in villages was a valuable resource for their survival in enabling a flourishing brick industry that created livelihoods in a context where agricul-ture was becoming increasingly unviable, their economic needs did not displace their sacred imagination. For them, earth and sand were not mere natural re-sources to be exploited for their needs, but sacrosanct nature, whose violation people reluctantly participated in and paid an outsider to do. As a result, no brick kiln was ever fired without a prayer and this provided a moment of reconnection with an enchanted universe within which the struggles of daily life continued. This brief example demonstrates that even a small event like the firing of a brick kiln reinforced some of the most profound values of life such as collective action, division of labor, and the value of natural resources. It is by unpacking such small and everyday events over a period of time that it is possible to build a picture of the social imaginaries of village life.

The four events that I have chosen to present in this book combine the techniques of the extended case study method in which the anthropologist is interested in "a sequence of events sometimes over quite a long period, where the same actors are involved in a series of situations in which their structural positions must continually be re-specified and the flow of actors through dif-ferent positions specified" (Gluckman 2006: 28–29, quoted in Englund 2018). Curiously, such an approach has seen remarkably little application in the study of India. F. G. Bailey was the most prominent and possibly the only member of the Manchester School to have applied its methodology to research in India, and he followed the spirit of the School in connecting the micro with the macro by presenting his study of village-level politics in Bisipara as intertwined with politics at levels beyond the village—namely the block, district, and the state of Orissa (renamed Odisha later).[3] His prodigious writings (two trilogies) on this one setting was faithful to the ambition of his tradition of providing data in excess of what an argument may require to enable future analysis by others. A recent study did just that and included re-visiting his research site and bore out a number of his projections (Otten and Simpson 2016). In this, Bailey met the Manchester School's commitment of the extended-case method to provide anthropologists with the means "to recover the antecedents of future crises" (Englund 2018). While in agreement of Bailey's commitment to the study of the village as part of a macro universe, I, however, diverge from his particular portrayal of politics which was in the late Machiavellian vein—namely, a rational and transactional activity that was marked by stratagems and spoils, envy and avarice, poisoned gifts and intrigue. My interest in politics, on the other hand, is as much in its potential to create collaboration as in its cutthroat, competitive nature and is directly the result of observation of how politics works at the village level. As will be evident, for instance, in the analysis of the first of the four events—that of a sexual scandal—political activity encompassed both the fissures caused by scandal itself and the process of repair that followed it. It is this second aspect of political activity that one does not encounter in Bailey, but one does in the early writings of Machiavelli and the Republican tradition in which politics is as much about deliberation and consensus building to effect collective action (Skinner 2010). These values were also the essence of the political in Spencer's analysis of an election in a Sinhala village, which he presents as moral dramas that revealed fundamental ideas about cooperation, competition, redistribution, and faith (Spencer 2007). In such a tradition, politics is as much about accommodation and cooperation for the sake of the common good—that is, the "whole-sum" (much like the navigation of the vessel for Aristotle's sailors in the epigraph to this book)—as it is about the zero-sum game of power and status. Bailey's discussion politics is largely dominated by the latter. It is true that politics in popular perception is invariably associated with dirt, with the unclean. In Bengali, the word used is *nongra* (filth), a sentiment that is shared by Spencer's Sri Lankan informants, as indeed many across the world. But Spencer's caveat to this characterization is worth bearing in mind: "What I think the village interpretation of politics as material self-interest really means was that politics had become the arena of life within which egoistic displays and naked self-interest were not merely expected, they were in a sense also produced" (Spencer 2007: 86). Our task, I suggest, is to take the moral evaluation of politics as "dirty" and test its trajectory against political action outside electoral times to observe if the values of self-interest and competition in electoral politics compete with the opposite and cleaner values of cooperation and civility. I will return to the theme of how to constitute "the political" later in the chapter.

Methodologically, the accounts of the four events presented in this book— a scandal, a harvest, a sacrifice, and an election—combine the techniques of situational analysis of a single event followed by an extended case study in which we follow the protagonists beyond the single event. Each event has a "social drama" at its heart, the term coined by Victor Turner to characterize the theater of conflict as well as its location in a temporal frame. I present these four events as a combination of situational analysis of a social drama in a single day, followed by an extended case to reconstruct the actions of the actors beyond it. Bruce Kapferer, drawing on the Manchester tradition of which he was a part, has observed that such events are important to study "as a singularity in which critical dimensions can be conceived as opening to new potentialities in the formation of social realities" (2010: 1). A situational analysis of such events thus revealed a substratum of shared understandings and common values formed the bedrock of everyday life and everyday ethics, but were only expressed as desirable in these extraordinary moments. For the anthropologist, these values that existed in everyday agrarian life were not always available for ethnographic observation—but in such events, the unspoken aspirations of social conduct were brought to the surface and made available for study. Consider, for instance, the second event presented, that of the harvest, which was a highly concentrated and somewhat ritualized activity in which the crop was cut, collected, and distributed. It was a complex drama not only because it encoded regimes of work and labor, but it also reacquainted each participant with the vital relationship between individual and collective effort. It was a communal activity par excellence that could never be achieved by a single individual and therefore reinforced the weight of the social. Similarly, the scandal that rocked the two villages over a period of nearly three years showed how seemingly intractable fault lines between groups along loyalties dictated by kinship, caste, and party-political loyalties needed to be repaired to keep the community together. To achieve this, cross-cutting ties of friendship and courage to challenge the status quo had to be found and ethical red lines that could not be crossed had to be identified. Both the scandal and the harvest situations reinforced the power of the collective and the importance of the social.

Thus, events that occurred periodically lent themselves to be analyzed as rituals that stood apart from and outside of the ordinary, allowing their participants to experience transcendental truths that were normally hidden in the everyday life of the transactional social. Victor Turner's work, also in the Manchester School tradition, is helpful as it brought together Durkheimian approaches in the anthropology of religion to the study of ritual to explore the importance of ritual in generating meaning considered valuable to society. Each ritual was analyzed through its tripartite structural form—separation, liminality, and reincorporation—as also its symbolism. Thickness of ethnographic description was key to truly appreciating the power of symbols evoked in each ritual as their meaning across a variety of contexts also outside the ritual was uncovered to show how resonance is created across spheres through each iteration and is thereby enriched. Adopting such an approach allows us to explore the potency of each event and its afterlife over a fifteen-year period. While these moments displayed many aspects of the transactional and conflict—Islamic cattle sacrifice was conducted amid widespread nervousness about offending the sentiments of the Hindu majority population of India, and elections were as much about money and violence as they were about citizenship—they were nevertheless able to create a realm of experience that transcended the everyday reality of life to generate profound meanings. It was the generative capacity of such events to overcome the frisson of the everyday that made them highly anticipated moments. It is such moments that make social life possible, for it is here that "human beings construct and reconstruct themselves in order to eliminate or otherwise cope with the problem of creatural existence" (Evens and Peacock 1990: 1). As Maurice Bloch has argued, it is the ability for imagining a world in which we are able to suppress the transactional in order to assert transcendental values that makes us human and distinct from other species (Bloch 2008). As I will show, each of the four events in this book creates moments of transcendent truth in a manner that all religion does in its commitment to another reality. By considering their resemblances in their commitment to the transcendent, the non-religious events of the scandal, harvest, and elections are closer to Robert Bellah's characterization of "civil religion" or "secular rituals" and can be placed alongside more overtly religious ones, as that of *Qurbani* (animal sacrifice). Robbins proposes "to sketch a picture of how religion informs ethical life in ways that do not explain away or traduce its everyday qualities, but that at the same time do not leave them to stand wholly on their own" (Robbins 2016: 771). By placing religious and non-religious "events" contiguously, we are able to lay bare their common achievement as "the key social form in which exemplary representations of values are made socially available" that Robbins argues about religious rituals (Robbins 2015: 18). K. Sivaramakrishnan does something similar in the context of his work on environmental politics in India, arguing that religion and its ideas of sacrality and auspiciousness should encourage us to examine the role of "religious ethics to the political ethics of nature" (Sivaramakrishnan 2015: 1303). In a similar move, I do not pose religion and everyday ethics as opposed to or exclusive of one another—one standing for the transcendent and explicit, the other as immanent and tacit—but I propose an accommodation of the everyday and the religious in the creation of desirable values.[4] As Evens and Peacock argue, the study of the transcendental realm alongside the social is productive because the former is where "society everywhere develops and proceeds. To a degree unmatched in any other animal species, the human being systematically exceeds itself to create and recreate its self and its world. The resulting world is social, since transcendence describes the self as ever reaching beyond itself, and therefore as intrinsically open to its other" (Evens and Peacock 1990: 3). The four major events in the life of the village presented here—a scandal, a harvest, a sacrifice, and an election—each have elements of the agonistic and transcendental, and each generates social imaginaries of the divergent impulses of the political.

To examine how the event and the everyday are connected, I draw on another tradition of the study of the event in anthropology, pioneered by Veena Das, that is distinct from the way in which I have discussed the event thus far.[5] Das's initial characterization of a "Critical event" was one in which "new modes of action came into being which redefined traditional categories" (Das 1995: 6). In her work, these refer to instances of extreme and unimaginable violence in urban India, such as those that occurred during the anti-Sikh riots following Mrs. Gandhi's assassination by her Sikh bodyguards in 1984. Such events of extreme violence were "critical" because they were ruptures of the ordinary and could not "be comprehended within the available categories at the time of their occurrence." In developing her ideas since, her attention has been on events and their relationship to the everyday and it is these ideas that I have found most productive in thinking with my own material. In her own words, Das explains, "There is a double register in which the event presents itself in my work. On the one side is its capacity to rupture the known coordinates of the everyday, and on the other side there is the simultaneous absorption of the event into the everyday" (2015: 382). But this isn't a simple dichotomy of ruptures and continuity, and in asking how the event is "anchored to the everyday" Das forces us to confront that the event is not set part from sociality but is "joined to the everyday by its tentacles," making the everyday itself evented. In exploring the afterlife of the values produced during the four events in village life, it is this idea of the evented everyday that is productive to think with, for my interest lies in how events such as harvests and sacrifices create social imaginaries that guide social action beyond the temporality of the event itself. Brighupati Singh's thoughtful analysis of Das's work is helpful for he directs our attention to the two tendencies that the event and the everyday contain. While the former is life-denying and agonistic, the work of the everyday in folding these into itself is through what he calls "reparative impulses." Das more often than not, Singh observes, is concerned with the reparative which, as Singh reminds us, is also political and is concerned with "how we might continue to live together" (Singh 2015b). While Das is concerned in particular with the everyday ethics of healing, repair, and knitting back together of social life after the ruptures created by critical events, for my purpose of thinking about the social life of a village community, these two registers of the agonistic and reparative are valuable frames through which to think of events that I present here, as generative of different impulses that lie at the heart of social life.

The Political

This type of study thus runs counter to the convention of studying "the political" by bracketing it off from the rest of society, what Kaviraj characterizes as the "underlying logic of modern societies of a *separation of spheres*" (Kaviraj 2011: 4; emphasis in the original).[6] Such a separation drew a distinction between politics and anti-politics, such that the latter invoked " 'religion,' 'community,' 'family,' or 'nation' as the necessary antithesis to the political" (Hansen 1999: 229, quoted in Spencer 2007: 177). Instead I aim to build a picture of the social imaginaries of democracy through a holistic account of political life. Such a portrait of the political draws on Jonathan Spencer's characterization of it, as a field that contains within it "politics and anti-politics, the agonistic and the altruistic, individual interest and collective morality" (Spencer 2007: 177). This characterization is a departure from the political anthropology from the 1940s and 1950s and its "indifference to the moral evaluation of political action" (Spencer 2007: 176) and takes seriously the "symbiotic connection" between the political and the anti-political. This connection, Spencer argues, is the "exploitation [by anti-politics], for *political* purposes, of popular unease with the moral implications of actually existing politics" (Spencer 2007: 177; emphasis in the original). But such a characterization of the anti-political—that is, those institutions that are not political in a formal way (religion, kinship etc.)—has to contend with the truth that while it challenges the political status quo, it remains within its grammar of agonism and thus produces a new political crafted on the same logic of agonism. Instead Spencer's attention, as mine, is directed at those moments in society that turn on a different logic, one that he calls the "counter-political" to identify those activities that "defuse the effects of the political" by aspiring to "avoid the divisive heart of the political altogether" (Spencer 2007: 177). We may call this "reparative," "collective," or "cooperative," but it is this cluster of non-agonistic values of politics that interests me here, as these are germane to the construction of the republic, as ideals of fraternity and mutuality are impossible to achieve only through agonism and competition. These counter-political values, I will demonstrate, are to be found in a range of events discussed here, in both those that are overtly political and those that are not.

Consequently, my analysis of democracy as a political system does not, and cannot, adopt a formalistic account of democracy either, because associating it only with a set of institutions, such as elections and elected politicians, would be to disregard democracy's ethical project that requires republican values. These values, I aim to show, are generated during the social dramas of significant events, both overtly political and/or counter-political (in the Spencer sense), and so the cultivation of democratic values happens as much in non-electoral times outside the realm of formal political institutions as it does within them. It is by paying attention to the creation of democratic and republican values outside of elections, when dogma and difference are put to the side, that we can hope to capture a sense of how citizens behave politically outside the formal structure of democracy. At the level of the village this entails studying their activities in between elections alongside their actions during elections.

In such an approach, it is therefore critical to place elections, which are the usual focus of the study of democracy, alongside other social dramas. Our assessment of elections for their generative capacity for a wider democratic context is helped by a wider anthropological literature, in which elections are "not epiphenomenal to the world of real politics" but are "crucial sites for the production and reproduction of the political" (Spencer 2007: 78). The potential of the political in Spencer's account is its ability to create the unexpected, to unleash forces that may be hidden in normal non-electoral times, but once produced can affect all areas of social life. Elections, therefore, while momentary and stylized in their performance of a democratic moment, contain within them a "corrosive power" of overturning the status quo, or challenging dominance, and of giving voice to those who otherwise remain silent in non-electoral times (Khilnani 1997). This capacity of elections to produce the unforeseen is what Hansen calls the "ubiquitous contingency" of democracy, and Spencer persuades us to pay attention to electoral moments in social life because they allow the expression of sentiments that may otherwise remain hidden (Hansen 1999).

The study of social institutions in the spheres of the economy, kinship, and religion can help us to understand how a notion of the political collective, of "we the people," is produced. In turn, overtly political institutions, such as elections, through their repetitive performance strengthen solidarity further. As Calhoun notes, "a democratic public is not merely contingent on political solidarity; it can be productive of it" (Calhoun 2007: 153). In West Bengal, a small but significant fact illustrates this. Throughout the electoral dominance of the Left Front for thirty-four years when they won every election, the main opposition party Congress, and after 1998, Trinamool Congress, continued to register consistently high vote shares (1977, 23 percent; 1982, 35 percent; 1987, 41 percent; 1991, 35 percent; 1996, 39 percent; 2001, 39 percent; 2011, 48 percent). The figures indicate that voters who did not support the Left Front continued to vote for the opposition even though they had no hope of their party winning in the face of the Left Front's formidable election machinery. But by doing so, they used the advantage of the secret ballot to keep alive the idea of political competition that is germane to democratic politics. It also helped these voters to imagine themselves as a group and over thirty-four years to begin to share a sense of solidarity with others like them who stubbornly refused to give in and support the incumbent government. The silent but collective support of the opposition party thus provides an illustration of how a democratic public can produce political solidarity. This resulted in the electoral rout of the Left Front after their debacle in the Singur-Nandigram issue in 2008 because it could build on this existing support for the opposition.

The Agrarian Life-World and Cultivation

The popular image of the agrarian life is dominated by the figure of a male farmer involved in agriculture, who lives in a village and earns a livelihood by cultivating crops on his own land. However, for India, this image is restrictive and misleading. According to the last census (2011) only 21 percent of the total workforce, so just under 50 percent of the workforce engaged in agriculture, were owner cultivators and most were in fact farm laborers. Less than half of the average monthly income (₹6,440) of a farmer family comes from cultivation of crops, and time-use surveys show that farmers spend only a small part of their time in cultivation (National Sample Survey Office 70th round for income and time-use study). Thus, the terms *agrarian* and *farmer*, and their association with agriculture, are not as self-evident as is assumed. This difficulty is reflected in official definitions where a *farmer* is defined by the National Policy for Farmers as "a person actively engaged in the economic and/or livelihood activity of growing crops and producing other primary agricultural commodities and will include all agricultural operational holders, cultivators, agricultural labourers, sharecroppers, tenants, poultry and livestock rearers, fishers, beekeepers, gardeners, pastoralists, [and] non-corporate planters."[7] How then do we summarize this all-encompassing descriptive list of the activities of a farmer? David Ludden provides a useful core definition of agriculture as "the social organisation of powers to produce organic material for human use," and this pithy summary is useful for enumerative practices that require farmers to be distinguished from non-farmers (Ludden 1999: 18). On the basis of this minimal condition, it is possible to construct the life-world of the farmer which includes overlapping regimes of the production of organic material for human use that share a family resemblance to the others. This tie to the organic is reflected in the words that are used to describe the "agrarian" in multiple Indian languages—*vivasaayam, kisani, kheti, khetihar, kheti badi, krishi, vyavasayam, krushi, gavai, zerai*—all of which are associated with land.

The agrarian setting interacts with the non-agrarian rural and urban in multiple ways. Non-agrarian settings in India are, first and foremost, populated by those who rely on the agrarian for their supply of food and animal products but always have higher social distinction. Non-agrarian settings in India, on average, have better roads, drainage, electricity grids, mobile phone signals, public transport, public institutions, and better access to consumer goods. They, however, also afford greater possibility of nucleated families and anonymity despite often cramped and crowded housing. The agrarian setting, on the other hand, even for those who live in small houses made of organic materials such as thatch and mud, provides access to open space that fields provide. Divisions between the inside and outside of the house are less sharply marked, and the material culture of the agrarian citizen tends to be less dominated by man-made fibers, technology, and mass consumption.

The life-world of the agrarian[8] is continually pushed to the margins by the project of modernity. In India, despite the agrarian being numerically dominant—60 percent of land is cultivated, agrarian citizens constitute a third of the rural population, and over a fifth of the total population and agrarian outputs counts for over 17 percent of the total GDP of India (much higher than the global average)—agrarian issues are very rarely accorded their commensurate importance. In his comprehensive *An Agrarian History of South Asia*, David Ludden demonstrates how and why "agrarian history is submerged in the historiography of nations and states" despite intersecting with the history of modernity everywhere (Ludden 1999: 1). Largely caused by a lack of first-hand experience, a stereotype of the farmer as a figure frozen in time and without history, and the rendering of the agrarian through official statistics, "the urban middle classes invented an agrarian discourse that was preoccupied with matters of public policy" (Ludden 1999: 8). The villages are seen mainly as a source of labor for the manufacturing markets and urban development, and the large number of workers has ensured that their wages have always remained low. Given this paternalistic marginalization, in contemporary India it is the classic modernism of democratic politics and elections that have come to be the most efficacious way to highlight the issues of farmers' rights, unfair trade practices, or the impact of fuel prices on irrigation and fertilizer prices. Despite the social marginalization in national discourse, the equal opportunity to vote has provided agrarian citizens with a sense of equal political citizenship, which would explain a Dalit official's remark to Robinson in the 1980s, saying, "progress starts with elections" (M. Robinson 1998: 264). Turnout rates in elections in rural areas have always been consistently high, and until recently significantly higher than urban areas, and the electoral choices they make at the ballot box can also be tactically insignificant (Chibber and Ahuja 2012). In 2018, for instance, the agrarian vote in certain states emerged as a critical voice against an increasingly authoritarian central and state government led by the same party.[9] It is thus critical that we have a deeper understanding of the interface of democracy and agrarian dynamics in order to fully understand how democracy works in the lives of over half the population of India.

For an examination of the linkages between democratic politics and the agrarian, it is therefore essential that we go beyond the minimal, marginal, or negative characterization of the agrarian that is reductively economistic and propose instead a definition that is more textured, and one that takes into account the culture and distinct ontology of the agrarian. Firstly, economic activity in the agrarian in India is rarely exclusively confined to farming but often includes diversified enterprises in addition to agriculture such as hatcheries, sand mining, brick manufacturing, crafts, and investment, for these often come from agricultural surplus. Thus, the economic life of the agrarian is varied, and while agriculture itself contributes relatively less to the growth rates of an economy, a whole range of related small and medium enterprises facilitated by agrarian productivity and profit contribute more. Socially, there is a sense of community in which everyone in the village is known by their name, where they live, and who the members of their family are. This close-knit set-up can lead to a claustrophobic atmosphere marked by gossip and judgment, and requires a certain civility and accommodation in inter-personal interactions in order to maintain a cheek-by-jowl existence. In an agrarian setting, anonymity is rare despite social distance between castes, and there is familiarity with the identity and circumstances of those who live within the setting. Alongside agriculture, there is a close human–animal relationship through sharing of space with animals, and while only some can afford to own and maintain livestock, a wider network of labor is engaged in their care, nutrition, and maintenance. This can include children who are frequently entrusted with grazing or rounding-up duties, distribution of milk and eggs, or locating strays. Animals are thereby equal inhabitants in a shared landscape and are individually known to its carers through their particular idiosyncrasies, and often affective bonds exist between people and animals. Adults who live in agrarian settings therefore worry about the crop in the field, the animals in their care, and their children in equal measure as requiring constant vigilance, care, and attention. While both men and women are involved in all activities, the primary responsibility for livestock usually rests with women, and with men for the crop. There is also a shared understanding in the agrarian that attentiveness to crop and livestock supersedes all other responsibilities, sometimes even those to children. The reason for this is that neglect of the first sign of disease or abnormality in a field or animal can cause it to escalate quickly and can have devastating effects on the family's income and survival. In agrarian India, knowledge of treatments for afflictions in crops and animals is often held within the community itself rather than a class of professional specialists, and this knowledge is shared and coveted by an agrarian community. There is an overall sense of precarity in the agrarian as agricultural profits are entirely at the mercy of inclement weather, unreliable infrastructure, and a discredited agricultural market system whose dynamics are invariably skewed against the producers.

Temporality in the agrarian is regulated by at least three different calendars—the agricultural calendar, the religious one, and the official Gregorian one. The first regulates the work of farming—preparation, sowing, growing, and harvesting of the crop—and this dominates all other subsidiary work. The religious calendar is firmly observed, and while all festivals may not be marked by holidays and consumption in the same manner as in the non-agrarian, they are observed in some fashion and provide brief reprieves from the quotidian. The official Gregorian calendar regulates the life of children and schools and those of all state-owned institutions that observe a seven-day week that separate working days from weekends. A typical inhabitant of an agrarian setting thus constantly juggles the demands of at least three different temporal cycles and their demands. Finally, the effects of climate change are more acutely experienced in agrarian settings than in non-agrarian ones. Depletion of water resources directly affects farming choices, the use of fertilizers has a direct impact on health, and even the smallest changes in weather are more acutely felt in an agrarian environment in India that is more in sync and vulnerable to them.

The agrarian life-world is thus distinct and dominated by land and farming, it has an intimate relationship with nature, it is regulated by multiple calendars, is susceptible to environmental change, and is marked by a diverse economy and sociality that is shaped through its processes of "cultivation and circulation" (Ludden 1999: 31). These twin processes, Ludden argues, connect the site of production in a particular location (e.g., cultivation) with much wider processes of state and market that "organise the movement of materials and activities into and out of farming and thus agriculture" (Ludden 1999: 33). The agrarian ethic is also a "moral economy in which critical redistributive mechanisms nonetheless do provide a minimal subsistence insurance for villagers" within a precarious environment (Scott 1978: 5). While agrarian life by definition has deep social divisions on the basis of ownership of land and labor, rural living requires a certain reciprocity and a sense of community that discourages extreme individual self-interest. As Karl Polanyi notes, "It is the absence of the threat of individual starvation which makes . . . society, in a sense, more human than market economy and at the same time less economic" (Polanyi 1944, cited in Scott 1978: 5). The villages of Madanpur and Chishti are representatives of such a setting and are where we will explore the processes of cultivating democracy.

The idea of cultivation in this book works in at least two different registers. First, this study is set within an agrarian ethic, in which the cultivation of crops was still the defining and dominant activity despite a recent diversification that included new mercantile businesses. Agriculture took place within a context of institutional change by land reforms that created an unprecedented rebalancing of hierarchies among castes and classes that in turn generated ideas about the division of labor and cooperation. This book will probe the affinity between this altered scenario and democratic values. Second, in a wider and related sense, the activity of cultivation generated practices of nurture, patience, vigilance, and hope—democratic values that are perhaps essential for the cultivation of democracy anywhere. These two registers of cultivation works are similarly present in

Anand Pandian's work among a Kallar community in south India in which he explores the contradictions and overlap between the apparatus of a developmental state and the legacy of a moral tradition of cultivation in south India. Here cultivation comes to stand for two meanings, and is both "an operation on the land and an operation on the self" (A. Pandian 2009: 19). While the former refers to a set of agricultural practices introduced as a "civilizing" mission for the putatively savage Kallars, his study shows that for them, agriculture emerged as an activity that required and stimulated the production of not just crops but also certain selves. The agricultural environment thus emerges as a "didactic environment of moral pedagogy" for the creation of a certain kind of "agrarian citizen" (Pandian: 44). While the historical context in West Bengal and my research site is significantly different from Pandian's, the notion of an agrarian civility that is associated with certain values of patience, accommodation, toil, and restraint are common and allow us to propose something of an "agrarian ethic" or even an agrarian ontology. The Tamil word *Kutiyanavan* that Pandian presents us with as "a name for an agrarian citizen, one that relied upon shared moral conduct as a basic foundation of rural belonging" has no Bengali linguistic equivalent but is a valuable descriptor for the citizens I present here (Pandian: 69).

During the fifteen-year span of my study, values came under strain as the circumstances in which people lived were challenged in multiple ways and in turn so did their responses. The long-term immersion and engagement and the nature of anthropological research allows us to chart these shifting contours, and to study the constantly evolving nature of the "social" and the moral complexities of cultivation.[10] An anthropological engagement also has the advantage of generating intimate knowledge of specific individuals, and by tracing their growth and development over this period it is possible to outline the processes of self-cultivation of these democratic values.[11] On the basis of evidence gathered over this fifteen-year period in one rural location, I attempt to deepen our understanding of how ideas about popular participation and an ethics of civility and citizenship—key ideas associated with a democratic ethic—are sustained in the soil of India. By examining key social institutions that regulate economic, political, religious, and familial life, the aim is to uncover the processes through which ideas of ethics and doing the right thing in public and private life are cultivated. These shared ideas cannot be presupposed to exist in a society; rather, their creation relies on social organization and practices that generate them.

Democracy, Republic, and Citizenship

Democracy exists in a tension between two opposing tendencies—one strain allows the expression of difference in points of view and creates division and competition between citizens. This is the aspect of democracy that contains within it the possibility of violence. At the same time, democratic culture also requires, in its choice of "ballot over bullet," an ability to deliberate, argue, compromise, and agree (Dewey 1939). "The substitution of ballots for bullets, for the right to vote for the lash, is an expression of the will to substitute the method of discussion for the method of coercion" (Dewey 1939: 128). This in turn requires a certain civic-ness and civility on the part of citizens that includes social solidarity created through the values and emotions of cooperation, the capacity to suppress individual self-interest for the collective good, an aspiration to egalitarianism, a commitment to redistribution, equal dignity for all, and the capacity for accommodation.[12] Anand Pandian, in his account of agrarian citizenship in south India, identifies empathy at the heart of such civility as it is the "ability to imagine oneself in place of others." This, he says, drawing on Adam Smith, is the "the well spring of virtuous conduct and moral improvement" (Pandian 2009: 183).

India's democratic life has had two strains running through it—the procedural and the substantive, or what Ramchandra Guha called the "hardware" and "software" of democracy. The first is composed of arrangements to make representative democracy work through the mechanisms of elections, the separation of powers, judicial oversight, and an independent media to enable all Indian citizens to participate in electing their government. India's "founding moment" in 1950 instituted universal suffrage and total political equality (Khosla 2020). Thus, independence from colonial rule was inaugurated by treating each and every Indian as a political equal by giving them all the right to vote in elections irrespective of any social or economic criteria (a right which they did not have during the partial democracy introduced by the colonial government). This complete political equality for all Indian citizens was intended to enable the more elusive project of social equality. As with all software, it required a re-programming of Indian social arrangements which in 1947 were deeply divided by caste, class, racial superiorities, and gender; and so was a revolutionary if audacious aspiration. Any stock-taking of India's democratic record thus has to take into account both of these aspects of democracy, the procedural and the substantive, and the verdict has consistently been that it is a case of a "battle half won" (Varshney 2013).

But what of India's record as a procedural democracy? In the mixed report card of Indian's democracy, the battle that has been half won has referred mostly to her record on conducting largely free and fair elections.[13] Given the scale and complexity of conducting elections in the world's largest electorate by far, the performance led by the Election Commission of India has been astonishing (Shani 2017). The response of the electorate in turn has been enthusiastic, marked by rising levels of voter turnout at every election (Banerjee 2014). The career of electoral democracy in India has been characterized as occurring in different "phases"—the first dominated by the Congress Party, the second by the formation of political parties that challenged the Congress hegemony, and the third in which political representatives began to be drawn from a much wider social base allowing for non-elites to occupy political office. This widening of the social base has been characterized as the "democratic upsurge" when procedural democracy and elections were wrested away from traditional political parties by newer ones (Yadav 1999). Impatient with the stranglehold of established political parties like the Congress, "backward castes" and Dalits formed their own political parties to represent themselves. The names of these new parties included words such as *Bahujan*, *Samajwadi*, and *Janata* that reflected caste identities and also a commitment to redistribution that would benefit the numerically stronger lower castes from which the leaders of these parties were drawn. The "democratic upsurge" was marked by a growth in electoral participation and the rise of caste-based parties in the 1990s onward and constituted nothing short of a "silent revolution" (Jaffrelot 2003).

Studies conducted by Lokniti in the late 1990s demonstrated that Indians who lived in rural areas, were poor, of low caste, and were marginalized communities were among the most enthusiastic participants of the electoral process, voted in high numbers, and attended political rallies and meetings (Yadav 1999). More than the level of turnout, what was most striking about the Indian elections was that the pattern of political participation defied commonsense expectations and academic theories alike in at least three respects. First, turnout in the Indian elections defied the general trend, especially in older democracies, of decline over time. In the last seven decades the overall pattern was that of stable and increasing turnout in elections. Second, the turnout tended to go up as one went down the tiers of democracy. As noted previously, the turnout in the local and state elections tended to be substantially higher than that in the national elections. Finally, the turnout was not lower among citizens at the lower end of the social and economic hierarchy; if anything, the reverse was true, since a poor, low caste person is more likely to vote in India than an upper caste, upper class person. In this respect the underprivileged groups have turned out stronger supporters of the democratic system than before (Linz, Stepan, and Yadav 2007).

Did this democratic upsurge create a better democratic culture in India? It is undeniable that the entry of lower caste parties which wrested control away from existing elites created access for a wider range of actors to enter the electoral arena. But did this enable an emancipatory transformation of Indian society from social inequality to a social democracy in the manner in which the Constitution had imagined? Public policies during their stints in power did not translate into better lives for their followers; instead, public spending was targeted more at the symbolic assertions of their presence in the public sphere through statues and buildings, capture of public bodies by members of their castes, and petty corruption by those who used public office to channel public funds for private use (Banerjee and Verniers 2020). Jeffrey Witsoe, who studied the rise of one important example of this politics in the northern state of Bihar, called this "democracy against development" (Witsoe 2013).

Further, was this "democratic upsurge" successful in creating democratic spaces within political parties? Did the lower caste parties generate a new kind of politics that not only mobilized electoral support from their fellow caste members during elections, but also provided new opportunities for them to gain prominence—that is, did these new political parties enable a wider dispersal of opportunity for their members? The answers to these questions are in the negative, for if anything, the new political parties resulting from the second democratic upsurge saw the entrenchment of dominance of only some individual leaders and their families. Gilles Verniers's work in Uttar Pradesh, India's most populous state of over 200 million, for instance, in which the second democratic upsurge has been the most pronounced, in these new low-caste parties candidate recruitment remained elitist, while power was concentrated in the hands of a few families (Verniers 2018). Thus, while these new parties mobilized the support of their caste members behind an emancipatory agenda, they did not create avenues for their participation in politics beyond delivering electoral victories, and coveted political offices were kept within a small circle of networked families. Verniers characterizes this as a "broadening of caste but narrowing of class" as parties that "claim to have become more socially inclusive . . . tend to enrol their candidates from among the new business elites of the state, who seek to further entrench their domination through participation in the democratic process" (Verniers 2018). The democratic upsurge was therefore a rise in the participation of lower castes in elections, but only as voters, who "vernacularized" democracy through social and cultural idioms and created a dominance of these parties in governments (Michelutti 2008). But ten years later, the same scholars identify the costs at which these elections are won and money and muscle and the ubiquity of violence are the mainstay of electoral politics (Michelutti et al. 2018). This scenario forces us therefore to ask if greater democratization can be said to have occurred as a result simply of a rise in the numbers participating in elections? Can the waxing or waning of democracy be charted through the growth and fall in electoral turnouts? And perhaps most importantly, can simply winning elections be a sufficient condition for greater "democracy"?[14]

For B. R. Ambedkar, the chair of the large and diverse Constituent Assembly that debated the Indian constitution and as the foremost spokesperson for India's socially discriminated castes, India's choice of democracy was not simply democracy as a form of government but democracy in society itself; as he put it, "a democratic form of government presupposes a democratic form of society [and what this required, among other things, was] a social organization free from rigid social barriers" (Ambedkar, quoted in Khosla 2020: 244–245). But he did not mince his words (see the epigraph to this book) when describing Indian society, which he characterized as "essentially undemocratic" and on which the constitution was only a "top-dressing." To address this challenge, the new constitutional provisions sought to replace the existing modes of thinking and communication with new ways of deliberation and consensus building, making it not just a "constitution of democracy" but a "constitution *as* democracy" (Khosla 2020). The constitution of India was designed, therefore, as a document that would enable a transformation of an undemocratic India into a democratic one, empowering through its laws each new citizen by making the individual rather than a community the primary political agent. The rights and duties and system of reservations were designed to allow full expression of individuals' rights, and for each citizen to be able to fully realize the potential of political equality without being held back or discriminated against by historical social injustices of caste and religion. In this sense, as Khosla has argued, the Indian constitution was more a "textbook" than a "rulebook," in three key ways. First, "it could provide the grammar for citizens who were required to speak a new language" of rights and liberties. Second, "the constitution empowered the state to counter the pressures by society and be the agent of material transformation," and finally, it made "the individual the focus," not community or other social groups, for freedom and stability. According to Khosla,

> These three features of India's founding vision were held to make democratic citizenship possible. Within such a framework, a person would be unshackled from extant forms of reasoning and association. It was this liberation which made self-rule possible. Without it—without speaking a new language or being under a new kind of authority or remaining under the pressure of existing groups—one could not truly rule oneself. To be part of a democracy thus meant being part of a new way of relating both to every other person and to the state. It was an egalitarian promise that extended far beyond the casting of the vote. (Khosla 2020a)

Khosla argues that these features make India's democracy audacious in its founding moment, because it is able to imagine not simply re-shaping India's political system as an electoral democracy but transforming the very nature of her society from deep social inequality and hierarchy to a social democracy. The quest for social democracy, which Niraja Jayal characterizes as a "quest for citizenship [that] has been conducted in tandem with a quest for democratic modernity," and the creation of a "civic community" has, she argues, remained an "unfinished project" (Jayal 2013: 274). At the heart of this incomplete realization lies the tension between two aspects of citizenship—the relationship between the individual and the state, mediated by community, and that between citizen and citizen, mediated by social inequality. On the first, that is, "formative citizenship," her assessment of India's achievement is "reasonably positive," but on the second, that being substantive citizenship, her assessment of India's record is "poor." It is to this relationship between citizen and citizen, what Ambedkar called "associated life," that I will devote much of my attention in this book.

In order to engage with the concept of "associated life," we return to the second form of citizenship outlined by Jayal, namely "substantive" citizenship that exists between citizens (rather than the citizen and the state) in the creation of which, in her assessment, India fares poorly. Much of the reason for this is the "undemocratic soil of India" in which, as Pratap Bhanu Mehta reminds us, a basic form of recognition and "moral standing" is denied to members of certain sections of society (Mehta 2003: 40). Such inequality and the consequent devaluing of others, he argues, remains one of the biggest "burden[s] of democracy" (Mehta 2003: 39). The ambition of the new constitution was to begin by providing each citizen with one vote, as the first step in recognizing that everyone had the same value, regardless of any other criteria, and so each election would reinforce the experience of this equality. It was Ambedkar's ambition, right from early discussions with the colonial government in 1919 when partial democracy was considered, that participation in elections "could itself serve an instructive role and that participation in political life would bring about consciousness among the lower castes" (Khosla 2020: 10). Participation in elections was therefore more than window dressing for democracy; rather, the experience of being a voter was expected to play a formative part in creating democratic citizens. It is therefore important to investigate the relationship that elections have with non-electoral life to explore what role elections/political democracy/formative citizenship plays in the creation of "civic community"/social democracy/substantive citizenship. The rewiring of the relationship that existed between citizens was of supreme importance for the creation of such a civic community, for the human self was constituted in, and through, social relations. Social relations shaped personhood in fundamental ways, and reimagining them was critical for the formation of the citizen-subject. Ambedkar, through his own "untouchable" caste identity, had first-hand experience of discrimination to recognize how corrosive social practices of untouchability could be. By giving each man one vote, the hope was that each vote would also have equal value. Fraternity was thereby included as one of the goals of the Indian constitution as it best described the newly reconfigured social relations of a democratic India, in which the relationship between citizens would be one of equality, and this was for Ambedkar a "first order consideration rather than a second order consideration" (Rodrigues 2011: 165). Thus, democracy in India could successfully lift its burden only when civic-ness and fraternity formed the basis of social relations.

An India based on the principles of fraternity was represented by the word *republic* in the preamble to the Indian Constitution, although the introduction of this word was not without contestation, as Ambedkar insisted on changing "independent, sovereign, republic" to "sovereign, democratic, republic" to describe India's new identity. By doing so, he wished to draw attention to the distinction between a democracy and a republic and the need for *both* democracy and republicanism in independent India to achieve the social justice that the Indian constitution hoped to produce. The word *republic* was used not merely to connote India's anti-monarchical stance but also to stress the agentive nature of citizenship in the new nation. India's new citizens would, it was hoped, aspire to create a new community of equals to replace the old divided one, helped by political equality of democracy to create a fraternity of citizenship that was the hallmark of republicanism. While there was a history of European and American political thought on this tradition, Ambedkar's inspiration for this idea came from the Indian intellectual and social reformer Jyotirao Phule who had argued that "the spirit of republicanism vanished from India with the rise of monarchy and its entwinement with Brahminism, and resurrected itself in the West" (Rodrigues 2020). The political philosopher Quentin Skinner dates this resurrection to the European Renaissance, when a neo-Roman concept of citizenship via Machiavelli's early writings in *Discourses on Livy* was critical to shaping political theory.[15] In the Indian colonial context, social reformers such as Phule and Ambedkar believed, active citizenship needed to be revived as it was a critical requirement for the fight to create a more equal society that would uproot pernicious social distance between castes and create instead "fraternity [which] was communication, participation, and interaction between groups" (Khosla 2020: 145). Thus, the legal provisions for political democracy (such as universal franchise) and constitutional norms were provided to all Indian citizens to struggle to achieve the much more elusive ideal of social democracy. The function of the Indian constitution was to create the legal and moral scaffolding to build this new social order; and for Ambedkar, at least, democracy without the republic, or elections without active citizenship, or elected leaders without the solidary sense of "we, the people," would be a failure of India's democratic experiment.

In social life, one way to study the juxtaposition of political democracy, on the one hand, and social and economic democracy, on the other, is to view electoral and non-electoral temporalities within the same spatial context. In such a study, it is possible to assess the forms of participation in two different modes— that is, citizens as voters and citizens as participants in non-electoral social and other political activities—and to test whether Ambedkar's expectation that participation in elections would be "instructive" in shaping a wider political consciousness came to pass. Elections, therefore, should be considered alongside other social activities in community life and voters should be studied in multi-dimensions, not simply as individuals who make a choice at the ballot box. By placing knowledge about the same actors in Madanpur and Chishti inside and outside electoral time, I propose to examine how formal politics exists contiguously with other areas of social life, and how the non-political and political interact with each other, and assess the afterlife of the political of electoral times in generating more enduring moral standards.

What I attempt to do in this book, therefore, is to bring together two strains of India's democratic republican life, the electoral and non-electoral, in the following ways. I will seek to demonstrate how the two are deeply interlinked as parts of a single universe, for the contention here is that the practice of electoral democracy in India has, over seventy years, impacted how Indian citizens behave politically and how they imagine the social universe. As Indian voters went through repeated cycles of elections, organizing, campaigning, and voting for political parties and candidates, these experiences had an impact in turn on how they lived outside of electoral times. The process of acting as political citizens, in which they had a right to equality, had an impact on their lives as social citizens based on civic reciprocity in which it was possible to at least imagine association with others on egalitarian terms, for as Mehta notes, the radical promise of democracy was that by affirming human dignity it granted them civic standing. "In a democracy, the desire for having one's moral worth affirmed, for emptying social space of humiliation, is given open legitimation and expression" (Mehta 2003: 44). By presenting both electoral and non-electoral times in the same frame, thus, we can begin to see the overlap between the dynamics of procedurally induced formalist citizenship of political equality in which one's moral worth was affirmed and the workings of the hierarchically divided undemocratic soil that needed to be turned in order to create fraternity. Second, it allows us to unearth any sources of democratic values that exist even within India's undemocratic soil, such as the egalitarian space of collective prayers in a mosque or the hush of collective guilt when the earth was set alight in a brick kiln that contributed to the cultivation of the self.

Methods

The initial provocation for the study was provided by the results of Lokniti's National Election Study which revealed that poor marginal and rural voters consistently voted in high numbers (Palshikar and Kumar 2004; Yadav 1999). While a survey was useful in revealing this large-scale trend, it required qualitative and ethnographic research to explain the reasons for it. The survey revealed that a low caste woman living in a village was more likely to vote than an urban upper caste male, but we did not know *why* she did. My collaboration with Lokniti was therefore to try to identify the factors to explain this enthusiasm for voting by studying the voter herself in greater depth. The study followed the classic conventions of anthropological research in which all aspects of village life—the social institutions of religion, politics, economy, and kinship—were considered as a whole in order to analyze and explain people's engagement and enthusiasm for voting and democratic politics. It approached the voter in Indian elections as a person who existed within, and was shaped by, a wider context of family, work, and belief and allowed a study of events from both political and non-political, electoral and non-electoral life alongside each other to evaluate their roles in generating values shared by the community.

With the intention of providing some consistency to the survey data that had been a catalyst for this project, I visited all of the dozen or so rural sites that were part of the random sample of sites covered by the National Election Study in West Bengal, and settled on these two adjacent villages as sites for in-depth ethnographic investigation. I chose them for several reasons. I had chosen the state of West Bengal as I spoke the lingua franca Bengali fluently and although I had visited the capital, Kolkata, throughout my life I had never lived in the state, thus providing a good combination of distance and familiarity to make ethnographic research productive. The district of Birbhum—known in Bengal as "Red Earth" (*Laal Maati*) was prominent in the story of revolutionary politics in the state, especially during the 1960s and 1970s, and there was thus much historical depth to the extant dominance of the Left Front in these parts. By locating my two research villages in the district of Birbhum, in a continuing bastion of Left Front power, I was able to observe the workings of the communist parties at close range, to understand how they maintained their influence at elections and to understand the texture of lived communism. The villages of Madanpur and Chishti were easy to access as they were located by the side of the highway and this cut down on travel time. The majority of the population was Muslim and that allowed me to further my understanding of Muslim societies that had begun with my doctoral research.[16] And, most important, these two villages perfectly illustrated the broad findings of the survey—namely, voters in rural sites with high levels of illiteracy were enthusiastic voters. These two villages had turnout rates of about 90 percent, a sparse supply of electricity and running water, houses made of mud and thatch, and a population that was socially depressed and marginalized; taken together, these factors perfectly represented the setting I wished to understand further. My aim was to get to know the voters who lived there as people, in all the myriad aspects of their lives, in order to understand why they were interested in democracy, elections, and voting.

My choice of research site to study a macro phenomenon (voter turnout) in a micro setting (village) is part of a long-standing discussion by social scientists on how to scale their studies. Arjun Appadurai's essay in an important and unusual volume entitled *Conversations between Economists and Anthropologists* (1989) addressed the challenges of studying economic change in the villages of South Asia, and he identified three key issues of methodology for the study of rural economic change. First was the issue of studying small-scale changes versus large-scale changes; second was the type of evidence and data, that is, qualitative versus quantitative; and third was the mode of analysis, namely aggregative versus non-aggregative. The debate as presented by Appadurai was about "what constitutes certainty in science, about the deep problem involved in separating epistemological *conventions* from ontological certainties, and about the relationship between numerical precision and the analysis of living forms, whether these are human or non-human" (Appadurai 1989: 258). My own response to this issue has been to take the certainty of quantitative data produced by surveys as a starting point for an ethnographic investigation. The 1998 National Election Study survey was the first to provide hard numbers and clear trends on a national scale that indicated that the most structurally marginal members of the Indian electorate were her most enthusiastic voters. Like any well-sampled and well-executed survey, it gave us a snapshot of the big picture and in this case provided a startling finding that observers of Indian politics did not know before. To understand *why* they were keen on voting was, however, beyond the scope of the survey and required a more qualitative investigation. As an anthropologist, the most credible way in which I could investigate the reasons for voting was to identify a research site where the macro phenomenon was reflected and where it would be possible to study the everyday alongside the electoral to gain an understanding. This methodology reflects Appadurai's recommendation that one builds "on the assumption that social life is constituted by a series of small-scale interactions in which large-scale factors are embedded, rather than by large scaled factors as such" (1989: 258). This book is an example of the benefits such a combination of the small and large scale can provide.[17]

By training our eye on the local detail of Madanpur and Chishti, I hope to show through the minutiae of ethnographic data how power is gained, maintained, and lost in social life. Such power is the aspect of political life, of course, but as we shall see, it is true as much in religious life, economic life, and in the realm of kinship and friendship. My aim is to attempt an explanation that will show how these struggles for power are interlinked such that influence gained in one aspect of life is the result of machinations elsewhere. By laying bare these workings, I would also like to demonstrate how ordinary people learn the modus operandi of doing politics in their own familiar setting (*lokniti*) before they use it in more public electoral contexts (*rajniti*). Each power struggle, however seemingly petty, equips the participants with the skills required to play a political game. It teaches political judgment, the importance of timing, techniques to build alliances and solidarity, ways to demonstrate power to one's followers, the importance of performing this power to opponents, and devices to quash opposition. Together, they form the basis for an "active citizenship" as defined by the neo-Roman tradition and the one that Jyotirao Phule and Ambedkar advocated for India, as essential to the proper functioning of democracy. These skills can be observed in play in completely non–party-political settings—such as negotiating a wedding alliance or managing labor arrangements for a harvest—but I hope to show that they are also demonstrably the same skills that are used for overt political activity. It is therefore both non-political and political contexts that shape the politics of the people of Madanpur and Chishti, and ultimately shape their ideas about democracy and participation. While distant observers and surveys are only able to note the presence of voters when they showed up in queues at the polling booth on election day, this book will take us into their everyday lives when seemingly nothing much at all is happening. An ethnographic approach—distinct from "fieldwork" which often counts as "qualitative research" but mainly consists of asking people questions—is key here, as it is reliant on observing and listening. It recognizes that ideas sometimes are discursively articulated and at other times need to be observed. And it is by being ethnographically present at all times that it is possible to show how the ideas and imagination are crafted in moments of the village's life. Thus, while the initial impetus for this study was to understand the reason behind high levels of voter turnout among rural Indian voters, the study has grown into a broader discussion of politics, citizenship, and democratic values in agrarian society in India.

The villages of Madanpur and Chishti have grown to become not just my research site but my research home for the past twenty years. My familiarity and engagement with people who live there over this period of time has also meant that I have learned to try to see every issue in contemporary India from their point of view. Thus, when pondering any national issue, such as agricultural policy or the electoral ambitions of Hindu right-wing parties in West Bengal or the need for better primary health care, my understanding is shaped significantly by the perspective of my interlocutors in these two villages. It is for this reason that when the Gujarat pogrom against Muslims occurred in 2002, my image of "the Muslim" was largely shaped by those who lived in these villages and I felt it important to publish a volume of essays by other anthropologists who too had worked in Muslim societies in India. *Muslim Portraits* (was the result of that exercise, profiling ordinary Muslim lives in India, much like those of my friends in Madanpur and Chishti (Banerjee 2008). Similarly, while writing a book on Indian women and their ideas of modernity expressed through their choice of wearing the sari, my co-author of *The Sari* (2003) and I began our research in Madanpur and Chishti to understand what the sari meant to my friends there (Banerjee and Miller 2003). Thus, these villages for me are not simply a fieldsite but also an intellectual home where all my subsequent ideas about India's rural life have developed. As Veena Das puts it eloquently, "we produce knowledge in a mode of intimacy with our subjects" (Das 2015: 404).

Organization of the Book

The next chapter (Chapter 2) situates the villages of Madanpur and Chishti within the wider context of twenty-first-century India to locate its particular story of electoral politics, Islam, and cultivation within national and international trends. The state of West Bengal in which they are located has been dominated by the politics of communist political parties and their allies that won all elections between 1977 and 2011. The first ten years of this study were thus conducted during the heyday of the communist period, when all local village affairs were dominated by the figure of the "Comrade," and the latter years saw the rise of the new Trinamool Congress, a breakaway party from the original Congress party. These villages are in the district of Birbhum that saw some of the most violent conflicts during the Naxalite movements of the late 1980s that ultimately led to dramatic land tenancy reform measures. The reforms in West Bengal were extremely uneven, but in this part of the state they were highly effective and saw the dramatic reconfiguration of land tenancy and shifted the balance from landowners to sharecroppers as each were given an equal share of the harvest. In this village, as elsewhere, this also led to realignment of caste hierarchies, as it made the elite Syed abhorrence for manual agricultural work unsustainable, forcing them to perform agricultural tasks for the first time while simultaneously also highlighting the superior agricultural knowledge of the lower caste Sheikh sharecroppers. Older humiliations of lower caste members being beholden to the patronage of Syeds for wages and work were radically erased and a newfound self-respect, strengthened by communist agitprop of local Comrades and a mandatory rise in the daily wage tenfold, changed social dynamics visibly. In this context, the village itself also transformed. In 1999 most of the fields around the two villages were covered by paddy cultivation and were double cropped. "For the first time since anyone can remember, no one goes hungry anymore" is how people put it. However, by 2013, less than a quarter of the fields were cultivated for paddy, such cultivation being replaced by various informal enterprises involving the sale of sand, poppy seeds, and pilfered coal—each an illegal trade but more lucrative than traditional agriculture. The story of these two villages is symptomatic of a much wider change in agricultural practices and the growth of alternative businesses that were responses to climate change and water crisis and the fading arc of the much-touted Green Revolution and high-yielding varieties of grain introduced in the 1960s and 1970s in India. These villages are thus a site of the inter-relationship of the changing dynamics of Islam, paddy, and politics, within a moral economy that has evolved over a period of nearly five hundred years.

The first of the four events is an account of a scandal that lasted for nearly three years in the villages of Chishti and Madanpur (Chapter 3). At the heart of the story is the figure of the Comrade, who represented the powerful party-state at the local level and who, up until this point, seemed invincible. But this particular scandal saw him cross an ethical red line, and that gave people the courage for the first time to challenge his hegemonic hold over village life. By examining the way in which the scandal was resolved, it is possible to identify how participants learned to behave politically to resolve the matter themselves and use ties of kinship and friendship to create horizontal alliances with others. The account of the scandal introduces the cast of major and minor characters who feature in the following chapters of the book, and shows their linkages through kinship, shared agricultural work, neighborhood, and political affiliations to political parties. In Chapter 4, the second event, a highly concentrated activity over a period of a few days that is a paddy harvest, is presented. In communist West Bengal, the harvest brought into the open a number of different sources of tension that the radical land tenancy reforms of the 1980s had ushered in. The reforms were the culmination of nearly two decades of revolutionary violence, meetings, and demonstrations that had ultimately led to a rebalancing of power between landowners and sharecroppers. Sharecroppers were given a more secure tenancy, greater crop shares, and higher wages for labor and so to avoid escalating costs, landowners had to put their own labor into agriculture to make it viable. As a result, for the first time agriculture had become a joint activity between landowners and their sharecroppers, with the latter often playing a dominating role in decision-making, owing to their greater technical knowledge, despite being of a lower caste status. During the harvest this asymmetry was magnified: decisions about when and how much grain would be harvested, how much labor was required, where the ripe paddy would be stored, where the threshing machines would be set up, and who would guard the grain through the night were made as much by the sharecropper as the landowner. This meant that the two had to work closely together, with the sharecroppers often calling the shots. The elite Syeds, who until a decade prior had acquired their social distinction from eschewing manual labor, were now to be found in the fields, covered in paddy dust and indistinguishable from everyone else. The classic anthropological drama of the division of the grain heap here played out in new and unexpected ways caused by the egalitarianism brought by land reforms, but it also harked back to older social inequalities of space and power. The harvest emerged as an activity that was generative not only of potential wealth but also of a renewed consciousness of the relationship between individual participation and the common good, a crucial ingredient of a democratic sensibility. The third event of the book (Chapter 5) is an account of a religious festival of *Qurbani*, or animal sacrifice, that demonstrated the emphasis placed on the purity of intention of the person offering the sacrifice, the attachment to the cattle being sacrificed, and the generosity and precision of rules in the distribution of the sacrificial meat. The festival of *Qurbani* (sacrifice) was conducted with complete commitment but not without nervousness about how the news of their sacrifice would be received by the majority Hindu population of the state. At the start of the research in the first years of this century, most members of the two villages were Barelvis and shared a common set of practices of daily prayers, Eid, Qurbani, and Muharram festival.[18] Fifteen years later, this scenario had begun to change. Some young boys had been sent to residential madrasas for their education, the neighboring village had turned to reformist Deobandi Islam and stopped participating in the Muharram procession, and at least one family in Chishti had been to the Haj, resulting in the wife now choosing to eschew the traditional draped sari for tailored clothing and covering herself from head to toe. Islam and its practices were therefore no longer uniform and consensus-based, and this raised questions about whether it had ever been so. The "event" of animal sacrifice had to be read against such a shifting sense of what it is to be Muslim within such mutability of religious beliefs and practices as well as a wider politics of growing intolerance of minority rights in India. The analysis of cattle sacrifice in this chapter explores the values that this ritual produced—of renunciation (offering a favorite animal for slaughter), of redistribution (only a few households can afford to offer the sacrifice, but the meat was distributed widely along kin and social networks), of egalitarianism exemplified in Eid prayers and the idea of giving without expectation that animated a wide range of Islamic practices and festivals. The final event presented here is an election (Chapter 6). While this was the only officially "political" event in village life, the family resemblance to the other events is noticeable. It was eagerly anticipated like the others, the rhythm of the day was much the same as it was for other festival days, women wore the same "best" sari as they did for a religious festival, and it provided a pause from humdrum daily life when people stepped out of a quotidian experience to participate in an event that was clearly special to them. Each election, and there were nine held during the research for this book, brought with it a discourse about the duty of citizens to participate in an exercise that was free and available and without which a democracy could not function. As a result, it also brought with it a reacquaintance with the core democratic ideas of citizenship, equality, and rights during the process of casting one's vote. The final chapter (Chapter 7) provides a common framework to evaluate the values produced in each of these "events" in the life of a village. The discussion of the resolution of the scandal and the elections that followed it will show how political competition was managed during a conflict and the unprecedented political opposition to the Comrade that grew out it. The harvest and sacrifice created imaginaries that went beyond the immediate purpose of these events, to also create and inculcate ideas of cooperative action and accommodation that contributed to understandings of citizenship as a collective identity more generally. In the concluding discussion, the emphasis will be on demonstrating the similarities between the four "events" presented in the book to identify moments that reinforce similar ideals in diverse settings—for example, the solemnity of Eid prayers, division of the grain heap, silence inside the polling booth—that shared similar characteristics and produced similar affect. The chapters will have demonstrated that the values that are produced in social life—cooperation with others to attain a common goal, willingness to renounce selfish interest for collective interest, a commitment to redistribution to those who have less, the ability to suppress difference to create consensus when necessary—are also central to shared and active citizenship. It will thus also be possible to demonstrate the organic relationship between the political and non-political aspects of social life and the potential of the non-political as generative of political values and the affinity of the imaginaries that are created in each event with those required for a democratic republic.

2

Context

The Village in a Democracy

Cultivating Democracy covers the period between 1998 and 2013, during which there were three key stories of change—in Islam, in paddy cultivation, and in politics. In 1998 people were devout Muslims but were relaxed in their practices of Islam; by 2013 a more austere and exacting Deobandi Islam was beginning to threaten these older syncretic forms. In 1998, the state of West Bengal was the highest producer of paddy cultivation, but fifteen years later, relying on agricultural income was no longer economically viable. In 1998, the Left Front, a coalition of communist parties, had been in power for over twenty consecutive years, but by 2013, they had lost the local panchayat elections in a dramatic defeat to the opposition led by Mamata Banerjee's Trinamool Congress, having already lost power in the state assembly two years before, in July 2011. Richard Eaton noted in *The Rise of Islam and the Bengal Frontier, 1204–1760* that "the interaction between the delta's Sanskritic, political, agrarian and Islamic frontiers forms one of the great themes of Bengal's history" (Eaton 1993: xxv). As this book will show, this complex interweaving of Islam, paddy, and politics has remained an important theme right up until the present day in Bengal.

The villages of Madanpur and Chishti were of modest size that could be traversed in under five minutes each to reach the green paddy fields that encircled them. According to the 2001 census, Madanpur had 53 families living in it and Chishti had 108 families and the total population came to just under 900 souls; by 2011, that number had risen to over 1,300. Of these, over three fourths were Muslim, belonging to all four castes of Syed, Shekh, Mughal, and Pathan, and the rest were Hindus from the Dom and Bagdi castes. Over the fifteen years during which this study was conducted, as the villages grew and crossed the 1,000 population mark, they became eligible to have their own polling booth for all elections. Housing in each village was a mix of mud huts with thatched roofs belonging to the lower castes, daily wage laborers, and sharecroppers. The wealthier Syeds had houses made of concrete with two floors. Unlike villages elsewhere in West Bengal and India, there were no caste-based neighborhoods, except for a "Bagdi para" (Bagdi neighbourhood) in Chishti. Houses belonging to all castes stood cheek by jowl with others, and Syed homes stood in between other castes. The use of tanks, or *pukurs*, was also mixed and while everyone had a preference for which one they used for bathing and washing, these were not determined by their caste identity. This may have been the result of the absence of any upper caste Hindu families and while some rules of caste endogamy and shared commensality within the upper caste Syeds was maintained, this exclusion did not extend to residence patterns.

Over the years that I worked in these villages, anyone who was able to afford it replaced their thatch with tin and mud for brick. Building two floors was beyond the reach of most, however, though some successful sharecroppers, like the low caste Hindu man called Okho Dom, had successfully achieved it. Each village had a mosque and Madanpur also had an *imambara*, a structure where the martyrdom of the Imam was marked during the activities during the festival of Muharram. Most economic activity centered around paddy cultivation, brick kiln work, and paid manual labor for sand and hatchery businesses. At the start of the research, Syed households employed lower castes for domestic work of cattle care, popping rice, boiling paddy, fetching water, and so on, and gradually members of other castes who could afford to pay for such work did. Each village had about a half-dozen small grocery stores that sold mostly food and comestibles, and itinerant salesmen with stocks of a variety of items from bangles to buckets came around on cycles regularly and did brisk business. People went to the market in the nearest town of Dubrajpur for everything else. There was also one fixed-price "ration" shop for the government's Public Distribution System for basic cereals and pulses in Chishti to serve both villages, though its offerings could be varied. It was routine for traders to arrive in the village on "ration day" and sit at some distance from the shop. They provided credit to those going to the shop to buy fixed-price grains that they did not want for themselves, which the traders would then "buy" back from the shoppers as they emerged from the shop, to sell at commercial rates in local markets. Each ration-card holder made a small profit in this transaction, thereby incentivizing their willingness to participate in this subterfuge. The villages lay on either side of a smart two-lane highway, funded by the Asian Development Bank in the early 1990s but were linked by kin, a shared primary school, a polling booth, and commercial enterprises. Households across the two villages were linked through marriage and blood, for rules of village exogamy that exist elsewhere in India did not exist here. Therefore, it was common for women to have their natal kin across the highway in the other village and for brothers to be based across the two villages. Older maps showed a smaller road dividing the two villages cleanly, whereas now a small part of Madanpur lay on the Chishti side of the highway. This Madanpur rump was also the site of the large sprawling house of the most prominent local political leader, "Comrade" (both a term of address and a term of reference), who was a member of the Communist Party of India (Marxist), the party which, along with other Left Front allies, had formed the state government of West Bengal since 1977. He had a wife in each village. Over time, I got to know the people who lived there intimately, participated in all their major festivals and harvests, witnessed several elections, and won enough trust to be told some well-kept secrets. While conducting this typical small-scale anthropological research, I was nevertheless mindful of a broader agenda of interests. The initial motivation for my research had been the high voter turnouts in villages such as these and I was keen to understand social life between elections, to grasp the lived experience of politics in the intense and unusual combination of hegemonic, but not totalitarian, communist politics in democratic India. I aimed to capture the social and cultural contours of change and continuity in the wake of the land reforms in the past, the communist leadership of the present, and the political possibilities for the future. What is presented herein is a textured portrait of agrarian life and its capacity for creating democratic life.

This monograph is located within an older tradition of "village studies" that flourished in the twentieth century but have more or less disappeared in the last two or three decades in the anthropology and sociology of India.[1] The reforms to the Indian economy in the 1990s introduced a narrative of economic growth in which the story of agriculture was marginal and villages were portrayed as the sites of subsidies and welfare rather than productive sites for food, commodities, and indeed political ethics. But two-thirds of India's 1.3 billion population continued to live in rural areas and, contrary to trends in older industrialized countries of the West, in India "there is no indication of the rural population declining in absolute numbers" (Jodhka 2012: 17).[2] Instead, the rural and agriculture re-entered the national imagination through a narrative of crisis and farmers' suicides rather than as a subject for sustained academic investigation that might have paid attention to, for instance, the changing dynamics of the "internal inequalities in agrarian India" (Jodhka 2018a: 45). This disappearance of the Indian village from academic work was framed provocatively by one commentator as the physical disappearance of the village itself under the title "Whither the Indian Village?" to point out that diversification of non-agricultural activity and increased mobility had called into question whether the village as a unique identity tied to the land could still be said to exist (Gupta 2005). Older representations of the village as "republics" (Metcalfe), "authentic" (Gandhi), "backward" (Nehru), or "oppressive" (Ambedkar) had all been proven true and false in equal measure, but they needed to be addressed afresh amid the changes brought by technology, state interventions, and the blurring of boundaries between the village and its surroundings and between the rural and urban. This study aims to redress this gap in the anthropology of India.

Some recent studies on West Bengal, in particular, have made the work of writing this monograph much easier and have allowed me to build on and expand on their scholarship. Of these, Dwaipayan Bhattacharya's *Government as*

Practice (2016) provides the most comprehensive account of West Bengal communist politics available. Tracing its origins from immediate post-independence India right up to its electoral rout in 2013, this historical and nuanced analysis proposes the term *party state* to characterize the hegemonic hold of the Left Front government in West Bengal and shows the erosion of credibility of the Communist government after its disastrous flirtation with big capital in Singur and Nandigram in attempting to build industries that caused its downfall. Bhattacharya shows how the governmental left not only did not have an "an effective strategy to deal with the complex demands of capital and of popular politics" (p. 47), its failure to take into account that large-scale dispossession of rural population within the framework of democratic politics could have very severe consequences, as it did. This work has not only been a valuable scholarly reference point, it also allows me the freedom to take the analysis as available for any reader who wishes to know more about the broader trajectory of the Left Front government in West Bengal. Further, Arild Ruud's *Poetics of Village Politics* (2003) is a study of two villages in Bardhaman, a district that is adjacent to Birbhum where my study is set. Ruud's study helps explain the reasons for Left Front dominance of West Bengal's politics and the "emergence and sustenance of rural communism" (Ruud 2003: 23). Using an account kept by a local historian and Ruud's own fieldwork from the time in which he lived in these villages, the study presents the minutiae of village politics and changing alliances and mobilizations, with a firm eye on wider political processes. Like my study, his is also an ethnographic and anthropological account of two nondescript adjacent villages in West Bengal whose residents lived within a broader framework of rural communism. Ruud's study provides a credible analysis of how rural communism came to be constructed in places like his research villages of Udaynala and Gopinathpur, or mine of Madanpur and Chishti. His study is rich in detail of political parties, electoral results, and shifting alliances in the formation of the Left Front and concludes in the late 1990s, at a point where my study begins. In particular, he shows how communist ideology was introduced and interacted in a society that "was already occupied by values, identities and contesting ideas" and the importance of symbolic processes such as poetry in capturing the political imagination of ordinary people (Ruud 2003: 211).

Most scholars of village India have argued that the classic hallmarks of rural life have undergone a radical change in recent years, and essays in the periodic "Review of Rural Affairs" published by *Economic and Political Weekly* chronicle this. A repeat study fifty years later of F. G. Bailey's Bisipara village in Odisha revealed that the village economy was no longer exclusively agricultural but a combination of agricultural and mercantile activities (Otten and Simpson 2016). Conceptually, while the rural remains opposed to the urban, in reality, vast areas of the country are in fact a continuum of agrarian-rural-semi/peri urban-urban-hyper urban, causing what Vasavi calls "the involution of the rural" (2018: 4). Within such a landscape, a village exists firmly within the rural, not as an isolated island but linked to wider networks of politics, commerce, trade, state surveillance, and tax. But "the triangulated structuring and the processes of separation-integration, differentiation, and erosion, place the rural into conditions of subordination and subsumption to the demands of capital, market, and political regimes" (Vasavi 2018: 24). These three processes, Vasavi shows, "make the rural a site of deep contradictions" and create a rural citizenship that is simultaneously threatened, impoverished, surveyed, ignored, and ruptured (Vasavi 2018: 24). If not all, many of these processes are a result of the changing dynamics of the agrarian within the rural, with 70 percent of the rural population in India dependent on agriculture as their primary income and 82 percent of farmers being small and marginal. Agriculture, the mainstay of any minimum definition of the rural to distinguish it from the urban, has become an altogether different occupation from before. Successive legislations on land ownership and credit pathways, the adoption of high-yielding varieties of wheat and rice, the resulting environmental degradation, the neo-liberal agenda of special economic zones created through land dispossession, and the inadequacy of public policy to address farmers' interests have all played their part. Among these, social differentiation has increased to create classes of landowners who use (or do not) hired labor, wage labor in state institutions, daily wage labor in a variety of small to medium industries, landless laborers who work seasonally, migrant labor, owners of small commercial enterprises such as repair and grocery shops, and so on. Across India the particular patterns of labor and capital arrangements vary, but there are trends that are reflected in studies across the country. As Jodhka concludes, "Thus, the agrarian economy is not an autonomous world, nor is its social landscape confined to the village. The agrarian village economy is an integral part of the larger economic process, regionally, nationally, and globally" (Jodhka 2018a).

But among other changes, the consistent organizing principle of village life has remained caste distinction for as long as Indian villages have been studied, and hierarchical caste distinctions have determined rules of social interaction, agricultural work, ownership of land, and marriage practices.[3] Yet anthropologists who have revisited their original rural research sites after a period of time have reported that the past three decades have brought in some significant changes. In north India, in the states of Haryana and Punjab, Surinder Jodhka reported that the "social and political grammar of village life has changed a great deal" through a process of what he calls "dissociation, distancing and autonomy" (Jodhka 2018a: 466). The main driver of this process was the Green Revolution, which forced a number of groups to withdraw from agriculture for the following reasons. There was a new reliance on a migrant labor force who possessed the skills to cultivate new crops, such as paddy, which was promoted through the Green Revolution and ones which the local labor groups did not have. This new migrant labor was casual and contractual and worked on a fixed cash rate basis and were not tied to the village through social ties, residing outside the village (Breman 2018; Chopra 2018). This led to the traditional labor force, dominated by Dalits and other lower castes, having to look for employment outside the village. Further, common lands had also been increasingly brought under cultivation during the Green Revolution to maximize farmed areas, and this led to diminishing space for grazing animals and a consequent dip in livestock ownership. The work that was traditionally available to women and other castes in the maintenance of cattle disappeared, increasing their precarity, and led to even greater dissociation of these groups from the village as they were forced to look for work elsewhere. As a result, during harvests when the demand of labor of all kinds was at its highest, there were few options available within the village and this led to increased mechanization of harvesting. The resulting scenario meant that "Dalits had completely withdrawn from the agrarian economy" and were instead occupied in a diverse range of work in nearby towns and industrial sites (Jodhka 2018a: 462). These new jobs brought with them new wages and a growing consumer culture and, crucially, less ties to the village itself, even when they chose to continue to reside there. What the village meant to them changed, and their choice of living in the village no longer implied "any kind of commitment to, or identification with, the village and its ethos. The social order of caste hierarchy is a thing of the past, and the collective identity of the village is fragmented" (Jodhka 2018a: 463–464). For Dalits and other lower castes for whom the village had been a place of social oppression where they lacked dignity, status, and resources, the distance from it was also an emancipatory process as it brought greater autonomy and a new "sense of individuation." But the precarity of the new employment opportunities and lack of welfare infrastructure also brought with them attendant anxieties evidenced by the growing membership of religious cults in the same areas of Haryana and Punjab. The collective identity of the village itself thus stood weakened with the disappearance of not just "the physical, but also social and emotional commons that are rapidly disappearing from the rural landscape" (Jodhka 2018a: 468). In the eastern state of Odisha, the repeat study of Bisipara revealed similar trends by which the combination of state intervention measures, such as abolition of untouchability and entry for all castes into temples and land reforms, when combined with increased autonomy from the village economy led to reduction in poverty and increase in self-esteem. This resulted in "Many families of the former untouchables [having] actively turned their backs on the local associations of their caste habitus, in favour of acting and imagining themselves as citizens of India" (Otten and Simpson 2016: 31).

The imagination of citizenship was, of course, possible principally through the procedural mechanism of universal adult franchise, which by definition did not discriminate against village dwellers or low caste members. While the right to vote had been legally available to all Indians since 1950, it was the cumulative impact of the repeated practice of voting and the increased institutional efforts to making the right to vote available to each citizen, especially to those from lower castes who were not always "free" to vote because of pressure from the upper castes, that helped constitute the rural citizen as equal to any other. One of Jodhka's respondents said to him: "Every individual began to matter and everyone had a single vote" (2018a: 464). The right to vote created a new politics of recognition for such citizens and went some way in explaining the enthusiastic embrace of electoral participation that was reflected in all India data. The National Election Studies conducted by Lokniti reported that the most socially disenfranchised sections of the population—women and members of tribal and Dalit communities—were its most enthusiastic participants during elections (cited in Yadav 1999). Gooptu calls this a "politics of presence" in which marginalized groups found that voting gave them "a sense of agency and affirmed their citizenship" (Gooptu 2007). Electoral politics, in turn, also changed the authority structure for the powerful whereby the ownership of land and high caste identity were no longer the sole markers of elite status because political power became less reliant on caste status or land and became more fluid and available to a wider group of political entrepreneurs. The increase in the number of players on electoral battlegrounds and regular elections also meant that the players had to work hard to maintain and grow their power and could no longer rely simply on traditional hierarchical and economic structures.

The dynamics of the processes discussed earlier—namely, the Green Revolution, changing labor arrangements, and the impact of the right to vote—manifested themselves in similar and different ways in West Bengal because there, there was also the additional factor of a continuous thirty-four-year tenure of the Left Front government. The alchemy of the ideology and practice of communism and the right to vote had its own particular impact on the social practice of caste. It should also be noted, however, that while caste has dominated discussions of Indian politics elsewhere, in West Bengal it has remained curiously and persistently absent (Chandra, Heierstad, and Nielsen 2016). This remained especially the case during the Left Front years when in fact all social conflict was re-cast in class terms, subsuming all other social cleavages of caste, religion, and gender. Throughout its tenure, the Left Front maintained its Marxist claim that the politics of "class" had managed to displace the "regressive" idea of caste (Bhattacharya 2016: 20). But a look at the leadership of any of the political parties in the Left Front coalition, or indeed of the list of members of the Politburo of the Communist Party of India (Marxist), revealed an overwhelming dominance of upper caste Brahmin and Boddi names. In a recent essay, Partha Chatterjee argued that this dominance is precisely the reason that caste is not explicitly discussed in West Bengal: "Therein lies the mystery of the absence of caste in West Bengal politics: the immensely superior control exercised by the upper castes over the mechanisms of electoral democracy through their dominance of the party system. That dominance is not in any serious danger now" (Chatterjee 2016: 101). In my research site, the villages of Madanpur and Chishti told their own story of caste dynamics as there was an absence of any upper caste Hindu communities and they had all four castes of Muslims as well as a Dom and a Bagdi community. Demographically, therefore, together they represented a significant part of the state's population, for "a majority of the population of the state is either Dalit or Muslim" (Chatterjee 2016: 98). But these are two groups that have never had a seat at the table in any of Bengal's political parties and have instead always formed part of a support base of a political party. Dwaipayan Sen recalls Dr. Nazrul Islam, a senior IPS officer and Additional Director General of the WB Police's statement: "Not only Muslims, not one SC or ST sits on any important post in WB . . . but whenever there is a clash between groups it is always Muslim or SC/ST who get killed. If we can sit together, we can launch a new political party for Muslim along with SC and ST" (Sen 2016: 119). A political party built on such a pact is yet to emerge, but the threat of such an alliance on a wider scale and its potential heft explained some of the machinations of Left Front politics at the village level.

For Madanpur and Chishti, the two key Left Front representatives were the Comrade and the local Pradhan Nathu Dom, who occupied a seat "reserved" for lower castes in accordance with the West Bengal Panchayat Act of 1992. But while a low caste man officially held the post, the real power lay with the Comrade, who was an upper caste Syed Muslim, and he took decisions that the Pradhan was expected to rubber-stamp. The Comrade was drawn from a section of society that Bhattacharya characterizes as "a class of petty capitalists, owners of non-corporate capital . . . local traders of fertilizer and pesticide, agents of ponzi companies, local transporters, suppliers of building materials, owners of brick kiln or rice mills, labourers and ration shop dealers" (Bhattacharya 2016: 40). But even this kind of tokenism of lower caste representation in jobs of Pradhan remained confined only to local levels of government. By comparing caste representation data at the higher levels of Left Front government and those of local bodies, Bhattacharya shows how lower castes were notably absent from any political leadership positions above the village panchayat level. At the state level, the entrenched elites, drawn from among the *bhadralok* [educated upper caste members], continued to dominate (Bhattacharya 2016: 19–21). Bhattacharya's thesis therefore is that while there was a governmentalization of the locality through the panchayats, this did not produce a simultaneous localization of the government.[4] And this was because "the Left in West Bengal pressed its government into the crevices of the social without socializing the government," which is to say the wide social base of a multiplicity of caste and religion was simply not reflected in its leadership that continued to be dominated by upper caste Hindu *bhadralok* (Bhattacharya 2016: 18).

Ruud's essay "From Client to Supporter," in the same path-breaking volume that examined the issue of caste in Bengal, provides a fine-grained overview of changes in his research villages from the late 1950s until the state assembly elections in 2011 (Ruud 2016). He traces the changes from the 1950s and 1960s, when there was a close connection between caste and patronage relations, to the present, during which he reports there have been "tremendous diachronic changes" (Ruud 2016: 196). The two factors he identifies behind these changes, similar to Jodhka's observations for Haryana and Punjab, are "the delegitimization of caste as a pillar of society" (Ruud 2016: 195) and "the introduction of adult franchise" as a result of which "the ideals of equality have become central to the political relation-building" (Ruud 2016: 196). He reports that, owing to a considerable reduction in the gap between rich and poor and the changed socio-economic conditions, this has led to a reduction on clientelist dependencies on upper castes. The factors behind this change were "advantages of the CPI(M) raj, including sharecropper rights and higher wages, and massively increased irrigation on lands they owned or sharecropped" (Ruud 2016: 211). Additionally, again in similar trends to the rest of India, greater access to education, travel beyond the village, and a more diverse range of employment options beyond agriculture had weakened land-based wealth of elites and they were no longer able to control patronage as they did before. "Process of reduction of landholding has been even and uninterrupted" from 1977 onward (Ruud 2016: 201–202). While inter-caste marriages still did not happen, social intermingling between castes was much higher. "These developments have undermined the clientelist relationships of agricultural society and weakened caste as a social indicator and as a practice" (Ruud 2016: 194). It is a great advantage to be able to compare my findings with Ruud's to build a picture of rural communism and its fate from 1998 onward as this study is able to present the legacy of rural communism, the fate of paddy cultivation, and the changing electoral landscape until 2013.

The dominance of upper caste leadership in West Bengal politics has continued to be reflected in the newer Trinamool Congress that replaced the Left Front, and yet few would suggest that political parties in West Bengal have represented only upper caste interests. The reason for this is that communist politics led to a reimagining of dignity of work and labor of the lower castes which, when combined with the changes brought by the Green Revolution and electoral politics as elsewhere in India, generated some long-term changes in the social practice of caste. The editors of the volume mentioned above summarize this process thus:

> The stark inequalities and agrarian impasse that had characterised rural West Bengal for a very long time gave way, from the 1970s to pro-poor land reforms and a period of sustained and high agricultural growth, living standards improved considerably and later, many rural Bengalis—almost from across the caste spectrum—have successfully diversified out of agriculture and now derive their livelihoods from a variety of sources. As a result, the very hierarchical land-based patronage relations of old between upper-caste landlords and lower-caste dependents have crumbled. Today, the core of patron-client relationships is neither caste, *jati* nor labour, but rather "politics"—that is, the distribution of protection and access to state resources and programmes, mediated by political parties. In this radically changed economic and political context, the socio-political salience of caste identities is both transformed and increasingly withering away. (Chandra et al. 2016: 14)

Ruud's recent portrayal of the dynamics of rural West Bengal marks a significant shift away from earlier descriptions from the 1960s of "factions" based on vertical ties between leaders and followers. In such accounts, Ralph Nicholas's for instance, "political activity" in these villages was "organized conflict over public power." By implication, "the question of the broader goals of political activity . . . which we would call political ideology or political values, is left unconsidered" (Spencer 2007: 37). Thus, the realm of the political was narrowly defined as a contest for instrumental power, leaving little room for a more expansive understanding of "the political" as containing within it the capacity for both agonistic and reparative politics, as would be more empirically accurate to do. As a result, as Spencer points out, such studies reported factional politics as some sort of "trans-historical essence" of Indian village politics and completely failed to account for the "horizontal solidarities which can be found behind alleged factional alignments" (Spencer 2007: 36, 37). Drawing on the historian David Hardiman's work on colonial Gujarat, Spencer illustrates the need for attention to such horizontal solidarities because of the "little effect the control of patronage had on political action" which was based instead on factors that went beyond caste or class to create much broader-based mass political groups. As a consequence, political action in the twenty-first century, as in the colonial period, needs to be explained as a much more complex process than factions based on vertical hierarchies formed around an upper caste leader; as we have seen, the empirical reality is a complicated interweaving of upper caste–dominated electoral politics in which access to political power, rather than caste status, dominates all other earlier sources of power even while the social practices of caste "wither away."

Paddy and Politics

At the turn of the century, the dominant occupation for both villages was paddy cultivation in the fields surrounding the villages. Traditionally, land belonging to the two villages was owned by the Syeds, and the remaining Muslim castes of Shekhs, Pathans, and Mughals, along with the Hindu Doms and Bagdis, provided the labor.[5] In Madanpur and Chishti, the land reforms of the 1980s had been very rigorously imposed and had led to a dramatic redistribution in class and caste dynamics. This had in turn had a palpable influence not only on cultivation but also on local politics, caste dynamics, changing value structures, and the nature of everyday life. But as agriculture and, in particular, paddy cultivation became less and less economically viable, people had turned to other activities. The "sand" business was the most lucrative, as was the clandestine cultivation of poppy (the seeds were used in cooking) and the sale of pilfered coal from faraway mines. Pilfered coal was transported by young men who cycled under cover of darkness with the heavy bags to avoid detection, and one such load fetched Rs. 400. During the same period, one quintal of paddy fetched Rs. 600 to Rs. 700 (half the profits from some years ago), thereby making the risk and labor of one night's work attractive when compared to several months of agricultural work to produce paddy. As a result, despite the illegality of trade in sand, pilfered coal, and poppy, in some years, these had come to dominate the already precarious economic existence of these two villages.[6]

In light of diminishing returns and small landholdings, the Syed landowners of Madanpur and Chishti decided to forego the taboo against manual agricultural work and took a collective decision to invent a small ritual to mark this transgression. They had gone down to the riverbed behind Madanpur in a solemn procession with their bullocks and ploughs and recited a collective *namaz* (prayer) before ploughing the riverbed as the first earth that Syeds would ever turn. Ever since, Syed men of these two villages had begun to perform agricultural labor in their own fields, ending a proscription that had been maintained for generations of Syeds. The ritual described here had been performed some years before I started my research, so in the present, it was normal for Syed men to work on the fields themselves, totally involved in all the manual work and the hard grind that it took. Given the rising cost of labor, Syed landowners also drafted any available sons to help, but only as a last resort. As far as possible, Syeds continued to aspire for education and white-collar work, maintaining a distance from manual labor and so most of the young Syed men who worked on family land during my research were those who had tried and failed to get such jobs. The most coveted of all jobs was to be a schoolteacher, as the Left Front had raised their salaries considerably and it was enough to sustain a family. The money was good, but even more coveted was the guaranteed income, unlike earnings from agriculture. Profits from small landholdings, especially as paddy cultivation in Bengal was subject to the vagaries of the monsoon, fuel, fertilizer, and market procurement prices, were notoriously small and unreliable. A salaried income, in contrast, was a valuable insurance. Further, regular school holidays meant guaranteed rest, which again for any farming community was a rare luxury because a farmer did not get a holiday from cultivation for any reason, and not even a wedding or festival allowed him to not inspect the crops or tend to its needs. Even one day's neglect could lead to catastrophic consequences, as disease could spread quickly, water channels could get blocked, animals could stray, and so on. Thus, even among the Syeds themselves, a subtle hierarchy had emerged between those who had jobs (*chakri*) and those who did not. While most of the jobs were those of schoolteachers, any job that was a "government job" (*shorkari chakri*) was considered to be the best. So, for instance, two Syed men had jobs in the Public Works Department (PWD) and another was a "compounder" in a primary health center—and these were equally good for the money and security they brought. But given the high status that education had in Bengal generally, a schoolteacher's job also brought with it a status that no other *chakri* could bring. Such a job also allowed the Syed to attend to farming matters before and after his official working hours, and most of them continued to own and cultivate land. The ones who worked for the PWD simply did what many in that department across the country did, which was to report for work and then abscond for the rest of the day to engage in other sources of income to supplement their salaries. The remaining Syeds tried to supplement their agricultural income with petty and medium businesses. Across Madanpur and Chishti, there were at least a dozen convenience stores that sold everything from cooking oil to fresh vegetables, and each of them was owned by Syeds. They were able to do this mainly because they had some sort of *pucca* structures for their homes and could afford to give up some space, usually a room adjacent to a public path or open area, to turn into a shop, and one that could be made secure against the elements. The low levels of disposable income of their customers meant that most of the sales were made on credit and debts were settled only at the end of the financial year. The Syeds therefore had to have enough capital to keep going for the year and the shops, more than anything else, gave them something to do during the day when even agricultural work had to stop in the midday sun and allowed them to stay connected with a wide network of people through daily interaction and obligation. Other Syeds had ventured into the business of making and selling bricks, and in Madanpur where the river bed provided a source of sand, there was always one kiln on the go, either being built or being baked; these were variously owned by younger sons of the Syeds. In 2012 two new shops were opened in Madanpur—a tailoring shop and a "computer" shop—by the side of the highway, powered by electricity drawn from the wire on the main road. Thus, Syed families tried to maintain a diverse portfolio combining agriculture, a job, and a business to ensure a healthy and guaranteed income. But amid all these new initiatives one final bastion guarded their caste identity: their women were not allowed to work for wages. Daily wage labor by Syed women and also men was unthinkable, and even work on their own fields by Syed women was still considered taboo. But some of them often helped out in the small grocery stores that their husbands and fathers ran. The shops could be accessed from within the house and their dimly lit interiors provided enough privacy (purdah); their children were often drafted in to help with stock taking, delivering bills, and keeping accounts. Shekh, Pathan, and Mughal families, on the other hand, worked as agricultural workers, brick kiln laborers (where even children contributed their labor), as domestic servants in Syed households, as animal carers for the livestock owned by the Syeds, as fisherman in the numerous tanks across the villages, or, more rarely, as political workers. But as with other social dynamics of caste, these too changed over the years. In 2011, one of the first measures of the Trinamool government was to ensure that the interior of villages was electrified. This led to simple creature comforts such as electric fans in the heat of summer which in turn dissuaded people from working in the fields. Anyone who could, and this included many Shekh and Pathan families, looked to lease their cropping arrangements to others to avoid having to do agricultural work.

The dynamics of paddy cultivation were therefore constantly shifting, as were those of politics. The left's radical reformist agenda of the early years gave way to the sole objective of winning elections, and it became the "political work" of millions of Comrades to deliver victory in elections by using state benefits that government brought as inducements to build their political capital through social networks. At the same time, they also cynically "used the party as an instrument for private gains, and exploited its vast network for advancing personal interests. . . . They supplied the cogs and wheels in the CPIM(m)'s legendary election machine" (Banerjee 2010; Bhattacharya 2016: 41; Chatterjee 2016). This "strategy of clientelism," using public goods for a politically targeted population while personal enrichment of the Comrade, accounted for the Left Front's continued electoral dominance for three decades, but this was ultimately also the reason for their undoing (Bardhan et al. 2012: 4). In a survey conducted by the same economists after the Left Front's defeat in 2011, the results showed that voters had gotten increasingly disillusioned with local leaders for their excessive interference in village matters and their own record of corruption.

The growing disillusionment at the local level was of course compounded by developments at the state level in 2008 when the Left Front government, in a desperate bid to address the need for industry and job opportunities in the state, forcibly dispossessed agricultural workers of land in Nandigram and Singur. This was in keeping with a wider national trend of the aggressive entry of commercial interests into agrarian land markets through such devices as Special Economic

Zones and development corridors, exemptions, and licenses, as studies show (Cross 2014; Levien 2018). In each of the cases studied, the state and the government in power often emerged as the key broker that acquired land forcibly in the service of commercial interests. It was exactly so in West Bengal. But here, the betrayal by the State was far greater, led as it was by communist parties whose main electoral base were the same agricultural workers who they now sought to dispossess. Thus, political opponents of the Left Front wasted no time in utilizing this opportunity to mount a robust protest against this naked betrayal of trust. As Kenneth Bo Nielsen's (2016) account shows in some detail, Mamata Banerjee's Trinamool Congress rose to prominence as a result, maintaining pressure until Tata Motors was forced to withdraw from completing the car plant on the forcibly acquired land and had to move its operations elsewhere. Mamata's Trinamool Congress won the next elections in 2011 and the electoral rout of the Left Front government after thirty-four long years was a combination of agitation politics, weak leadership in government, and a complete misjudgment of the public mood. The rise of Trinamool in the West Bengal imagination, and the national one, demonstrated how the politics of social movements, protest, and mobilization interacted with electoral politics. While the Singur and Nandigram agitations may have precipitated events and proven beyond doubt that the Left Front government was no longer a champion of the rural poor, the electoral reversal of 2011 was possible because a nascent political opposition to the Left Front had been quietly cultivated even during the years of the hegemonic party state. The switch in the public mood reflected in the electoral result was possible because the roots of this opposition had already dug deep.

Islam

The Syeds of modern-day Madanpur and Chishti claimed descent from a holyman (*pir*) from Iran, and counted themselves as the elite *ashraf* classes, a category that "included those Muslims claiming descent from immigrants beyond the Khyber—or at least from beyond Bengal—who cultivated high Perso-Islamic civilization and its associated literatures in Arabic, Persian and Urdu" (Eaton 2000: 249). As a nod to their foreign origins they still, rather uniquely in Bengal, continued to speak Urdu among themselves. In addition, historically, what had served to distinguish *ashraf* identity alongside their foreign origins and cultivation of high Perso-Islamic civilization was their refusal to engage in agricultural operations. Whereas local Bengali paddy farmers defined their Muslim identity around cultivating the soil, the *ashraf* maintained a disdain for the plow, which they refused to touch. This continued into the twentieth century, and a 1901 survey among the Muslims of the Nadia district in Bengal found that "the

Ashraf will not adopt cultivation for their living. They consider cultivation to be a degraded occupation and shun it for that reason" (Eaton 1993: 311). And in the Census of the same year, H. H. Risley recorded that "like the higher Hindu castes, the Ashraf consider it degrading to accept menial service or to handle the plough" (Eaton: 311). This *ashraf* disdain for the plow and manual work continued into independent India and defined the Syeds of Madanpur and Chishti until the land reforms in the 1980s. This disdain was also, according to Eaton, an important defining feature in the spread of Islam in Bengal, for while Muslim regimes had ruled over Bengal since the early thirteenth century, Islam itself had not spread in the region because the ruling classes, the meat- and wheat-eating *ashraf*—administrators, soldiers, scholars, or merchants from Western India— held the local effete, fish- and rice-eating Bengalis, in disdain and kept their distance from the local population. Eaton points out that "in the period between 1342 and 1574, under the rule of a succession of Muslim dynasties, Bengal became isolated from north India, and immigration from points west was largely curtailed. . . . For them, a rich tradition of Persian art and literature served to mediate and inform Islamic piety, which most of them subordinated to the secular ethos of Mughal imperialism. In particular, the ashraf classes refused to engage in agricultural operations and some Mughal officers even opposed the Islamization of native Bengalis who did" (Eaton 2001: 249). Consequently, even though the Bengal delta was ruled by Muslim kingdoms, the spread of the religion of Islam was limited. This changed dramatically in the late sixteenth century when "a noticeable community of Muslim cultivators" emerged and cleared forests to bring new land in the delta under the plow for paddy cultivation (Eaton 2001: 259). By the seventeenth and eighteenth centuries, therefore, owing principally to phenomenal levels of agrarian and demographic expansion in East Bengal, the dominant carriers of Islamic civilization in the delta were no longer the aloof urban *ashraf* but peasant cultivators of the eastern frontier, who took on the task of proselytizing their religion. Eaton's thesis demonstrates, therefore, that the spread of paddy cultivation was germane to the spread of Islam as a popular religion in the Bengal region. But the growing number of Muslims also created greater pressure on the elites to maintain their distinction, and we have seen how the Syeds in present-day Madanpur and Chishti achieved this through a variety of practices. Although they never self-identified as *ashraf* per se, they nevertheless attributed their ancestry to Iran, and establishing the details of this story was one of my early fieldwork challenges.

It was evident within the first few weeks of research in Chishti and Madanpur that the Syeds seem to have very strong bonds with a village called Tilaboni, in the neighboring district of Bardhaman. Most Syed families had relatives there, daughters had been given or taken in marriage, and people frequently went on visits to attend weddings and funerals. These visits were usually heralded and concluded with eloquent paeans of praise for Tilaboni; I was told repeatedly that the houses there had two stories, people had jobs (*chakri*), and coal was delivered free to each home. Their accounts seemed effusive considering that the Syeds of Madanpur and Chishti were reasonably comfortable compared to the other castes in the village as most had pucca houses, some of which even had two stories, they had enough to eat, and their children were beginning to go on to local colleges. Many of them, especially in Chishti, had jobs which brought in regular salaries, and the remaining Syeds had petty businesses and/or some land that allowed them enough income to host celebrations and feasts at weddings and festivals. But their houses were rarely properly finished and had exposed brickwork; the interiors were sparsely furnished with very little furniture, usually simple beds and a plastic chair or two. Rooms were not assigned as private and public spaces as such; "bedrooms" were where the family happened to sleep at night, and the main focus of the house tended to be one room which had a ceiling fan, where meals were taken sitting on the floor, and where the family watched television if they owned one. Daily rhythms of family life rarely allowed for everyone to congregate at once, but when they did it was in such a room. The rest of the rooms in these houses seemed to be mostly used for storing grain, agricultural implements, fodder for cattle, cycles, trunks, mattresses, and general paraphernalia. Some, but not all, had one outdoor flush toilet for the whole family but water had to be pumped from the nearest tube well and stored in containers as there was no piped water in the village. Tilaboni, in comparison, was Eldorado. There people had time to have leisurely baths in proper bathrooms, cook in properly equipped kitchens with gas cylinders, and watch television sitting on sofas with cushions while sipping cold drinks stored in refrigerators. There, I was told, people had proper houses, the daily business of living was not a grind, and there was time for leisure and comfort. The reason for this prosperity was coal that had been discovered in the area, and people were given land-losers jobs in the colliery when the colliery was established on their land. The financial reward of the compensation and the secure jobs that ensued put all inhabitants of Tilaboni, the ex-owners of land at least, in an altogether better position than their poor relatives in the neighboring district of Birbhum, who toiled in their paddy fields and could only admire them from a distance.

I would have left the story of this prosperous village at that if my ethnographer's curiosity had not been roused by the intermarrying of people of two villages so far apart. The distance from Madanpur and Chishti to Tilaboni was about 120 km (about 75 miles) and involved a change of two buses, a journey that took several hours. It seemed odd, therefore, that people continued to perpetuate such close kin links with one particular place that was at such a physical distance. The opportunity to visit Tilaboni came unexpectedly one day during Ramzan when we received news of the death of an elderly relative in Tilaboni. An elderly woman,

Manohara, who usually did not much stir out of the village, was strangely resolved to attend the funeral which was to be held within a few hours, as was normal Islamic practice. The deceased was her father's sister Rabia. Given how little time she had to make the journey and in deference to her age and in return for her warm hospitality when I was new to the village, I offered to take her in my car. The vehicle was soon filled with all manner of relatives who all expressed a sudden desire to pay their last respects to the dead, and we set off for Tilaboni with about a dozen people.

Tilaboni indeed had an air of prosperity about it. A lot of houses had their own wells, the Syed houses all were over two floors, and though notionally a village it looked nothing like Madanpur and Chishti. The main road was paved, the houses were finished with plaster and paint, and some even had gardens. Every house I visited had furniture that people seemed familiar with using; tables, chairs, and sofas were everywhere, and all the Syeds, at least, looked very comfortable indeed. After offering my condolences, I watched the mortuary rituals while the body of the deceased was washed and wrapped in a shroud. The burial itself took place in an area at one end of the village among other gravestones. It was clearly not the village's main cemetery, for the tombstones were sparsely spread out and the deceased seemed to be one of very few women to be buried there. This struck me as odd, but it was not the right moment to ask questions so I simply watched the burial from a distance and was grateful that I had been allowed to watch the proceedings, as women rarely, if at all, do. I spent the rest of the day visiting the relatives of people from Madanpur and Chishti, anxious not to omit anyone for fear of recrimination on my return. On one such visit, someone casually asked me if I had visited the "dargah" in Tilaboni yet. I had not heard a shrine mentioned before and so quickly leapt to my feet to make the visit, my eagerness meeting with their approval. As I walked to it, accompanied by others, I learned that it was the shrine of Kamaal Baba from whom the Syeds claimed descent and the significance of Tilaboni dawned on me as the site of the shrine of the ancestor of the Syeds. Kamaal Baba was well known in the area, and an annual fair was held and happened to be in progress at the time of our visit. The enthusiasm of the mourners climbing into my car now became clearer. The funeral had provided them with the perfect pretext to avail of a free ride in a private car to Tilaboni and they were all planning to stay on a few days afterward to enjoy the fair. The shrine itself was in the middle of the village and was an elaborate structure surrounded by railings to which pilgrims had tied charms and threads as they made wishes. They fluttered weakly in the warm breeze as several holy men (*fakirs*) from different parts of the country sat enjoying the shade and chatted among themselves as others dozed. It was a peaceful spot, and as I went in, the fakirs engaged me in conversation as I covered my head in preparation to visit the shrine, telling me stories about the saint who was buried there. I heard stories of the miracles performed by Kamaal Baba and of his final days on earth. In a trope familiar across the Islamic world, anticipating his own death, Kamaal Baba had sat down in final meditation in a walled-up space, requesting a single cup of milk to be placed in a small gap in the bricks once a day. Every day the empty cup was returned through the small opening by the saint, but one day the cup of milk remained untouched and people knew that the saint had left his mortal body; the gap was walled up and the shrine was built around it. The quiet of the afternoon and the wise and welcoming smiles of the fakirs made the story a powerful one, but it was still unclear why the descendants of this saint buried in Tilaboni had come to live in Madanpur and Chishti, a hundred miles away.

My persistent questions made my friends take me to a wizened old woman with bright green eyes draped in a black sari who they promised would have answers. And Shamma Bibi did indeed throw light on the subject. It turned out that the woman we had buried that morning was the great-granddaughter of Kamaal Baba's great-grandson.[7] According to custom and in deference to her lineage, she had been buried alongside Kamaal Baba's other direct descendants in the special cemetery reserved for them where I had watched the proceedings. She had died on the twenty-sixth day of Ramzan, which was considered an auspicious day, and was buried after 1:00 p.m. that afternoon, making it the twenty-seventh day of Ramzan, which made it even more auspicious. Thus, Rabia was six generations removed from their original ancestor and given that her great-great-grandchildren had been born, my friends in the village were only eight or nine generations removed from Kamaal Baba. So it was likely that Kamaaluddin had come to visit Bengal over two centuries ago, from Kirman in Iran where he left behind a wife who was also his first cousin, who could not give him children.[8] In India, it was believed, he had traveled across the northern Gangetic plain and used to labor by day but meditate by night. The story went that in Bengal, the Raja of Burdhwan was impressed with his powers and gave him some land which he could cultivate to make a living and invited him to travel around the region. He came across a Hindu village in Mira forest where there had been a cholera epidemic which he felt he could cure. So the people there invited him to stay and he sat in meditation (*chilla*) for forty days and the epidemic ended. He married a local woman and had one son. While this is a story that has been passed down for generations, it is possible that Kamaal Baba was among those who arrived from Iran as part of the second wave of Muslim settlers in Bengal after the Mughal conquest of 1574 and confirms Eaton's thesis about the spread of Islam through forest clearance and proselytizing by small Muslim cultivators. Kamaal Baba did not appear to have belonged to the original urban *ashraf* classes, but his origins in Iran provided sufficient reason for his descendants to acquire the elite status of Syeds and the gene for green eyes that expressed itself in some served as a reminder of their Persian ancestry .

By the time we traveled back from Tilaboni to Madanpur late that evening, the links between my Syed friends in these two villages and Kamaal Baba were now clearly etched in the genealogies I had drawn with Shamma Bibi's help. But the questions about why the links existed with such far-off villages remained, and the answers to those emerged over the next few years, again through pure serendipity rather than through precise accounts. What I learned was that Kamaal Baba had four brothers who either accompanied him or joined him later, and it was their lives that provided the link between distant Tilaboni and my fieldsite. For instance, one of Kamaal Baba's brothers, Shah Pahadi, had found his way to our very own village of Chishti during his travels and he had died there. When I asked to be shown to the grave, friends pointed to an unusual clearing among a cluster of huts to indicate it, a spot I had passed by several times, unaware of its importance until the chance visit to Tilaboni had triggered a whole new line of inquiry. His grave was yet unmarked, and a shrine would be built only if someone "had a dream" instructing him to do so. While they collectively waited for this dream, the space itself was considered to be sacrosanct and left clear, and I was told that those who had tried to build over it or desecrate it had suffered the consequences. Once, a young boy was said to have bled from his nose for three days after he tried to nail a tethering peg on the ground. Further questioning about Kamaal Baba's other brothers revealed that they too were buried close by: Syed Shah Pahad was also buried in Chishti, Fazle Rahman's grave was in Madanpur, and Syed Shah Sultan in Turulia which was about a kilometer (just over a half-mile) away and the fourth Syed Shah Abdullah Kirmani in Kushtigiri, also nearby. The bonds between Tilaboni and Chishti had been furthered when a grandson of Kamaal Baba called Amir Ali had married a woman named Shamma Bibi from Chishti and from then on such alliances had continued into the present.[9] The area around Chishti must therefore have been something of a magnet for holy men, for I learned that there were two other graves of notable *pirs* in the village itself: Dorbesh at the end of the main village lane, right on the edge of the fields, and Pather Tola, whose grave also lay close by. Once the discussions got going, it was evident that these saints were well known among most people in the village and their stories were told to children. Each saint seemed to have their own characteristics, in the ways in which they made their presence felt. So, for example, Shah Pahadi was known for giving people a scare, Dorbesh for saving them from disasters, and Pather Tola showed himself as a snake from time to time. These saints, collectively known as the "kirmanis" or "the people from Kirman," from where Kamaal Baba, the ancestor of the Syeds, came, were known locally as Sufis in places under Ilambazar, the nearby center of Islamic learning.

Needless to say, this aspect of Madanpur and Chishti was unknown to me when I had chosen them from the random sample sites for the NES survey; at that stage their generic Muslim identity and the ensuing marginality but robust electoral participation were the main reasons. But, as we shall see, the fate of the Syeds, their elite status and its loss resulting from the communist-led land reforms, came to have a pivotal effect on the life and politics of the village. The remaining three castes—Shekhs, Mughals, and Pathans—were always named in that order to indicate a hierarchy among them. It was evident that the Shekhs were considered to be placed higher than the others as their women could marry into Syed households. Though no Syed would agree that this was desirable, it was possible and increased in frequency. But intermarriage between Syeds and the bottom two castes was still unthinkable. It was held by local historians that the members of the Pathan caste in villages like Madanpur and Chishti were descendants of the soldiers and henchmen for the *rajas*. These rajas were Muslim landowners in the fourteenth and fifteenth centuries, such as in Rajnagar, within which Madanpur and Chishti would have been included. Indeed, in nearby Hetampur (about 2 kilometers, or approximately1.25 miles, away from the villages) lay fairly intact ruins of a palace of the Raja of Hetampur, and in Bolpur, the closest railhead town, there existed a house called Mughal badi, which most probably belonged to soldiers associated with Raja Mansingh's army. It was believed that most Muslims in Birbhum were converts from Buddhism.[10] The primary cleavage between the Syeds and the rest in the present thereby rested on the former's ownership of land and their descent from an original Muslim from Persia rather than the result of conversion. They were thus considered to be more authentically Muslim than the rest and this social distinction was maintained in several ways.

As noted before, the use of Urdu as a private language and fairly strict endogamy were critical boundary markers. Further, using the cousin-preference marriage rule, Syeds married their children to those of their siblings, thereby creating a dense web of kin networks across villages. Alongside these rules regarding kinship and language there were also specific Islamic ones, such as particular ablutions that only Syeds were associated with, such as washing with water during every toilet trip. Or being so strict about rules of "nothing ingested" during the thirty-day dawn-to-dusk Ramzan fast that even saliva was spat out at periodic intervals. These visible and less visible practices for many Syed women, in particular, was the bedrock of their ritually superior status and on which distance was maintained with other Muslim castes. This boundary maintenance was, of course, especially significant in a small rural community where there was constant interaction across castes. Syeds employed a number of workers from other castes to help with a variety of household tasks. Children of the lower castes were contracted to look after cattle and livestock through what were called *mahinder* arrangements. They also helped run errands between houses or buy provisions from the village stores or carry light loads from the fields to the homes. Women helped husk and clean grain, wash clothes, prepare fodder, prepare puffed rice (*mudi*)—some of these were specialist tasks, and different labor arrangements were made for them. But these arrangements meant that there was constant mixed-caste traffic in and out of Syed homes. While eating meals in Syed homes never happened, laborers were often offered cups of tea, and the "two-cup" system that had pretty much disappeared in other parts of India was still in practice here. This meant that a separate set of crockery was used for "non-Syed outsiders" from those that were used for domestic and Syed persons; I was myself the recipient of these in some strictly religious homes. Although my upper caste Hindu Brahmin status was established very quickly, as a non-Syed I was assimilated among all other lower Muslim and non-Muslim castes and was served in crockery reserved for "non-Syeds." As with such hierarchical arrangements, the flow of water and cooked food within the village was always in one direction, and Syeds never accepted any of these from non-Syeds. These rules were, however, much more relaxed in more public settings such as tea stalls and nearby towns where men and young people ate and drank freely. Thus, up until recently the Syeds might have resembled the "dominant" caste of Indian villages, displaying all the characteristics of intra-group rivalry and patronage links with remaining castes, until the government of the Left Front and its modes of "government as practice" established the Party as the sole dominant force in the village (Bhattacharya 2016). Caste, of course, continued to play a role, but its dominance itself was challenged quite substantially by ideas of communism.

There was another added layer of complexity to the Muslims of Madanpur and Chishti, and this was about their particular brand of Islam. At the start of my fieldwork, I had been struck by the *imambara* in Madanpur village that was the focus of the festival of Muharram and had asked if the villages were Shia. People had looked at me with baffled expressions, and it was evident that while they knew what the terms "Shia" and "Sunni" indicated, these had little relevance to them. Over time, it transpired that Madanpur and Chishti were part of a cluster of neighboring villages—Rengna, Shimuldi, Turulia, and Mohammedpur—that all lay within a two-mile radius and with whom they shared Muharram observances. Toward the end of my research period, people had begun to explain to me that they were tied together by their membership in the Barelvi School of Islam. The *tazia* (float) procession, a final stage of the festival of Muharram, passed through each of these villages and each added their own tazias to it until they all congregated together in a clearing in front of the *imambara* in Madanpur. Here the crescendo of the festival, the Game of Sticks (*lathi khela*) between teams made up of young men from each of the six villages, took place.

But during the course of my research, Rengna and then Turulia dropped out of this network, and the explanation offered was that they had now changed over to Deobandi Islam. While the Deoband School was also part of the Hanifi School in Islam like the Barelvis, there were some significant differences between them that my informants described to me. Most of these revolved around the emphasis placed on the importance of the Caliphs. While they all celebrated Milad ul Nabi, the Prophet's birthday, the Barlevis believed that the Quran was received through the Prophet and therefore praised him while also remembering the martyrdom of the *char yaar*, or the Caliphs.[11] The Deobandis, on the other hand, my respondents said, placed greater importance on the supreme authority of Allah and did not believe in joining processions. This difference was also manifested in numerous daily practices. For instance, they explained, Deobandis didn't observe the practice of *key am*, in which everyone in a congregation stood up as a sign of respect for the Prophet. Nor did they symbolically offer sweets in the name of the Prophet at celebrations before distributing them to the community. Further, Barelvis took about ten to fifteen minutes to say their prayers, as they believed in prophets and offered prayers in the name of the dead, whereas the Deobandis took only about four minutes. They had also seen Deobandis shake their arms during the *salat* before placing them by their sides. The reason for this gesture, I was told, went back to the time of the Prophet when new converts (from other idolatrous religions) had to prove their complete commitment to the new faith and show that they were not hiding any idols under their arms or their tongues. It is for this reason they also said *Amin* very loudly at the end of the prayer opening their mouths wide. In their strict adherence to Allah and no one else, they did not believe in *pirs* and *mazhars* (saints and their shrines) and believed these to be *haram*, or taboo. These and other differences between the Deobandis and the Barelvis, I was told, led to the people of Rengna withdrawing from participating in the *tazia* procession of Muharram in 2002, saying they were now Deobandi and they found it distasteful to join a procession.[12]

In this tiny corner of West Bengal in India, global shifts in hierarchical membership of Islam have played out their story. The growing awareness and proximity of Deobandi Islam, which also purported to be superior and based on greater education and understanding, created a sense of shame and embarrassment among others, as with my friends in Madanpur and Chishti. These were, after all, villages where the graves of men who had traveled from Persia lay, where shrines could only be built after receiving a message through a dream and where stories of saints were told to children and Barelvi practices were still conducted. Initially, the daughter of a man in Chishti who had become Deobandi told me, he was socially ostracized for this and "treated like a dog" and could only re-establish his credentials when he had a dream and accurately foretold his brother's death. But as Deobandi Islam gathered new members, its status also rose, and they began to dissociate themselves from Madanpur and Chishti. To compound the growing Islamic schisms, there were also two important administrative factors that deepened the divide between these contiguous villages. Until the 2001 elections, the polling station for voters in Rengna, Madanpur, and Chishti used to be located in Rengna. This forced a mingling of people from these villages in a non-religious context too. But from the 2006 elections onward, Madanpur and Chishti between them had over 1,000 voters and so were given their own polling booth. As a result, this enforced link between the villages also disappeared, accentuating their already growing distance on religious matters.

These developments, in this particular corner of India, were symptomatic of a much wider tension that has existed in South Asian Islam for the last hundred years or so. The Deobandi movement originated in a center of learning in a place called Deoband in northern India in 1866 (Metcalf 1982). This was a sort of puritanical revivalist movement within Sunni Islam that sought to propagate the essence of Islam against the corrupting influences of British colonialism and the accompanying English-language education. Like other revivalist movements, they proposed the stripping of religion of all non-doctrinaire beliefs, such as the belief in saints and their *barkat* (blessings), mystical elements, and Sufi poetry and music. But given that these beliefs were in many ways the characteristics of South Asian Islam and made it distinct from its Arab counterparts, the Barelvi School was established to retain them. For this reason, the hardline Deobandis despised the Barelvis and all Shia sects of Islam that were associated with mystical Islam. In my fieldsite, the tension caused by Rengna switching to Deobandi Islam, in contrast to the more common Barelvi beliefs of Madanpur and Chishti, was therefore at least a hundred-year-old phenomenon in the Indian subcontinent. It is possible that the identification of groups under these different Islamic schools was a post facto mechanism to match their existing religious practices with the labels that matched them most closely. Kamaal Baba may not have identified himself as Barelvi, but his latter-day descendants thought it best to define their particular practice of Islam in commonly used categories. In the present, the rivalry had been further exacerbated, however, by the imbalance of influence of Deobandis who had set up seminaries across India, providing education and jobs to many and providing students with free board and lodging and several years of education after which they could leave with reasonable prospects, as clerics and teachers. In a political context in which Muslims had been routinely neglected by the state and fell way below the national average on all social indicators, such opportunities were golden (Sachar Report 2002). On every visit that I made for research I heard of another young boy or two who had been sent away to these seminaries, sometimes located at a considerable distance. The families rarely got to see them during these years but lived with the relief of having secured the future of at least one son. I had the experience of meeting one such young man when he returned for Eid one year. He belonged to a Shekh family

I knew well and at whose home I had spent many hours chatting, sharing meals, and helping with cattle. I noticed him immediately, simply by the whiteness of his clothes, the slightly hitched up trousers, and the covered head. While I greeted him with a smile as I hugged his mother, his gaze remained stern. He asked his mother who I was, whether I was Muslim, and what my caste was. He then told me in no uncertain terms that it was not suitable for a woman to be gadding about on her own. He clearly disapproved of his family's easy familiarity with me and left soon after, saying it was time for his prayers. Such reserve from one of their own was deeply embarrassing for his family, but it was also evident that they were torn between their love and pride in their son becoming a "real Muslim" and their confusion at his open disapproval of me. For me, this was an encounter that confirmed what I knew of the growing influence of a new and more austere Islam in south Asia—one that was at stark variance with more moderate attitudes of subcontinental Islam that I was familiar with in the 1980s and 1990s in India and Pakistan. The new ways of being Muslim required a greater fluency in Arabic, more pronounced demonstration of individual piety among men (exemplified by beards and exposed ankles), and the corresponding covering up of the female form with all-enveloping hijab. I had begun to note an internalized shame among my friends about their bodies exposed by saris and their admiration for my modest and "proper Islamic" dress of kurta and trousers. But I had not appreciated the depth of the politics of their shame until the changes over the years unfolded before my eyes. The young sons returning from madrasas were the new proselytizers of Deobandi Islam.

Thus, over a period of fifteen years of this study, the story of Islam and politics underwent many changes in the villages of Madanpur and Chishti. As we saw, at the beginning, the Syeds of the two villages shared a common ancestry from Kamaal Baba, a *pir* who had traveled from Kirman in Persia, and they maintained their ties through kinship and marriage and celebrated the key festivals of Qurbani, Eid, Muharram as well as others together. They were also part of a wider network of villages that belonged to the same Hanifi school of Islam as them. But by the first decades of the twenty-first century this picture had changed considerably. As new Islamic identities were adopted by neighbors, categories of identification were entangled at the local level and an attempt was made by my respondents to fit their diverse practices of Islam under recognizable labels that they hadn't needed before. Increased funding for Deobandi schools of Islamic learning had led to an erosion of the numbers of Barelvis and a growing sense of insecurity, even shame, about their beliefs and anxiety about being "proper" Muslims. This had led them to draw further into themselves, which was reflected also in their marriage practices. "We take women from the Deobandis but don't give our daughters to them" was how they put it. But greater prosperity among some of the Syeds had also seen at least one Syed and his wife make the Haj pilgrimage and another had been to Ajmer Sharif in Rajasthan, thereby opening them up to other foreign experiences of Islam which in turn led them to question their own belief and practices further.

Conclusion

By 2013 people in the villages like Madanpur and Chishti had had a long engagement with both democracy and communism. Since the first elections in 1951, over thirty elections had been held in West Bengal for three different tiers of government, and each had brought into power a variety of governments, chief ministers, local MPs, MLAs, and village Pradhans. The average voter in Madanpur and Chishti had thus developed a thorough familiarity with the structures of institutional democracy and elections. And for over three decades of these, a Communist Party–led government, via a deep and extensive network of local comrades, had dominated the lifeworld of every citizen in West Bengal. Prior to these decades, social movements over land dispossession, of the Naxalite-led "land-grab" in the 1960s and 1970s and more recently the Singur-Nandigram in the 2000s, had also led to a thorough familiarity with a politics of protest and mobilization. Their enthusiastic participation in elections, the evidence of which prompted this study, was thus shaped by this history and context.

By the time the land reforms were introduced by the Left Front government in the 1980s, there had therefore already been some cultivation of political activity: an awareness of laws passed by the Congress recommending a redistribution in the ownership of land. The Communists had mobilized agricultural tenants to demand the implementation of the law that existed on paper by evoking a language of rights and entitlements, and this awareness of rights would have been, at least in part, a result of the growing awareness of the meaning of democratic citizenship enacted during each prior election. The thirty-four years of communist politics that followed overlaid a language of rights and duty of formal citizenship with ideas of dignity and self-respect. The institutional change of land reform gave impoverished sharecroppers the right to half the harvest and security of tenancy, and their superior agricultural knowledge meant that they had the upper hand in the knowhow of cultivation. The rise in the daily wage for agricultural workers meant that they were no longer destitute, and a fairer wage led to greater self-respect. The Communist legacy in West Bengal was thus to change the habitus—"system of durable transposable dispositions"—of the lifeworld of agricultural workers. A shared understanding about how to conduct oneself, speak in a certain way, show deference—all of these changed as a result of the struggle of land reforms and then later with the altered scenario that the reforms brought.

The activity of voting from 1952 onward, on the basis of universal suffrage, had also created ideas about political participation and ideas of citizenship among the electorate in West Bengal, changing "the relation of Indians to themselves" (Khilnani 1997: 17). Institutional democratic politics created political capacity in specific ways as voters were recognized as individually sovereign and were treated without discrimination at polling stations, and these new experiences—despite the continued inequities of wealth and caste—contributed to altering the very habits of the rural world. This was what Spencer states is the potential of democracy to "to transform other areas of life, but not in any particular or predictable way" (Spencer 2007: 74). Thus, a critical new ingredient was the growing experience of voting in elections that brought with it an altogether new recognition of being identified as a citizen like anyone else. Deference to the landowner was thus no longer required, eyes were no longer lowered when speaking to upper castes, nor did workers have to wait outside the door of landowner homes to be paid, and so the way in which people saw themselves and others around them, and those above them in the social hierarchy, was altered. All of these changes were effected and realized through practice. My friends in Madanpur and Chishti would often enact to me their changed posture from "before" and "after," by hunching or straightening their backs. And in this embodiment, a new set of rules for a more egalitarian social interaction was forged. As Taylor observed, a rule exists only in our "embodied understanding" and so "a bodily disposition is a habitus when it encodes a certain cultural understanding. The habitus in this sense always has an expressive dimension. It gives expression to certain meanings that things and people have for us, and it is precisely by giving such expression that it makes these meanings exist for us" (Taylor 1993: 58). Taylor, by drawing on Wittgenstein, forces us to think about the nature of rules as "the phenomenon of the unarticulated background" which points us to those shared understandings among the members of a society about the rules of social behavior (Taylor 1993: 47). That is to say, rules may exist to guide action but they only come to life when they are put into practice, and Bourdieu's path-breaking work drew our attention to the necessity of judgment and strategy in knowing how to apply these rules. It is this knowledge of how to act on rules, how to play with them to achieve desired goals, how to use them to create a finely altered scenario as a result of one's action that Taylor later formulated as an important aspect of "social imaginaries." The use of the word *social* was significant, as Taylor argued, because it indicated that the unarticulated background knowledge had to be shared among many and that it was the result of a dialogic engagement between an actor and others, rather than one that was confined to an individual's mind, as a "centre of monological consciousness" (Taylor 1993: 49). This dialogic engagement is more than mere coordination between one's actions and others; it is the knowledge of how to be in sync with them—Taylor provides the actions of sawing or ballroom dancing as illustrations. The role of imagination in social imaginaries is also critical and linked to the social. For if rules really come into force through practice, it is the awareness of how far one can bend the rule, or overturn a rule altogether but make it socially acceptable, that required imagination. Thus, both imagination and social practice are germane to the idea of habitus. In these sorts of social practice, it is an awareness of the unspoken but shared understandings that made a joint action possible, and it is to this aspect of the social that we will next turn our attention to.

*

3

Scandal

Cultivating Competition

There was great excitement in the village of Chishti. It was early morning in April 2001 and I had been away for a couple of days, so I stopped by the home of Tinkari Dom to catch up on news. Before I could even sit down, I was told I had just missed the departure of a bus full of villagers to the famous annual fair of Pathor Chapri, held 50 km (31 miles) away at the shrine of a Sufi saint. As I looked across the fields between the Dom household and the highway running alongside the village, I could see children hanging around, gazing longingly up the road where the bus had disappeared into the mist. Though it was customary for families to visit the fortnight-long fair, it was too expensive for many, given the travel, the offering at the shrine, and the spending money needed to have fun. Those who went kept it quiet, to avoid inviting envy, although their bleary eyes following late returns usually prompted friends to demand details the next day. So, I was surprised to learn that an entire bus full of people from the village had left for the fair.

By the time Tinkari's daughter-in-law brewed black tea with ginger, I had heard the details of what was clearly not a routine event. A man called Mansur, who ran the shop selling government price-controlled rations, had recently acquired a bus and its inaugural run was made auspicious by a journey to the shrine of the saint, and some fellow villagers had been invited along. He had clearly wanted it to be noticed and admired by all, and so the entire village had been alerted to the departure of the bus by musicians and dancers hired specially from the nearby town of Bolpur, and all the awestruck children had been given sweets. A grand picnic (*pheasty*), including 12 kilos (twenty-six pounds) of chicken and rice, was to be cooked for the guests at the fair after the traditional offering of a cloth (*chador*) at the shrine. For a village where most houses were made of mud and thatch, electricity was intermittent, and running water unknown, such luxuries outside of traditional ritual festivities was an unexpected treat.

These were still early days in my research, but I could sense that this was a significant event. The trip had been arranged on the day before the deadline when compensation money had to be paid by Mansur's family for their son's culpability in a sexual scandal. The two things were clearly linked, and so it seemed important to know who had been on the bus. I was told "everyone" had gone, that "the bus was full," and despite my repeated requests for specific names, I got none. "Everyone has gone!" remained the dramatic yet non-specific reply from the many who had not. Confirming my suspicions, it later transpired that two members of the three-member arbitration committee (set up for the scandal) had accepted the invitation, indicating that the gift had probably contained the poison of intrigue. Indeed, over the next few weeks, months, and even years, the events linked to the scandal and its resolution displayed all the classic ingredients of politics—as a game of deceit and lies, stratagems and spoils, played with tactical uses of passion (Bailey 1969). But there was also something else. This particular bus trip generated the beginning of a new political coalition of interests in a form that had never before existed. Unlike Bisipara, the village where Bailey gained his ideas on the nature of politics, Madanpur and Chishti could not be said to be dominated by *doladoli*, or factionalism. This was mainly because of the absolute dominance of Communist-led politics that violently stamped out any hint of opposition at the very root. At the village level, the Comrade, as a representative of the Left Front "party-society," was able to wield absolute control by ingratiating himself in all political and non-political matters, and in this instance had tried to control the problem but had caused a scandal and a grave injustice instead (Bhattacharya 2016). However, in resolving the scandal, debating the ethical implications of the Comrade's actions, and weighing the judgments made by those who did and didn't accept Mansur's invitation, a new alliance of actors took shape for the first time in Chishti. These were not a group of people who had come together before—and some of them even shared a history of enmity—but the need to settle the scandal in an ethical and transparent way had created the need to find the courage to challenge the Comrade's dominance, which required them to rise above their own differences to ally with those with whom they were in agreement, on this issue at least. This new alliance culminated in creating the victory of a rival political party, ten years after the scandal took place. In 2011, when the groundswell of opposition to the Left Front West Bengal was articulated by Trinamool Congress at the state level, the formation of the local chapter of Trinamool in this village was led by a young man named Majhi[1] and supported by Hakim, Mustafa, and Enayat (all school teachers) as well as other villagers who had been gradually won over in the intervening years. The capillary structure of the Left Front, with a "Comrade" in each village and a Communist Party office in each administrative block, meant that this kind of process was being more or less replicated thousands of times across West Bengal. That year, the Left

Front lost the state government to Trinamool, after thirty-four years in power. In retrospect, the event of the scandal could be seen as a significant turning point that had triggered a lasting oppositional force to the Comrade.

As noted earlier, the only expression of alternative political opinion during the Left Front years was to be found in the electoral results in every cycle, in which the opposition parties consistently registered an average of 40 percent of the vote share, which was made possible because of the secret ballot. While this evidential proof confirmed that the Left Front did not enjoy the whole-hearted support of the electorate, this alternative political loyalty could find no public expression, as the violence of local Comrades toward those who challenged the status quo was immediate and swift. In the scandal, therefore, any countermoves to the Comrade required secrecy and determination, and as we shall see, were executed successfully. More significantly, the victory of the new coalition sustained the group beyond the resolution of the scandal itself to create an unprecedented, nascent but lasting, formation against the Comrade. This gradual shift in opinion at the local level was reflected in the state results as the Left Front dramatically tumbled from a seat share of 80 percent to 21 percent. As Bhattacharya notes, "The scale of the decline, and its decisive character, can possibly be measured by the fact that never before since 1977 of the CPI(M)'s and LF's share of votes dropped continuously for 4 successive general elections as it did from 2004 to 2011" (Bhattacharya 2016: 215). This meant that as the anti–Left Front alliance grew, more and more voters used the secret ballot to vote for alternative parties, thereby reducing the Left Front vote share. As the anti–Left Front alliances at local levels gained momentum over the next ten years, drawing to it others who were also disgruntled by the Comrade's hubris and the Party's growing dominance, it eventually led to the routing of the communist parties in state-level elections. To understand the turn of the electoral wheel in 2011, therefore, requires recognition of how citizens in a democracy act in between elections to create a new political consensus that challenges the status quo. Electoral change at the macro level takes place when political opposition toward the incumbent is cultivated at the micro level in between elections, and finds expression at the ballot box at the next election. The discussion of the event of scandal here will show how the rupture caused by the Comrade's crossing of an ethical red line set in motion maneuvers that sought to mobilize the opinion against him, hitherto voiced only through the secret ballot, into a more overt political opposition. This chapter will demonstrate how the rumblings of opposition toward one corrupt Comrade in one particular setting, such as Madanpur and Chishti, when multiplied manifold across West Bengal's villages and their Comrades, can effect an aggregate change in elections.

The event of the scandal discussed in this chapter presents itself as a "social drama" that revealed what was not otherwise evident in the villages of Madanpur and Chishti. On the face of it, the Comrade's writ ran large; his party was in power and seemed to likely impossible to dislodge. But the reactions to the actions of the Comrade in this particular event revealed reserves of creativity of political action for the first time and thereby disclosed the social imaginaries required for it. It became clear that the idea of competition between political parties that is a key aspect of democratic politics was understood by all, despite the hegemonic hold of the Left Front's "party society" (Bhattacharya 2016). So far, multi-party had been a reality on (ballot) paper, but even so, people had clearly exercised their right to choose by voting for the opposition throughout the heydays of the Left Front. But what the scandal showed was the shared understanding that in order to translate a protest vote into change in government required much more active participation in "doing politics" to create a viable alternative electoral force. The detailed examination of the scandal allows us to witness this process as it happened. As Victor Turner observed, "the social drama is a limited area of transparency on the otherwise opaque surface of regular, uneventful social life" (1957: 93).

As with studies from the Manchester School, attention to social structure here is important, and as we shall see it is a combination of kinship ties, class divisions, and cross-caste solidarity that form the basis of social action. As Turner noted, "Social dramas occur within groups of persons who share values and interests and who have a real or alleged common history" (Turner 1980: 149). In Turner's *Schism and Continuity*, the tragedy of the protagonist, Sandombu, was the "result of the structural contradiction between virilocal residence and matrilineal descent" (Englund 2018). Here, we will see that the decline of the Comrade is effected through the mutual challenge of pre-existing ties of kinship and shared agricultural labor, on the one hand, and the ideas of political citizenship on the other. It was the awareness of their sovereignty as citizens (performed at least during elections) that provided the courage to challenge the grip on power by a single individual. In a sense, this challenge was a vindication of Ambedkar's aspiration that elections "could [themselves] serve an instructive role and that participation in political life would bring about consciousness among the lower castes" (Khosla 2020: 10). But to act collectively, rather than as in one's individual capacity as voter, had required wholly different skills of both compromise and cunning alongside communication and camaraderie. The resulting process revealed fissures of kinship, friendship, and partisanship that required creative use of cross-cutting ties to repair the damage. As a result, the plot of this social drama was entirely dependent on the creativity of the actors, who emerged from the performance very much like the "active citizens" in the writings of the young Machiavelli.

*

West Bengal, through the 1980s and up until the first decade of the twenty-first century, was completely dominated by the politics of the Left Front, a coalition of communist parties.[2] In my research villages, this dominance was personified by the figure of the local Comrade, Maqtool Hussain, who controlled all resources, opportunities, decisions, and people's lives. The slightest challenge to his hold was met with immediate and swift retaliation—an access to the main road was cut off, causing inconvenient detours, animals were let loose to destroy the crop on the fields of the offender, a son mysteriously failed his exams, or a bank loan was suddenly rescinded. People thus lived in constant fear of the Comrade and described the atmosphere as one of *shontrash*, or terror, in which it was best to keep one's head down and let the Comrade have his way. But the Comrade also stood for the positive changes that successive Left Front governments had brought about in West Bengal. He was the President of the Block Krishak Sabha, the farmer's union, which played a seminal role in the sweeping land reforms that were introduced by the Left Front government early in its tenure in the 1980s and remained the source of its continuing popularity and support in rural areas. These "Operation Barga" land reforms had provided a much-improved deal for many sharecroppers (*bargardar*) and day laborers. While the reforms' implementation had been uneven across the state, in areas where they did gain traction, as in Chishti and Madanpur, the results had been significant, indeed nothing short of a social revolution.[3] Any *bargadar* who had worked a piece of land for a landlord for more than three years could register his own name against it and thereby be guaranteed tenancy and a 50 percent share of the harvest and of secondary agricultural outputs. The landlord received the remaining 50 percent but remained responsible for the capital outlay for seeds, fertilizer, irrigation, and bullocks for plowing. The farming decisions thus came to be made jointly—in fact, they were often dominated by the *bargadar*, who had greater practical experience. Harvests flourished and West Bengal emerged as the largest rice-producing state in India. Meanwhile, daily wage workers (both male and female) enjoyed a new government-prescribed minimum wage of Rs. 50 per day (a fivefold increase over existing rates), which now had to be paid at the start of the day, ending the traditional humiliating wait at its end. This allowed even the poorest families to afford three meals a day, consisting of rice, dal, and vegetable and occasionally fish. Both sharecroppers and agricultural workers were recruited into farmers' trade unions. Overall, the poorer, low caste rural proletariat gained a new sense of self-worth, voice, and dignity and became far more self-assured in their dealings with the landlords.[4] They greatly appreciated the Communist Party's role in upturning the age-old status quo in this way and, as in the two villages, remained loyal to the Party and its man on the ground, the Comrade, across the state of West Bengal.

In contrast, local land owners bewailed the reforms as impoverishing. They lived in constant fear of crossing the Comrade, who could, for example, use the loyalty of the share croppers to turn against their landlord, or impose more sharecroppers on his land, or reduce his share of crop further to only 25 percent. Thus, the traditional land-owning class, drawn mainly from the elite Syed caste, found their influence in the villages checked by the Comrade (himself a Syed) and other Party members, in return for cooperation from *bargadars* and agricultural workers. As a leader of the district's farmer's union, the Comrade also had considerable powers well beyond the two villages, and it was this reach that made him a such force to reckon with for any inhabitant of Chishti or Madanpur. He lived right near the highway, with easy access for his loud motorcycle, the only private motor transport in either village. The Comrade had a vantage position from where he could keep his eye on both villages and bestride the affairs of both. The only local man with two wives, he had one in each village, which further entrenched him in the affairs of both through wide circles of relatives and retainers—though his scandalous elopement with the second wife, from Chishti, had given their women a lasting reputation of being "loose."

This reputation was particularly true for Feroza, the young woman at the heart of the scandal. She was said to have had a six-month affair with a young man only slightly older than her, Shohin. But Shohin was not just any man in the village, he was also her maternal uncle as Feroza's MFB (mother's father's brother) was Shohin's father, Mansur. Feroza's father, Amir Ali, was an impoverished Syed who struggled to feed his family and had none of the gravitas that some other Syed men possessed, seeming to be happy for others to speak on his behalf. His wife, Angora, was gregarious and widely liked, and it was striking that no one openly criticized her inability to control her daughter's romantic dalliances, of which there had been others before Shohin. In this instance, however, Feroza had become pregnant, though this was not the cause of the scandal. Rather, the scandal was caused by the Comrade, who had gotten involved in his capacity as self-appointed arbitrator of all village disputes and had unilaterally ruled that Shohin should marry Feroza but that the pregnancy should be terminated. This marriage is what had horrified the village, for while first-cousin marriage was common, inter-generational marriage, especially on the matrilineal side, was taboo (*haram*) and was the root of the scandal.

Turner notes that social dramas have four phases: "breach, crisis redress, and *either* reintegration *or* recognition of schism" (Turner 1980: 149' original emphasis). With the Comrade imposing his decision for the couple to be wedded, despite the Islamic proscription against it, the first phase of "breach" occurred. The marriage had taken place about a year before the bus trip. Shohin's family, as the rest of the village had anticipated, had treated the union as a mere formality and had locked Feroza up and denied her access to her husband. Finding this situation intolerable, after several months Feroza found a chance to break free and ran to the highway to throw herself in front of a truck. She was rescued just in time and taken back, humanely this time, to her parents' home. This time around, the parents sought a divorce for her, and the Comrade, stung by the disapproval of his earlier decision, convened an arbitration committee composed of those who would seem impartial and wise, thereby setting in motion the second phase of "crisis redress" of the unfolding social drama. Accordingly, he chose three schoolteachers, Mustafa, Hanif, and Lulu, and together they determined that Shohin's family should pay Feroza compensation money to settle the dispute and established the date by which it should be paid. But given that the settlement sum was large and the Comrade had avaricious designs on it, he had rather cleverly chosen three schoolteachers with whom he shared kinship and personal ties, ready to activate these if he needed to sway them to his side. And the first sign of trouble was when Mansur's bus trip to the fair took place on the day after the payment deadline, which had come and gone without any money being paid. Surely this was no coincidence? And to confirm suspicions, I found out inadvertently that the taciturn schoolteacher Mustafa, a member of the committee, had joined the outing. When I arrived at his house on the day of the trip, as I had been asked to lunch, I found no one there but his wife, who told me with studied casualness as she kindly wafted a fan over me while I ate, that her husband could not be present as he had gone on the bus trip that morning. It seemed odd to me that an arbiter had accepted a gift from the "accused" in a case, but I hid my surprise. Over the next few weeks, as I gradually learned the names of all the people who filled the bus that day—which included another member of the committee and the brother of the third one—the "event" slowly developed into a vivid snapshot of the micro-politics of the village, a picture which would have been impossible to piece together in more normal times. Mansur's audacity, with the Comrade's complicity, of hosting the bus trip the day after missing his settlement deadline, set in motion a series of political maneuvers that was to have far-reaching consequences. By providing the detail of this event, my aim is to provide an account which demonstrates the process by which "particular values and ends, distributed over a range of actors [is converted] into shared and consensual meaning" (Turner 1980: 156).

*

The "arbitration committee" appointed by the Comrade was made up of three upper-caste Syed men who, as noted, were all schoolteachers—Mustafa, Hanif, and Lulu. As throughout rural India, being a schoolteacher was a highly coveted profession as it brought respectability (they were addressed by all as "Mustafa Master" or "Hanif Master"), security, and an excellent salaried income, and also provided long vacations and short working hours that allowed spare time for agricultural work on the side. Unsurprisingly, all the schoolteachers were prosperous. But there was also resentment and jealousy among them, largely caused by varying degrees of favor granted by the Comrade. Salaried jobs, such as schoolteachers, belonged to the public sector which political actors like the Comrade could manipulate to reward loyalists with. As Madanpur was the village of his rejected first wife, there were no schoolteachers in Madanpur, despite having several educated and qualified Syed men who had repeatedly sought appointment. Indeed, the only two salaried people in Madanpur were the Comrade's brother and brother-in-law, both of whom had coveted posts in the Public Works Department. As the two villages were closely connected through marriage and kinship ties, resentments caused by this preferential treatment by the Comrade crossed village boundaries, causing rivalry within families and among brothers. The Comrade was therefore able to keep his detractors divided to avoid any cooperation among them.

The Comrade owned over 16 acres of land (50 *bigha*[5]), the largest holding in the village, on which he cultivated paddy and wheat. In the early 1980s, alert to the impending land reforms his party was about to introduce, he had pre-emptively gotten rid of his own sharecropper by switching to hired labor before the reforms came in. He thereby avoided the crop sharing and financial ruin which most middling landlords experienced. He also diversified into other businesses: he was the first in the village to exploit the nearby riverbed to extract sand, which he sold to building contractors; he also utilized it for a brick-making business, having set up the first kilns in the village, and later he had also established a lucrative fishery. The financing of these ventures was provided by interest-free loans from either the central and state governments, and he alone seemed to benefit from them. It was no surprise, therefore, that the Comrade was the most prosperous man in the village, and many of his relatives and political contemporaries resented his disproportionate and corrupt prosperity.

But the Comrade was more than a feudal patron. He was also a political entrepreneur who was a party functionary in an electoral democracy and utilized his ties to the Party to expand his personal networks of loyalty which he then deployed back into support for the Party. As the man on the ground, he was the representative of the party-state and his job was to implement its policies, increase its base of support and, most crucially, deliver votes to it during elections. In turn, his links to the Party provided advance information on available loans, and bureaucratic favors granting permits for his ventures or to those he favored. His activities thereby increased his wealth and widened the circle of those tied to him through obligation or loyalty. The Comrade conducted much of his ideological work among the lower laboring castes whom he referred to as "the poor" (*gorib*), and it was while sitting with them that he shared the Communist Party's vision of greater social equality and fairness and how support for the Party at elections would usher this in. For example, following party directives on a new scheme to encourage self-help groups, he used various forms of leverage to swiftly and efficiently persuade some women (and their families) that cooperative action was necessary and beneficial in the long run. And it was by listening to the *gorib* in turn that he could feed back to his party colleagues about the mood and demands of the electorate. He thus acted as the crucial go-between between party and people and facilitated the government's responsiveness to voters. The Comrade was thus a political entrepreneur, playing a delicately balanced game which, at its best, simultaneously increased his personal prosperity and his party's popularity.

However, other Syed landowners remained competitors, for despite their impoverishment following the land reforms they continued to have influence among the poorer laboring classes. While it was true that the landowning Syeds had less money in hand as result of having to share 50 percent of profits with the sharecroppers who in turn had a growing sense of entitlement and dignity, the latter still depended on the Syeds' resources for storing their share of the grain, for instant liquidity in an emergency, for help with their children's homework, and so on. Thus, Shekhs and Pathans were no longer at the mercy of the largesse of a particular Syed, but they continued to rely on their support. In turn, Syeds had themselves begun to do manual work on their own land to save on labor costs but had to defer to the superior agricultural knowledge of the lower caste tenants to create substantial crop yields. There had been, therefore, a rebalancing of power relations in which Syeds could still gain the upper hand if they could establish a reputation of respecting the lower castes by being generous with their assets toward them. Thus, if anything, the land reforms had ushered in a new moral economy in which older bonds had persisted despite the new realignments in hierarchies. As a result, despite his superior standing in the village, the Comrade had to be constantly vigilant about other Syeds potentially influencing or encroaching on his supporters. This became a growing possibility as, over time, more and more among the peasantry began to question whether the government was a one-reform wonder. The minimum daily wage, which had not increased since the mid-1980s, did not seem as radical or generous a measure in the inflated prices of the new century, and the coverage of the land reform program had remained patchy. Further, the much-needed reform of the agricultural markets had never materialized (see Harriss-White 2008), leaving West Bengal among the country's least prosperous states despite its high levels of rice production. Questioning the credibility of the Communists was thus a genuine and growing possibility made visible by the daily, shameless accumulation by the Comrade, and such dissent was most likely to be encouraged and provoked by the Syeds through the bonds with their poorer tenants. One such instance took place when the Comrade tried to turn one of the big communal tanks (*pukurs*)—a resource that was jointly owned by groups of Syeds—into a hatchery for his private fisheries business. Two Syed men, Enayat and Hanif, questioned his move even though at the time Enayat was a senior member of the Comrade's penumbra. His objection was on a point of principle, and it emboldened several poorer non-Syed men, who were otherwise loyal to the Comrade, to protest too. As one of them, Kalo, a Pathan daily wage laborer, explained, the customary leasing of a *pukur* was normally limited to only one year at a time, and it was given to a bidder from the non-Syed castes for fishing rights who could benefit from the extra income. This decision was meant to be made jointly by all the Syeds as the resource was a part of the village commons and not the private property of any individual Syed. The Comrade's attempt to unilaterally and permanently appropriate a tank for his private business provoked the village to unite across caste lines.

It was in this context of nascent resentment toward the Comrade from both tenants and the Syeds that the current scandal unfolded. Thus far, the Comrade's strategy had been to embed himself in the daily life of every household, allowing no matter too small to escape his attention, and his intervention in the affair between Shohin and Feroza was the latest instance of this. As one woman put it, "*Comrade daaley achey, bhaatey achey, machey achey*" (The Comrade is in the rice, in the dal, in the fish [that is, he has a finger in every pie]). In each case, he would seize on or create incidents, magnify and stir trouble around them, then restore order by issuing threats to the mischief-maker and mollifications to the injured party, thereby strengthening his indispensability. His interventions and decisions did not follow a principled policy of seeking justice and truth; instead, his punishments were arbitrary and often did not bear any relation to the seriousness of the "offense," and it was this unpredictability of outcome that helped create an atmosphere of anxiety and what was increasingly characterized as naked terror (*shontrash*). By behaving in this fashion, every dispute—genuine or contrived—became an occasion for the Comrade to entrench himself further in everyone's affairs, his capriciousness increased his hold over people, and he could use them to needle his enemies and reward his supporters.

In the normal course of things, dispute resolution in Madanpur and Chishti took one of two main forms. If it was a matter between two parties, say of disputed boundaries between properties or someone's cattle straying into another's fields, this was considered a domestic (*gresto*) matter, to be resolved at a meeting held in the village mosque by the families concerned, with some mediation by a neutral third party. In contrast, if an issue affected many people in the village, then it was considered through *bichar* (deliberation) with a meeting held in the school, which anyone could attend, with an elder appointed to arbitrate.[6] In Chishti this would be someone of Mustafa's or Enayat's stature, and in Madanpur,

Akbar's or Mukhtar's. However, in the years of the Left Front's dominance, the Comrade had insisted on escalating all traditionally *gresto* matters as requiring *bichar* arbitration. Further, he sidelined all others to appoint himself as sole judge and jury on all cases and his ruling as final and irrevocable. Thus, property matters, disputes between parents and children, or even the choice of groom for a young woman, were all turned into *bichar* issues, about which he would mobilize supporters from across the villages to support his ruling.[7] And each of his rulings was designed to further his own personal interests. The core of his support came from a penumbra of loyalists who traded their support for the Comrade in return for benefits of his largesse that he was able to accrue through his connections with the political establishment. Anyone anticipating the need for such largesse could be persuaded to join the penumbra of "supporters," and as the Comrade mediated even basic state services such as flood relief, such supporters were never in short supply. Thus, the Comrade was able to skillfully use each dispute to accrue loyalty to himself and weaken his detractors. As Akbar, an elderly Syed man, observed to me, politics (*rajniti*) in the village was a complicated business mainly because the only law (*niti*) was that of the Comrade's; so fearful were people that they might be overheard and be reported to the Comrade, they would discuss politics with me only in whispers in the quiet of the afternoon or the middle of a paddy field, while most would not discuss such matters with me at all. In Madanpur and Chishti, the arena of politics itself had come to be defined as the sum of the Comrade's actions.

In the case of the Feroza-Shohin scandal, the Comrade had ruled that the two should marry but with the pregnancy terminated. This ruling seemed to be driven by two important vested interests—first, that Shohin's father, Mansur (the owner of the bus), and his older brother, Munsab, had been long-standing supporters of the Comrade. They were relative outsiders to the village and had no close kin in the village so had found it beneficial to be in the Comrade's good books. Further, Mansur's *bargadar* was Nitai Dom, whose son was Shohin's best friend, and by letting Shohin off lightly, it was hoped that Nitai Dom could be brought into the Comrade's penumbra. This was deemed necessary because Nitai's older brother, Tinkari Dom, was a charismatic communist firebrand who was a staunch critic of the Comrade and had wasted no opportunity in fearlessly criticizing his corrupt ways. By ruling in favor of Shohin, who was Nitai's son's friend, the Comrade hoped to wean Nitai away from his brother, so that they did not stand united and provide a potential front against him. The tactic had worked; Nitai's entire family had been on Mansur's bus. Such machinations to keep brothers divided were typical of the Comrade's tactics, and as a result most brothers in the two villages were not on speaking terms. My inquiries revealed that in each case the roots of discord indeed lay in the prosperity of one brother—facilitated by a job, loan, or marriage arranged by the Comrade—and the less prosperous circumstances of the other, who invariably struggled to improve his fortunes. Aware that sibling solidarity could lead to alliances across families, the Comrade kept brothers divided, holding one in his constant debt and the other in continual sullen hope of becoming a likely recipient of the Comrade's favor. Some people could of course see through this strategy and warned against it, as an old woman did by saying, "*Ek bhai daley, ek bhai khaley, tomar shonger dekha hobey, oi moron kaley*" (One brother lives on a branch [like a tamarind], the other in a tank [like a fish]; they meet only in death in the cooking pot).

To foreclose the possibility of further outrage, the Comrade had taken great care in picking the arbitration committee. It was composed of Mustafa, Hanif, and Lulu, each a schoolteacher and a Syed. They were also related to the Comrade through marriage—Mustafa was the Comrade's brother-in-law; Lulu's wife was the Comrade's wife's sister's daughter; and the three men were also interrelated: Mustafa's wife was Hanif's sister, and Lulu was Hanif Master's mother's brother's son and also his assistant teacher in school. Clearly, the Comrade was banking on the loyalty of kinship links over political rivalry. And he was right to be cautious, because there had indeed been history of this before. Hanif had publicly challenged the Comrade on the water tank issue and was a truculent figure, who had been very active in politics during the land reform agitations. He had been an active member of the Forward Bloc party and had more or less inducted the Comrade into politics as his guru. But the Comrade had betrayed his trust and forced him out of active politics in the early 1990s by kidnapping him just before the panchayat elections, when Hanif's candidacy and potential victory was assured, taking him to a secret destination for three days, bringing him back only once the elections were over and after Hanif had signed an undertaking that he would never enter politics again if he wished to live. Ever since, Hanif had held a burning grudge and the Comrade never missed an opportunity to remind him of his promise by quiet intimidation. Hanif made his disapproval of the Comrade evident whenever we spoke but was clearly also secretly flattered to be asked to serve on the arbitration committee.

Mustafa, on the other hand, gave off the air as one who was above such petty emotions. He was one of the wealthiest men in the village and lived in a relatively large compound next to the Comrade's. He was widely respected for his learning in Islamic theology, fluent reading and writing of Arabic, and working knowledge of English. He displayed these skills daily, sitting next to the window of his house overlooking the main village lane and reading Islamic texts or writing treatises. He was known to attend *jolsas*—all-night gatherings of thousands before whom learned scholars from across India debated the finer points of Islamic theology—and was known to hold his own in those discussions. But within the village, he was taciturn and rarely to be found anywhere apart from his own house. Distinctively tall and erect, his involvement with farming appeared minimal, unlike the other teachers who did much physical work before and after school hours. His wife, however, mixed easily with the other women, where her superior status was implicitly acknowledged, and it was rare for anyone to gossip or speak negatively about her or to her. If a controversial topic came up in the afternoon sessions of talk over mat weaving or embroidery, she usually held her counsel and rode out the conversation in silence with a non-committal smile. She encouraged younger women to remain pious and say their prayers and was regularly consulted by them on matters religious and domestic.[8] Her regular attendance at these gossip sessions kept her informed about the goings on in the village and provided valuable information to Mustafa Master for his use at opportune moments.

Finally, Lulu Master, the youngest member of the arbitration committee, lived in the heart of the village, next door to his brother Mohit.[9] Like the other committee members, he taught in a primary school elsewhere, and his slight, light-skinned figure was rarely seen around the village, except on the most important occasions. His wife, Sabera, was a confident and outspoken woman from Tilaboni, and her dress and comportment indicated a more prosperous upbringing than those in Chishti and Madanpur. The Comrade had given his own daughter in marriage to Sabera's brother in Tilaboni.[10] To the village, overtly at least, the choice of these three men looked impeccable, for they had the right credentials of probity, education, and the lack of any shared kinship with either party in the dispute. Covertly, however, the committee also subtly shifted the center of gravity toward the Comrade, because each of them shared history or kin relations with the Comrade. While it was true that until this point Hanif Master and Mustafa Master had kept their distance from the Comrade in political affairs of the Party, by flattering their egos and inviting them into the arbitration committee the Comrade had hoped to effectively stifle any potential opposition from them. This had clearly been a successful strategy, as Mustafa and Hanif had been on Mansur's bus and Lulu Master had been represented by his brother, Mohit Ali.[11]

So, at this stage in the event, the Comrade appeared to have triumphed again. The arbitration committee did not seem to mind accepting hospitality from the defaulting party in the dispute, and this appeared to condone the non-payment. But when the money was not paid for several days well after the deadline had passed, it became obvious that Mansur had laid on the excessive hospitality during the outing to the fair not only to buy off the committee's objections to the delay but because he did not intend to pay the money at all. He had hoped that their acceptance of his invitation would consequently absolve him of his dues.

Feroza's household, on the other side of the dispute, lived in a state of stress and tension as the deadline came and went. Unlike other Syeds, Amir Ali, Feroza's father, had lost ownership of all his lands and now worked hard as a wage laborer but did not earn enough to sustain his family of three daughters and one son. He had the reputation of being a pious and simple man, who called the prayer at the village mosque for a small fee. He was tall, with a straggly beard and gaunt features, and was always busy, caught up in the daily struggle of work and making ends meet. When I was finally able to find a moment to talk with him, he was forthcoming, his eyes blazing with anger as he began to explain the causes of his declining fortunes. But as soon as others stopped by to join us, his demeanor changed dramatically as he reverted to the slightly hangdog air that made people affectionate toward him and sympathetic to the hard times the family found themselves in. His wife, Angora, had a ready laugh for everyone, but her torn sari and un-oiled skin told their own tale of want. I found her once at Mohit Ali's grocery shop, selling him a handful of rice to buy household items; something only the very poor resorted to when lacking cash. But Mohit Ali was a sympathetic friend, and once I got to know him it transpired that he was very resentful of having been press-ganged into going on Mansur's outing by his brother Lulu. He had seen it as a betrayal of his friendship with Amir to accept the hospitality of his enemy and resented the pressure deeply. Mustafa Master, too, seemed to be embarrassed to talk about the trip to the shrine, and Hanif waved my questions about his joining the trip away, indicating that it was more an unavoidable social obligation than a compromise of his neutrality.

In the days following the bus trip, as I visited each household in Chishti to piece together the names of those on Mansur's bus, I learned that most non-Syed families who had been on the bus had gone along mainly for the ride, as such a trip would be too expensive for them to afford otherwise. The fair was a famous one, and the luxury of being transported to it and entertained with a feast was simply too much to resist. Besides, in each case, it was the Syeds they had working relations with who had persuaded them to go along—Munsab, Mansur, Lulu, Hanif, Mustafa, and of course the Comrade himself. They were, of course, aware that their presence on the trip contributed to strengthening Mansur's hand in demonstrating the weight of the village behind him, but in the end they felt they were too distant from the scandal itself to consider their acceptance of the invitation as a complicity in Mansur's non-payment of the settlement money. What was seen as significant, however, was which Syeds had been on the trip and especially the fact that the ones on the committee had gone along. This explained why those who had stayed behind had insisted that "everyone had gone" when I had initially asked who had been on the bus.

In the days following the ignored deadline and the bus trip, one could not help but notice some odd conversations around Chishti as discussions about the scandal and its apparent resolution continued. Despite the sexual transgression at the heart of it, most of the gossip was not about the affair itself but about the way in which the elders, led by the Comrade, had resolved it. As noted, the need for the arbitration committee had arisen because of the scandalous imposition by the Comrade of a marriage between members of maternal kin from different generations. His disregard for Islamic rules of marriage and kinship perhaps reflected a communist disdain for such beliefs to be "the last vestige of feudalism," as a noted local communist intellectual had once observed to me. But even the members of the committee clearly demurred. On one occasion, I found Mustafa (from the committee), Noori, Mina, and Enayat standing by the main village lane, chatting among themselves. This was in the early evening when people are often seen in public spaces as cows return to their dwellings, kicking up the dust as they scamper home in the fading light. But it was very unusual to see a group of Syed men and women, especially Mustafa Master, chatting with those who dared to be volubly critical of the Comrade in private conversations at least. (Most people did not dare to do even this.) Noori and Mina were sisters who ran the only female-headed household in Chishti and had endless accounts of being harassed by the Comrade. To see Enayat with them confirmed that this was some sort of discussion about the Comrade, as Enayat had been unafraid to openly challenge the Comrade in the past. When some days later I found Enayat dropping in to see Mohit, probably knowing that he could meet Amir (Feroza's father) there, it indicated to me that some sort of critique of the Comrade was being cultivated. Enayat was also a good friend of Hanif, who was of course a member of the arbitration committee, and despite my presence I heard the two men discuss quite openly how the Comrade may have overplayed his hand this time. With Enayat, there had been serious history with the Comrade. His earlier challenge of the Comrade had led to severe repercussions that led to Enayat's near-public humiliation when the Comrade had mobilized his supporters to boycott Enayat's son's wedding, returning the sweets that had been sent to their households. He had also persuaded them to stay away from joining the wedding party. But in the end, his friend Hanif had stepped into the breach and saved Enayat's face by persuading enough people to make up a respectable groom's party. On the other side of the dispute, Lulu (also a member of the arbitration committee) broke off a conversation with me to have a hushed chat with Munsab outside the room in which we were talking; his reluctance to let me see Mansur's brother in his house was difficult to overlook. The Comrade's conduct through this whole affair over a period of several months was now being assessed in discussions across the village. Hushed conversations with Shekh families who lived among the mud huts at the end of the village lane where Munsab's house stood revealed that the Comrade could never be impartial in a case involving Mansur's son because he had longstanding affairs not only with his brother's wife but also with his daughter, Beli, and their neighbors had themselves seen the Comrade vaulting over Munsab's wall at dawn. But in all these conversations, the outrage expressed was not about the Comrade's own licentiousness so much as his claim to impartiality. Many pointed out that this time, the Comrade had been so focused on his usual game of realpolitik that he had failed to anticipate the moral red line he had crossed by forcing a marriage that was considered a social taboo for his fellow villagers. As before, his *niti* (law) had been solely to serve his own naked greed, but this time it had caused a moral transgression that had been too much for the community to ignore. In addition, the blatant use of the treat of the bus trip to coerce individuals into associating themselves with one party had led to the loosening of tongues, so far tied in terror of the Comrade's actions. And people utilized the ties of friendship such as that between Enayat and Hanif, or Amir and Mohit, to band together. Women too rose over petty differences to share stories of the Comrade's sexual excesses for the first time. Parasa lived next door to Noori and Mina, but this was the first time that the women could compare their similar experiences. The outrage thus began to cross caste, class, and gender lines as the seeds of discontent grew.

In his important paper on the role of gossip in creating and sustaining group values, Max Gluckman draws on the work of a number of anthropologists of the Manchester School to propose a general theory about this ubiquitous social activity, "part of the very blood and tissue of that life" (Gluckman 1963: 308). Drawing on examples from small towns in the United States to Welsh villages, he points out that gossip is a "culturally determined process, which has its own customary rules" (Gluckman 1963: 308). In Chishti, the rules of gossip became evident as the weeks rolled on, as more and more people came forward to share stories of their own experiences of the Comrade's reign of terror. These accounts were shared in the aftermath of the scandal but almost never referred to the affair between Feroza and Shohin and the young woman's consequent pregnancy. If people were shocked by those events, they did not speak about it. Rather, what they chose to share among themselves were accounts of the Comrade's own sexual and other transgressions. By doing so, they learned for the first time the harrowing experiences that others had been through and consequently their shared victimization by one man's depravity. In evaluating his behavior, judgments were made about acceptable transgressions, the limits of an individual's behavior, and the moral fiber of the Comrade. Gluckman's conclusions about the role of gossip and scandal in creating solidarity accurately describes what was happening in Chishti: "The process of scandal enables a group, to evaluate people for their work, their qualities of leadership, and their moral character, without ever confronting them to their faces with failures in any sphere. Thus animosities between individuals and cliques are built into the larger social order through the cultural techniques of gossip and scandal" (Gluckman 1963: 313). While this shared activity did not erase the differences that continued to exist between groups based on gender, caste, or class, these differences were nevertheless suppressed to create common ground of grievances against the Comrade.

A natural center of gravity of this groundswell of gathering resentment was the home of a young man called Majhi. He lived with his elderly mother, and his older brother Akhtar, dropped in on weekends. Both brothers were graduates and had trained to be schoolteachers but Majhi, despite repeated attempts, had failed to gain a post. In contrast, Akhtar, the most qualified person in the village with a master's degree in English, had started as a teacher in a secondary school in a nearby town and a few years later became the head teacher of a school in a neighboring village.[12] Majhi, by contrast, was restless and frustrated that his attempts at political work for the Congress Party, whom his family had traditionally supported, had been thwarted by the Comrade at every turn. On one occasion the Comrade decided to end Akhtar's open defiance by humiliating him and slapped him for a minor offense, in full view of his friends and neighbors. Majhi was cowed on that occasion, but the Comrade had made an enemy for life. Majhi did not engage in overt political activity again, but this incident made his antagonism towards the Comrade widely known, and he continued to look for opportunities for a breakthrough; in this he had the whole-hearted support of his widowed mother. She was an intelligent woman who, as a single mother, was progressive enough not only to have educated her two sons but was also the only one in Chishti and Madanpur to have given her daughter a university education. This gave their household an air of accomplishment and pride that was only slightly tarnished by Majhi's restless and unchanneled energy. So, when discussions about how Mansur and the Comrade had used the bus trip to buy off dissenters began to spread, Majhi's home became the natural hub for people to drop in and meet others who were in agreement.

*

Six months later, the harvest also coincided with Ramzan, the spiritual month of regular prayers and introspection, fasting, and feasting that precedes the festival of Eid. The dynamics between families during this month deepened the plot of the social drama further. From the fifteenth day of the holy month of Ramzan, prayer meetings called *milads* were held in the evenings. Traditionally, after the day's fast was broken and the evening meal consumed, these meetings were held in the roomier courtyards of Syed households, with agnatic kin (*kutum*), friends, and village folk (*gramer lok*) invited to listen to recitations of the Quran and join in collective singing and prayers, followed by sweets. The hosting household also sent sweets to the households of all those related through descent (*kutum*) who had been unable to attend. This gift of sweets was a useful way to maintain kinship links when political divisions or other disagreements of the type common in Madanpur and Chishti came in the way of attending a *milad*. Attendance at a particular *milad* by non-kin members held significance, for it demonstrated cordial relations with the household of the host, and people made the effort to go as the *milads* provided a public platform where their relations with the host could be noted by all. It was routine for people to discuss who had been seen at which *milad* the following morning for everyone to draw their own conclusions. In the past, Syeds hosted these meetings as a sign of their feudal largesse, when they opened their homes to everyone to pray together, paid a talented orator to entertain their guests, and provided them with the prized luxury of sweets. The assumption was that for all these reasons, anyone who had been invited would consider it a privilege and turn up. In the altered moral economy after the land reforms (discussed previously), however, the character of the *milads* had altered. Now, the increasingly impoverished Syeds could not always afford to host these prayer meetings, and when they did, there was constant comparative evaluation of their hospitality by the rest of the village. Even the choice of orator had become contentious as traditional Syed village orators had to be replaced by young men from lower Muslim castes who had been sent away to study at madrasas and had returned home for Ramzan bearing the signs of their newly acquired piety: an all-white attire, distinctive long beards, hitched-up trousers, and authentic Arabic pronunciation.[13] The older Syeds had to accommodate these young men as orators to prove their own commitment to piety even though they were often sons of an erstwhile *bargadar* or wage laborer whom they would have treated with disdain. Audiences were also no longer guaranteed, as non-Syeds did not rely on Syeds to provide entertainment and sweets, since they could increasingly access these through technology and earnings. Further, loyalty to the Comrade also implied that a laborer would not freely accept the invitation from one of the Comrade's opponents or someone with a reputation as a vindictive landowner. The newfound pride and dignity of the rural proletariat now meant that attending a *milad* was one he had some choice in doing rather than an obligation that he had to fulfill. Attracting a good-sized audience with the key actors of village life present was therefore something Syeds had to work hard to achieve. To make matters even more tense for the host, in the absence of any system of RSVPs, there was no guarantee of attendance until the time of the meeting itself, leaving the host to nervously scan the lane outside his home in the hope of spotting approaching attendees. But they made an effort to do this because a successful *milad* signaled strong friendship bonds with non-kin Syeds (substantial social and political capital), and an ability to attract new audiences of "the right sort" to attend his *milad* also allowed the host to expand his network of supporters. The Syeds used these gatherings—their timing, the guest lists, the choice of orator, and the size of the audience—to play their own political games.

If new invitees accepted the invitation, it implied the makings of a new alliance, and new bonds forged at one *milad* were reinforced by further invitations from Syeds who belonged to the same alliance. These prayer meetings were thus used as arenas where the contours of new groupings could be put on legitimate public display.

All these tensions and anxieties were on display at the *milad* hosted by Hanif Master. He had invited Syeds from the households where he had agnatic kin. But the rule of *kutum* also allowed Hanif to pointedly exclude the Comrade from his invitations, as Hanif was related to him only through his wife and was therefore not agnatic kin, and by not inviting him Hanif could send out the message that he did not count the Comrade as a friend. Hanif didn't invite Mansur either, even though he was distant agnatic kin, on the grounds that he had never responded to previous invitations.[14] Instead, Hanif sought to reclaim some of the credibility that had been compromised through his appointment by the Comrade to the arbitration committee and, more so, by his participation in Mansur's complementary outing by bus to the fair. He did this by inviting a large number of sharecroppers, not only from his own *bargadar*'s family, as was customary, but also from many others. They were initially hesitant, but after a complex process of persuasion by his own *bargadar* and the other Syeds, they all came in the end. This was something of a coup for Hanif, as these sharecroppers were fully aware that the Comrade had not been invited, but came despite the likelihood of his anger about their accepting the hospitality of his rival. This was, rightfully, read as a sign that something fundamental had shifted in the Comrade's standing in the village.

To make matters even more complex, three other *milads* were also scheduled on the same evening: the first one at the home of a woman called Paru, the next at Hilal's, followed by Mustafa Master's, and then, finally, Hanif Master's own. This packed dance card had been carefully sequenced by them and reflected intertwined agendas. Paru had rebuffed the Comrade's sexual advances many years ago, and she and her husband had suffered as a result, never receiving any of the benefits that her Shekh neighbors had received. But their hard work and lack of dependents had allowed them to build a house big enough to host a *milad*, and anyone who disapproved of the Comrade was welcome in her home. Hilal, on the other hand, was close to the Comrade, and his wife was Mustafa's sister; using this close kinship connection, Hilal had invited Mustafa to lead the prayers, in the hope of building bridges across the factions that had formed during the scandal. The gamble had been to see if members of Hilal's circle of fellow Comrade supporters would show up despite Mustafa leading the prayers. It was agreed that if they did not, then Hanif would bring the audience from his *milad* over to save face for Hilal (and Mustafa). By doing so, Hanif also hoped to win Hilal over to their side and bolster opposition to the Comrade. As feared, the turnout was indeed thin at Hilal's, and Hanif's extra guests were crucial in filling the courtyard. The significant strength of Hanif's audience, on the other hand, was evidence that more and more people were questioning the hold of the Comrade over them and were willing to literally vote with their feet by attending the *milad* hosted by someone openly critical of the Comrade. Hanif and Mustafa were by now allies, following their shared membership on the scandal arbitration committee, and it helped that Mustafa's wife was also Hanif's sister, so there was a close kinship bond too. In his effort to solidify the developing bonds of solidarity, Mustafa invited Enayat (who had abandoned support for the Comrade following the disruption of his son's wedding following Enayat's calling out of the Comrade over the water tank issue) to lead the recitations at his *milad*, in an effort to seal the new alliance against the Comrade and to make up for having gone on Mansur's bus trip himself. By offering to conduct his *milad* after both Hilal's and Mustafa's, Hanif was able to visibly present his popularity over all three Syeds. On hearing of thin attendance at Hilal's where Mustafa was the orator and then at Mustafa's where Enayat was the orator, he was seen to generously add greater entertainment of two extra *milads* for his own guests while also saving the face of the two Syeds.

Meanwhile, similar tactics were being used on the other side: Mansur invited Abu, another Syed from Madanpur, to do the recitation at his *milad*, partly because he was an excellent orator but also to draw him over to his side in support of the Comrade. Abu had recently been told off by Akbar, another rival of the Comrade, to tone down his *milad* recitations so as not to upstage other performers. Abu had taken umbrage at this, and Mansur saw an opportunity to wean Abu away from the Comrade's critics.

The *milads* were thus a performative expression of bonds of solidarity, as members of the village who had, until this point, discussed their opinions only in whispers in the safety of their homes now showed themselves publicly to others. What had been an initial casual chat among them by the village lane one evening in the days following Mansur's bus trip had generated further gatherings at Majhi's house and bolder conversations within homes, and were now put on public display throughout the evening as audiences moved from one *milad* to the next and assembled again at future *milads*. People worked hard at finding expressions for their growing solidarity, and the use of traditional forums such as prayer meetings reinforced their shared history and identity.

*

Following such challenges, the Comrade meted out various punishments in retaliation, but the challenges continued to put a dent in his seeming invincibility. If anything, his self-seeking aims and actions seemed, ironically, to provoke even greater cooperative action among the rest of the village. At this stage, such cooperation could still not take an overt political form, such as a rival polit-ical party, but it continued to strengthen the idea that political opposition to the status quo was possible and necessary. Each of his actions forced others to eval-uate the ethical basis of his actions and weigh how far they were willing to con-nive in them. Though the Comrade disregarded opinions about his greed—both economic and sexual—deliberating on his actions forced the villagers to con-front what their own ethical red lines were. And with structures of formal politics closed to them, they utilized non-political arenas to demonstrate their growing political cooperation, such as the carefully orchestrated *milad* gatherings just discussed, that were designed to consolidate the alliances formed in the wake of the scandal and its resolution. A couple of years after the scandal, the alliance was tested as Comrade tried to get out of paying a fine of Rs. 10,000 for capturing some of the zakat land that the village owned as 'commons'. But the coalition held strong and they were able to force the Comrade to pay.

Though these challenges had limited impact in the short run on the Comrade's dominant position, they gave hope to those who wanted political change. Among these were the Comrade's erstwhile allies, whom he had driven variously to si-lence (Akbar), poetry (Mukhtar), bitterness (Tinkari), wiliness (Hanif), or mad-ness (Shaker). The scandal caused by the Comrade hubristically overstepped the line by insisting on a marriage that ignored Islamic notions of *haram*, openly siding with one party, and attempting to manipulate and acquire the settlement money however provided an unexpected opportunity for bringing their resent-ment out into the open. His actions made the ethical red lines shine brighter and reinforced the need for change.

Phase 3: Crisis Redress

The growing clamor of criticism against the non-payment of settlement money made it impossible in the end for the arbitration committee to not insist that it was paid, and although they did grant an extension, a new deadline was fixed. On the newly appointed day, Feroza was summoned to the Comrade's house—the venue was changed at the last minute as yet another tactic of intimidation—and no one was allowed to accompany her. She reported afterward that she had felt awkward and frightened in the unfamiliar surroundings of the lion's den. She had been asked to sign in five different places, including for the divorce and the paperwork for the settlement money to be held in a fixed-rate bank deposit. We heard that the Comrade had unilaterally ruled that Feroza, despite being an adult, was not allowed to be the sole signatory for the money. Neither did the Comrade allow her father or anyone from her family to be a joint account holder. The Comrade had tried to persuade each of the members of the committee to be a joint signatory, no doubt hoping to maintain access to the funds through them, but both Hanif and Mustafa, by now thoroughly involved in anti-Comrade discussions at Majhi's house, declined. In the end, Lulu Master had agreed, to save the Comrade's face, and no doubt gained a favor he would call in later.

Amir Ali's family looked both relieved and exhausted when Feroza returned home. Her mother promptly began making plans for marrying her off and hoped that the fixed deposit, maturing in five years, would make for a handsome dowry. In the customary socializing after lunch, neighbors and kin offered their advice and were quick to tease, if slightly enviously, about the significant income that the family would receive as interest from the deposit in the meanwhile. Amir Ali told me in resigned tones that the months of tension had taken a huge toll on his health, and it was true that his strong and muscular body had visibly shrunk. He also took the insistence on a third-party joint account holder as a clear insult to his reputation for probity, and he rightly worried that Lulu Master's involvement left the account vulnerable to the Comrade's greed. The fallout of the bus trip had loosened tongues, and so now people openly speculated that the Comrade was trying to get his hands on the money for his son's expanding fisheries business. What was significant was that this was the first occasion on which I heard such speculation even among those who counted themselves as constituting the penumbra of acolytes around the Comrade. This included Bishwa Dom who, like other Dom daily wage laborers, was a fierce Left Front supporter, and who saw the Comrade as their champion against upper caste interests. So far, they had chosen to overlook the Comrade's excesses, not because they did not know about them but because they chose to focus on the Comrade's communist political work of creating a fairer distribution of resources and dignity. But Mansur's bus trip had changed something significant in the village when even those who had not personally lost anything from the scandal had come out and taken a stance against the injustice of how it had been resolved. This provoked the Comrade's supporters also to reevaluate their loyalties, and one day I heard Bishwa grumbling to his wife inside their hut, as I sat in their courtyard chatting with his father, that the Comrade had unnecessarily complicated matters by insisting on the joint signatory for the deposit. "This money was to pay for injustice, not to play politics with," he observed. To me he acknowledged for the first time since I had known him that the Comrade "could not bear to see anyone make too much of himself." This indicated that while the immediate scandal may have been redressed by the payment of compensation money to Feroza, a wider schism in the village, with far-reaching consequences, may have occurred.

The ever-vigilant and politically astute Comrade may have sensed this discernible shift in the stance of his supporters toward him and the momentum it had imperceptibly gathered. Thus, when the deposit matured some years later, Feroza was able to claim her money without interference from the Comrade, signaling a victory not just for her family but also for the Comrade's critics. The scandal and its resolution had therefore successfully brought together various detractors of the Comrade who until then had been disunited. The bus trip had provided an occasion for a moral evaluation of right and wrong—the disregard for ideas of taboo that the Comrade had shown by forcing the marriage, his obvious ties to one party in the dispute, his hypocritical attempts at neutrality while choosing the arbitration committee, his blatant use of the bus trip to make his supporters complicit by inviting them on a trip intended to absolve Mansur from paying the settlement money, and finally the Comrade's enforcing a joint signatory to the deposit in the hope of keeping access to it open—had at every stage provoked thought and reflection.

The Scandal and Democratic Citizenship

The scandal can be read as a significant event in the democratic life in the politics of the village, for it "enabled a group to evaluate people for their work, their qualities of leadership, and their moral character, without ever confronting them to their faces with failures in any sphere" (Gluckman 1963: 313). In retrospect, the true significance of the event was revealed through the sequence of events that followed it in the months and years to come. In the short term, the Comrade's designs were foiled when Amir Ali married his daughter off safely to a distant village, using the settlement money as her dowry. But in the longer term, the scandal helped coalesce opposition to him, which was able to provide local support for the political alternative of the new party of Trinamool Congress. It was a small but significant shift that contributed to the political earthquake ten years later.

In the essay "Social Dramas and Stories about Them," written late in his career, Victor Turner provided a comprehensive definition of "social drama" thus:

Big or small, a social drama first manifests itself as the breach of a norm, the infraction of a rule of morality, law, custom, or etiquette, in some public arena. . . . Whatever may be the case, a mounting crisis follows, a momentous juncture or turning point in the relations between components of a social field—at which seeming peace becomes overt conflict and covert antagonism become visible. Sides are taken, factions are formed, and unless the conflict can be sealed off quickly within a limited area of social interaction, there is a

tendency for the breach to widen and spread until it coincides with some dominant cleavage in the widest set of relevant social relations to which the parties in
conflict belong. (Turner 1980: 151)

As we see in the account presented in this chapter, the scandal was a social
drama par excellence, and reading small developments in this way provides a
valuable frame to make sense of such an event in the villages of Madanpur and
Chishti. As in Turner's definition, here too a minor transgression between two
young people became, through a series of ever-expanding events, the reason for a
cleavage between the Comrade and others, which then coincided with the dominant cleavage between the Left Front and its critics. As argued at the start of this
chapter, macro electoral changes, such as the loss of power of the Left Front after
thirty-four years, can often be understood better by looking at their workings at a
more manageable level of the village.

The scandal also revealed something fundamental about the nature of political activity itself and its role in creating social solidarity. A large part of what
people had observed as the Comrade's work is what they described as "O Party
korey" (He does Party) and what I have previously described as "political work"
(Banerjee 2010). As we have seen, this included doing the work of his political
party in the village, which included disseminating agitprop among the agricultural workforce about dignity and rights, marshaling votes during elections, and
also, crucially, impeding anyone else from usurping his role. He was what Weber
called a "professional politician" who lived "off politics." Through its reliance on
such political work by various Comrades, the Left Front government was able to
stay in power by limiting participation of ordinary citizens in politics to only the
act of voting in elections. While the Left Front was ideologically committed to
an emancipatory agenda for the agrarian proletariat, they did not tolerate citizens' interest in actively "doing politics" or aspiring for influence, which was kept
strictly as the preserve of a few trusted lieutenants. Active citizenship of the kind
required by the spirit of republicanism was therefore aggressively constrained
by closing off all avenues to political action, and political participation was confined only to elections. Democracy itself became increasingly narrowly defined
by electoral victories rather than the basic ideas of expression of dissent, peaceful
challenges to the status quo, or political competition, all of which were fairly germane to any definition of democratic politics. Voters, of course, saw and learned
much from this, and some of them expressed their dissent in the only safe avenue
available to them—namely, the secret ballot. But the event of a scandal created an
opportunity to alter this. The Comrade's actions causing the scandal highlighted
the modus operandi of how he "did" his professional politics and led to an intensive moral evaluation of this political work. While people may have made
such evaluations earlier, the terror tactics of the Comrade had ensured that these

remained confined to the privacy of their homes. At that stage any gossip shared was a "weapon of the weak . . . where power and possible repression makes open acts of disrespect dangerous" (Scott 1985: 282). In the past, therefore, criticism of the Comrade sounded like personal grudges and was diffused across the village. To convert such atomized, fearful, and silent resentment into an open but peaceful collective confrontation required an aggregation of individual grudges into a collective critique that could not be dismissed easily. For it to be effective, the only safety was in numbers and had to be based on solidarities that could be trusted and sustained over a period of time. Knowledge of political parties such as Trinamool Congress had also created awareness that while the united critique during the scandal was directed against the Comrade, it had the potential of also challenging the hegemony of his party and its government. This required an imagination of a larger electoral arena beyond the village where such a battle could be fought. Years of voting in elections had brought an understanding of the relationship between an individual vote and the final electoral result, and this knowledge served to sustain their courage at the village level. The inhabitants of Madanpur and Chishti were thus aware that while they were waging a battle, it could help win a war.

This new political action required, first and foremost, actors who would be fearless enough to voice their dissent publicly and who would also have the credibility to attract the support of others. Figures like Enayat, therefore, were key to the success, for although he was wealthy, he had maintained a reputation of fairness and generosity with his sharecropper and workers—unlike the Comrade—and he had also displayed remarkable courage in calling out the Comrade, despite knowing that it would cost him dearly. His throwing down the gauntlet attracted others, like Hanif, who brought with them their friendship but also crucially a nous for strategic thinking, as displayed during the *milads*. This led to others adding their weight to the growing opposition even if it meant only serving as a willing audience for the unfolding drama. This, in turn, encouraged the actors to come up with new strategies to challenge the status quo, especially those that would achieve their purpose without tearing apart the social fabric. Murdering the Comrade, for instance, was never, ever discussed as an option, even though some of his transgressions may have provoked such thoughts and it would have been relatively easy to achieve. Instead, creative use was made of prayer meetings and kinship links, which were customary arenas of cooperation, to aid the inhabitants of Madanpur and Chishti to suppress their individual desires in favor of a collective, non-violent action. This required much "off stage" activity of planning and strategy, negotiation and persuasion, and this process in turn forced participants to reflect on their ethical positions and the means they were willing to use to achieve the desired end. The *milads* were "sites of political vitality," in which new modes of political action were fashioned and the possibilities of new ones for future political action were created (Wedeen 2008: 139). Such arenas were not so much "rituals of rebellion" that allowed prescribed venting of frustrations as they were anvils on which the possibility of future challenges was forged.

As a result, political activity in the villages of Madanpur and Chishti was no longer confined only to the work of professional politicians like the Comrade, with his union activities and budget disbursements, but it also included discussions of the role that everyone could, and had to play, in such a politics. The new actors were Weber's "part-time or amateur politicians"—that is, those who "lived for" politics, rather than the Comrade who "lived off" politics and profited from it (Weber 1919). The contrast between the professional and amateur politicians raised questions about what politics was "for" and forced discussions about the nature of complicity and participation, competition and rivalry, and the need for cooperation across existing social divisions. It became increasingly clear even to the Comrade's supporters that he had turned all politics (*rajniti*) into his own law (*niti*). These questions were not directly concerned with elections so much as the kind of political life that electoral politics created in which power could be captured by some individuals over others. This led to reappraisals of the desirability of such a zero-sum game and the imagining of more whole-sum alternatives.

It can be argued that this evaluative process had ironically been made possible from the key messages of the communist vision that the Comrade had himself helped introduce; the dignity that had been bestowed on even the poorest and most socially disenfranchised in rural areas had been truly revolutionary and had created a sense of self-worth among ordinary people that empowered them to dream of change. Further, the Left Front's vigorous use of universal citizenship to ensure that everyone voted may have been cynically motivated to create their own electoral success, but regular voting had also brought to many a new and lasting acquaintance with the idea of citizenship. Emboldened by this sense of dignity and citizenship, villagers in Madanpur and Chishti were eventually able to use their imagination to create an alternative to the Comrade's dubious dealings, one that was based on a shared understanding of "doing the right thing." By debating these issues within their families and in hushed gossip sessions, people not only imagined alternative and more appropriate solutions to the scandal but also articulated the kind of moral community they wished their village to be. By being forced to evaluate the greed, lust, arrogance, deceit, violence, probity, integrity, and patience variously adopted by actors during the scandal and its aftermath, they had to define for themselves their own ethical aspirations. As the anthropologist Jarrett Zigon notes, "familiar moral concepts may be best considered not as moral aims, but rather as pointing or indicating an ethical problem or imperative that cannot yet be neatly conceptualized but nevertheless motivates action in the world" (2014: 761). The exchange of gossip allowed them to evaluate the Comrade and helped them to identify the village's values and identify others who conformed to this moral universe. By the collective sharing of their evaluations of the Comrade's actions, citizens were also able to bring into force a new sense of "we-ness" whose basis was not the formal affiliation to any particular political party nor caste or class, but a moral community.[15] This process is what Hannah Arendt would call "politics as action," an action in world-making and self-making.

I have presented this scandal, the first of the major events discussed in this book, as an example of how non-electoral events can be critical in shaping democratic subjectivity. As we have seen, this social drama and its moment of moral breakdown generated an evaluation not just of the rights and wrongs of the scandal itself, but of the wider realm of the political. A desirable politics was imagined in the process, as well as a recognition of the values that needed to be cultivated for such politics as action.

*

Coda

During another visit several years later, I learned that Feroza, following her separation from Shohin, had been caught with him again and this news had spread like wildfire across the villages. While Shohin's family blamed this on her bad character, most others concluded that Shohin had seduced her again at his family's behest, to try to recover the money they had paid in settlement. In response, Feroza's father, Amir Ali, who often traveled in North India on business, staying overnight in mosques and or making use of local hospitality, had decided to move his daughter far from the village, and had made a match with a young man he'd met in small town near Moradabad in Uttar Pradesh. I saw photographs of the wedding (which only Amir Ali attended due to the cost of travel) and was told that Feroza was now pregnant and would visit sometime in the future.

Later still, during the national elections in 2009, his wife told me that Amir Ali was away visiting his daughter but that he would return with her before election day, as he never failed to vote, seeing that as a shocking waste. Sure enough, on the day of the election, Amir Ali appeared with his daughter and son-in-law. Feroza looked happy and prosperous and was excited by all the attention she got on her return. For the first time we saw her wearing a tailored two-piece shalwar kamiz, not a sari, and enjoyed her many stories about the "North," where people ate wheat rather than rice, and enjoyed plentiful fruit and the comforts of running water. She didn't have to do manual work, she boasted, as her husband's salary as a driver allowed them to buy modern conveniences and hire domestic help. All in all, her bright pink clothes, plump figure, and confident manner contrasted vividly with the wiry, sari-clad figures of her kin and neighbors who sat listening open-mouthed, and suggested she had survived the scandal well enough.

*

4

Harvest

Cultivating Cooperation

The scene I encountered one December was extraordinary. The main entrance to Chishti was blocked by two bullock carts to which men carried and loaded bundles of paddy, stalks spilling out of bulging sacks. Squeezing past them, I found the village transformed—lanes were strewn with straw, sticks, and bits of rope, and in every courtyard and open space freshly cut paddy lay in tall piles creating a maze; it was as if the fields had marched into the village itself. The air was thick with fumes from diesel-run threshing machines and their noise, and the voices of people giving each other instructions were the best way to find one's way around. Everyone was busy, immersed in their tasks, working with a sense of urgency, and there was little inclination for small talk. After a cursory welcoming nod and grin as they spotted me, everyone returned to what they were doing, in marked contrast to the cries of excitement and questions and cups of tea that usually greeted my arrivals. Words remained at a premium over the following days. People rose early, went over the required tasks at the start of the day, designated groups to carry them out, and then got on with them promptly, stopping only when absolutely necessary. It was clear that any questions would have to wait, and without their usual helpful commentaries, I was challenged to observe and make sense of what was going on in light of the many previous conversations we had shared about the land reforms, changing labor relations, the challenges of agriculture, caste dynamics, and kinship networks. Sweat and paddy dust had a curiously leveling effect as Shekh and Dom sharecroppers were indistinguishable from the elite Syed landowners whose machinations I had watched closely during the unfolding scandal a few months ago.[1] But in this harvest season, work dominated everything, and every person worked as a part of a team.

In a rural agricultural community, a harvest is a key event and perhaps the most important annual moment outside the religious calendar. It lasts for a few short days and is a time of expectation and anxiety when months of hard labor, care, and cultivation finally bear fruit and can be materially assessed, collected, weighed, divided, stored, and sold. In the context of a region dominated by a communist government whose hallmark institutional policy had been land reform, any harvest was likely to carry even greater value as tensions around land, changed caste dynamics, increased wages, and a more confident labor force were likely to be more visible during it. This would explain why an elderly informant had suggested that I would not understand politics until I had witnessed a harvest. In Madanpur and Chishti, as in the rest of communist West Bengal, the harvest brought into the open a number of different sources of tension that the radical land tenancy reforms of the 1980s had ushered in. The reforms had been the culmination of nearly two decades of revolutionary violence, meetings, and demonstrations that ultimately led to a rebalancing of power between land-owners and sharecroppers. Sharecroppers were given a more secure tenancy, greater crop shares, and higher wages for labor, and so to avoid escalating costs, landowners had to put their own labor into agriculture to make it viable. As a result, by the twenty-first century agriculture had become a joint activity between landowners and their sharecroppers, with the latter often playing a dominating role in decision-making, owing to their greater technical knowledge which was required for the recently introduced high-yielding varieties (HYV) of paddy. During the harvest, this asymmetry was especially magnified.

The social structure of Madanpur and Chishti was closely linked to paddy cultivation practices. In the past, the Syeds had marked their distinction within the village social hierarchy by maintaining a taboo against their handling of the plow and, by implication, against manual labor. They owned the land, although the size of landholdings was never very large, 40 bighas (about 16 acres) being the biggest, and the average more likely to be between 10 and 15 bighas (4 to 6 acres). As Bhattacharya records, "In 1982, a whopping 81.6 per cent of West Bengal's agricultural households held less than 5 acres" (Bhattacharya 2016: 58); that is to say, there was a preponderance of small/medium tenants cultivating land belonging to small/medium landowners' (Bhattacharya 2016: 59). In Madanpur and Chishti, while the owners used to live in the village and supervise cultivation, they rarely stepped into the fields themselves. This manifested in a cleavage among the Muslims, between the elite Syeds who owned most of the land and the other Muslim castes of Shekhs, Pathan, and Mughal, who worked on their land. The relationship between the owner and the tenant farmer, though a relationship of mutual dependence, was vastly exploitative. The sharecropper hoped for secure tenancy but lived in precarity, beholden to the owner's capricious choice of tenant every year. The owner was dependent on the sharecropper for both his labor and his knowledge of farming, given that the owner himself was unable to farm as a Syed. But the Syeds set the terms of contract and labor arrangements, and the sharecroppers suffered precarious employment and pitiful wages that were paid mostly in kind and at the whim of the landowners. Memories of hunger and humiliation marked the life of those who did not own land.

This scenario began to change quite radically in the late 1980s, for two principal reasons. First, land reforms were brought in by the newly elected Left Front and second, High Yielding Varieities (HYV) of rice were introduced. The reforms, though uneven and incomplete across the state, nevertheless brought security of tenancy to sharecroppers in Madanpur and Chishti, and by the early 1990s "the number of recorded bargadars crossed 1.4 million and was still counting" (Bhattacharya 2016: 59). Additionally, the new HYV matured quickly, requiring about ninety days from planting to harvesting, compared to twice as long for the traditional varieties. As a result, double cropping became the norm with the Green Revolution as HYV of rice were cultivated alongside traditional varieties[2] and combined with reform in land tenancy and the statewide tenfold increase in the daily wage, addressed issues of precarity and impoverishment of tenants and agricultural work. It should be noted that this combination of institutional and political innovations in West Bengal made it distinct from other states in India where the Green Revolution was also introduced. Although it was considered "scale-neutral," it appeared to have a "pro–rich peasant bias" and had very little impact on alleviating rural poverty.[3]

Academic literature on the Left Front's land reforms was sharply divided on whether the land reforms had been radical enough or not and whether they had had an impact in creating the impressive breakthrough in agricultural growth that West Bengal had in the 1980s. Many had argued that they were not nearly radical enough (Mallick 1992), others had been in favor of the realistic path that the reforms took (Dreze and Sen 1989; Kohli 1987; Lieten 1990), others attributed other factors such as technological innovation and infrastructural change rather than institutional reform to growth in prosperity (Gazdar 1992; Harriss 1993), while still others offered counter-evidence to prove causal linkages between reform and growth in productivity (Banerjee, Gertler, and Ghatak 2002).[4] My fieldsite of Madanpur and Chishti was an ideal location to chart the impact of land reforms, as they had seen institutional change, technological innovation, and infrastructural change—the three factors that scholars variously attributed to the spurt in agricultural growth and change in West Bengal. Many in Madanpur and Chishti had been beneficiaries of Operation Barga, which introduced tenancy reforms and strengthened the security of the sharecroppers' tenancy, although transfer of ownership did not apply because even in the radical version of land reforms articulated in CPI(M)'s "Resolution of Certain Agrarian Issues," tenants who were leaseholders from small farmers (as in Madanpur and

Chishti) did not have the right to ownership. Both villages also cultivated the technologically advanced strains of HYV paddy that had a much greater grain output, and the use of shallow submersible pumps was common. As a result, support for the Left Front was solid in this area, and discussions about the rights of agricultural workers and tenancy were common. It seemed important to therefore observe a harvest in a context in which all the preceding factors had been in play—that is, where there had been land reforms, greater crop shares, technological innovation, and a growth in production. Each of these changes would have inevitably also impacted real lives in concrete ways, and I was especially keen to observe the non-quantifiable effects of the reforms and the impact that they had on social relations, hierarchy, and cooperation. A harvest would concentrate into a few days of activity myriad different aspects of agriculture and social relations, and prior knowledge about caste and class dynamics between the elite, landowning Syeds and agricultural labor drawn from Shekhs, Mughals, Bagdis, and Dom could form the basis of observing any change in the balance of power relations during the harvest. This was perhaps what an elderly sharecropper had meant when he advised me to be present for a harvest if I wanted to understand politics.

The politics of West Bengal since Indian independence in 1947 had been dominated by the issue of land and agriculture. West Bengal has been among the largest rice-producing states in India and successive governments had also attempted to address the issue of inequity between agricultural labor and land ownership through legal reform, especially to secure tenancy for sharecroppers. The West Bengal Bargadar Act of 1950 prohibited the eviction of a sharecropper (*bargadar*) except on the grounds of self-cultivation by the landowner, the Estate Acquisition Act 1953 aimed to limit the size of agricultural land by declaring holdings in excess of 25 acres illegal, and the Congress government in 1971 brought further modifications to the Land Reform Act of 1955 to impose land ceilings on families rather than individuals, to close a loophole that had been exploited by the landowning classes. As Bhattacharya notes, "Every new law after independence attempted to enhance the rights of the sharecropper, raising his share of crop while reducing his burden of input or leaving it unaltered" (2016: 64). But at every step, the laws failed in their implementation due to the entrenched complicity between the landowning classes and local administration, a lack of readily available information for sharecroppers regarding their entitlements according to the new laws, and a general lack of political will to mobilize them to claim their rights. The coming of the Left Front (a coalition of left political parties) to power after their comprehensive victory in the elections in 1977, however, proved to be something of a game changer. Their innovation was to not simply introduce legal reform but to also simultaneously bring in key political reform to achieve agrarian change. Thus, while the Left Front government introduced yet another West Bengal Land Reforms Bill in 1980 that led to Operation Barga to secure tenancy for sharecroppers, they simultaneously devolved political power to the village level through local tiers of elected government while introducing land reforms measures.

The CPI(M)-led Left Front were expected to implement the two policies they had always verbally committed to, namely abolishing landlordism and restoring land to the tiller. On the whole, Operation Barga itself has been widely regarded as a success, at least in terms of increase in registration and crop shares, leading studies to note that by the early 1990s, "the number of recorded bargadars crossed 1.4 million and was still counting" (Bhattacharya 2016: 59), which meant that "more than 65 percent of an estimated 2.3 million share tenants had been registered . . . [and] data showed that the proportion of tenants . . . getting more than 50 percent of output increased from 17 percent to 39 percent" (Banerjee et al. 2002: 243, 256). While these results were indeed impressive, it has also been pointed out that the comparative performance of the previous United Front government had in fact had been better than that of the Left Front. "The United Front managed to vest 0.5 million acres in its short tenure (1967–69) as against less than 0.3 million acres by the Left Front during the first 13 years in government" (Bhattacharya 2016: 75). In fact, the commitment of restoring land to the tiller through the transfer of tenancy land remained incomplete as "the CPI(M) in the Left Front suspended transfer of tenancy land until all the sharecroppers were recorded which it regarded as a vital security against their constant threat of eviction" (Bhattacharya 2016: 71). But the critical qualitative difference had been that land reforms implemented by the Left Front had "a political charge" created by a critical change that the Left Front introduced to the existing law, which was to move the burden of proof to the landowner if he wished to dispute the claim of a *bargadar* rather than the other way around. Shifting the onus to landowner thus liberated sharecroppers to stake their claims to tenancy, which, when combined with greater political voice and representation at the village level through decentralization, allowed for active political mobilization.

However, land reform under the Left Front, despite its potential to create genuinely radical change, remained ultimately conservative by giving in to the necessity of maintaining a wide support base for electoral victory that increasingly became an end in itself. Political pragmatism meant that radical revolutionary bark gave way to a more reformist bite, what the economist Ashok Mitra called "the feasibility frontier."[5] The Left Front's choice of tenancy reform, rather than the disbursement of "land-to-the-tiller" that was adopted by the communist parties in Kerala, could be read as a cynical compromise with an eye on creating enduring political gains. The implication of tenancy reform was that the sharecroppers remained "secure in the possession of land and payment of below-market rents *only* as long as the state sides with the tenants rather than the landlords" (Herring 1983: 90; emphasis added), thereby establishing a dependence on the Left Front government by its rural support base.[6] Further, it avoided the petty embourgeoisement of the poorer peasantry in case it reduced their electoral enthusiasm for the Left Front. In fact, the rights of the agricultural workers—who were always referred to as *gorib* (poor) by Comrades—were never fully fought for, and their wages were raised only enough to signal a change and buy their loyalty to the communists. The promise and hope for further reform and greater increase in wages kept both sharecropper (*bargadar*) and agricultural worker (*khetmujur*) loyal to the Left Front through successive elections. At the same time, wages were never raised so much as to frighten away the middle and rich peasants, nor were agricultural markets reformed, allowing the monopoly of mill owners to continue—thus allowing the Left Front to maintain a wide-angled rural electoral base (Harriss-White 2008). And this base was kept content through small benefits, as Bardhan and Mookherjee found in a large sample survey that showed that the drip, drip of short-term and personalized benefits, rather than big improvements in public services, helped keep the electorate loyal (Bardhan and Mookherjee 2010).

*

These villages, lying in the well-irrigated areas of Birbhum district, were able to grow two paddy crops a year, and many also cultivated a wheat crop, harvested in April/May, in between. The harvest I had arrived for was of the traditional swarna paddy, sown in the summer and harvested in the winter, although HYVs of rice were also cultivated since the 1980s when they had been eagerly adopted for their much larger yields. The HYV crop matured quickly in just three months, in contrast to the six months that the traditional varieties needed, but it was expensive to cultivate, requiring large amounts of fertilizers, pesticides, and water extracted by diesel-run pumps.[7] But despite these costs, HYV enjoyed enduring popularity because the returns from this crop were nearly three times as much as the capital outlay required. "The 'Highling rice' [HYV] is a lottery," people said. "The prize is much bigger than the price of the ticket." In contrast, swarna paddy was cheaper to cultivate, as it was fed by monsoon rains, but it took longer to mature but was still cultivated for a variety of reasons. It was grown mainly for food security but also because a number of the by-products it generated were not available from HYV rice.[8] For instance, the staple and ubiquitous snacks of Bengal, puffed rice (*mudi* and *khoi*), could not be made from HYV paddy, nor were ritual offerings of rice made with HYV rice as it was considered too synthetic, too manmade, too dry (*khora*), to be offered to the gods. There was an implicit reasoning that the success of the HYV crop was more reliant on money and capital inputs than on the labor of the farmers and was therefore less sincere a ritual offering than the swarna rice. For the same reason, HYV was never used for the pulao of wedding

feasts or for special festive foods such as pithey; instead people routinely cultivated swarna and other traditional varieties expressly for these purposes.[9] Also
significantly, the short stalks of HYV were no good for fodder for the considerable livestock in the village (all plowing was done by oxen), nor could it be
used for thatching roofs, as they tended to mold in the monsoon. But perhaps
just as important a reason for growing this less plentiful swarna variety was its
restorative quality for the soil. Earlier, the fallow periods between two swarna
crops removed the acidity of the soil, but the introduction of HYV had made this
impossible and instead had sapped the ground of nutrients, which only a vast
quantity of cow dung or swarna paddy could restore. All these factors meant that
the harvest of the swarna, as it was that December, was met with greater trepidation than the HYV; the yields were never very high and so not one grain could be
wasted; the by-products were precious and so had to be collected carefully, and
the grain had to be stored separately and set aside for festivals and consumption.
It was the rice they knew better and loved but also one that they had to work
harder for, and this added to the frisson of the harvest.[10]

The size of landholdings in Madanpur and Chishti was not very large, 8 to
10 acres (25 to 30 *bighas*) being among the largest.[11] This put the Syeds into the
category of mid-sized *moddhobitto* rather than large land owners or *zamindars*
(who typically held more than 16 acres/50 bighas) or small *pranti* farmers (less
than 1 acre).[12] The owners of land used to live in the village and supervise cultivation but rarely stepped into the fields themselves, maintaining their elite *ashraf*
status by eschewing manual work, especially handling the plow. The relationship
between landowners and sharecroppers was a permanently strained one, as each
was reliant on the other; the sharecropper had to watch out for the owner's capricious choice of sharecropper every year, hoping to win enough confidence to
secure continuity in his tenancy and, in turn, the owner was, while wholly dependent on the sharecropper for the farming, nevertheless free to set the terms
of tenancy. As sharecroppers reported, there was a greater supply of labor than
demand and that made them ultimately dispensable and put them in a position
of permanent dependency and at the beck and call of the owners. Until the late
1970s, when the Syeds owned most of the land and the Shekhs, Pathans, and
Mughal castes alongside the Dom and Bagdis provided the labor, sharecroppers
(*bargadar*) were entitled to receive a third of the yield once the requisite amount
had been put aside for the seeds (*bichon*) for the following year. In addition, they
were also meant to be paid a daily wage for their labor (about Rs. 3 in the 1970s),
but the sharecropper could not ask for any extra labor to help with his tasks and
only his wife, not even his sons, were allowed to help. But the injustice of the
system was not simply that this made the work quite literally back-breaking, but
that even the abysmally low wages were often withheld and workers were often
paid in kind with small amounts of rice to feed their family that provided only

for a meal of rice and not much else, just once a day. And even these tiny stocks dwindled when they needed cash, as they were forced to sell small quantities of it; given that there was only a single annual crop, this measure was highly risk laden. Any other work they found outside of cultivation was also paid the same low wage, and again it was paid at the whim of the employer, who routinely made the worker wait for days. As a result, chronic hunger, precarity, and humiliation marked the lifeworld of the sharecropper and agricultural worker.

This changed radically with the introduction of the Act of 1980 which, in its effort to protect poorer landowners (and call out spurious claims of "personal cultivation" by large landowners), made provisions to reclaim barga land if "the landowner could prove that he derived his principal income from that land and promised to cultivate the land himself or with his family members, not by farm servants or hired hands" (Bhattacharya 2016: 78). This piece of legislation achieved two principal aims. One, as observed earlier, it put the onus of proving their claim on the landowner rather than the sharecropper. Second, it forced the landowning class to cultivate the land with their own labor while also having to give up half the profits to the sharecropper working on it. By the time of this study, the Syeds had been doing agricultural work for well over two decades, but their resentment at this unambiguous loss of status was still fresh. It was evident that some of them were more confident in their agricultural knowledge and skills than others, but they seemed united in claiming that it was the addition of their labor to the cultivation process that had resulted in significantly higher crop yields at any harvest.

Crop Yields and Productivity

Anticipating the crop yield before any harvest was a delicate business as it depended on a variety of factors and could vary widely across fields. Since the introduction of land reforms, landowners and sharecroppers explained the variation in diametrically opposed ways. The Syeds, somewhat predictably, blamed the sharecroppers for low yields in the past and explained current higher yields as the direct result of the input of their own labor. They insisted that this explanation was not simply self-satisfied arrogance but the result of their need. One Syed woman defended this strategy by explaining that "the poor can go out and sell their labor and earn money, but we have few options other than to work on our own land. So we have to work very hard to make the yields good because we have no other sources of income." In contrast, the sharecroppers insisted that the landowners took even less interest in farming ever since their share of the harvest had been so radically reduced by the reform and didn't think that the extra labor (*shrm*) by anyone made the slightest difference to the final yield. Any increase in productivity, they argued, could be entirely put down to the introduction of HYV of paddy.

Research shows that both parties were partly correct. Evidence indicates that West Bengal's rice production soared from the 1980s onward, and scholars such as John Harriss and others have argued, like the sharecroppers did, that technological innovations such as HYV, combined with the development of irrigation infrastructure (essential for growing these varieties), were the critical factors behind this increase in paddy production (Harriss 1998). But given that land reforms had also come into effect during the same period as the introduction of HYV, the question was raised whether factors such as institutional change had had any effect on productivity or not. One study tackled this question by comparing agricultural productivity in West Bengal (before and after the reforms) with neighboring Bangladesh, which had also introduced HYV but where there had been no tenancy reforms (Banerjee et al. 2002). The evidence led them to show that "even though the rate of adoption of HYV rice was faster in Bangladesh than in West Bengal, the rate of growth in rice productivity was higher in West Bengal" (Banerjee et al. 2002: 260), and they attribute the higher productivity principally to institutional reform. The reason for this was that reforms in West Bengal had two direct consequences, which they call "a bargaining power effect and a security of tenure effect" (Banerjee et al. 2002: 240). Security of tenure was of course a direct consequence of Operation Barga, which through legal and political processes on the ground registered and recorded the tenancy rights of sharecroppers. This move removed the vulnerability of the sharecropper's existence which earlier always remained at the whim of the landowner as the latter could arbitrarily allow, or not, a sharecropper to till his land. Reforms did away with this precarity. The newfound security in turn gave the sharecropper a newfound confidence in his dealings with the landowner, what Banerjee et al. call the "bargaining power effect." The authors demonstrate, by holding other factors constant, that the combination of these two "leads to an increase in his share and his productivity" (Banerjee et al. 2002: 248). Thus it led them to conclude that land reforms "can have a positive effect on productivity" (2002: 277),[13] which is further proved by figures that show that in areas where there was greater uptake of land registration by tenants, the tenants were also more productive, and this led to higher crop yields. As they put it, "a district with a higher proportion of more productive tenants is likely to have high output as well as high registration" (Banerjee et al. 2002: 273). This study therefore leads to an important conclusion that was reflected in the discussions and disagreements between the landowning Syeds and the sharecroppers that I had been part of. And this was that while technological innovation had indeed given rise to greater crop yields (as it had in both Bangladesh and West Bengal), institutional change of land reform was the critical factor that had ultimately put West Bengal ahead of Bangladesh in paddy output.

From this study we can therefore conclude that even when technology plays a role in creating greater outputs, it is a sense of dignity and security that can increase the final output even more, which is to say, greater confidence made people better farmers. Let us turn next to examine how these values played out on the ground among the farmers we know in the familiar setting of Madanpur and Chishti.

*

Institutional reforms could thus said to have had a profound social revolution in these villages. The greater bargaining power in cultivation from gaining security of tenure, higher wages, and half the share of the harvest meant that the lower caste (Hindu or Muslim) sharecroppers could now demand labor commensurate with the work and this labor force increased fivefold.[14] This meant that in real terms, even though Operation Barga had principally benefited the sharecroppers more than the agricultural workers, the increased bargaining power of sharecroppers created more opportunity for them to create work for others and greater solidarity between the two groups. A new wage regime also meant that higher daily wages were fixed by the Party and had to be paid promptly at the start of the day.[15] Specific daily rates were assigned for specific jobs: plowing, done with oxen, was the most expensive at Rs. 70 (i.e., less than $2 in 2000), women planting rice got Rs. 40, men who sprinkled insecticide Rs. 60, and so on. All the costs of the initial capital outlay, which included the oxen and plow, seeds, fertilizers, irrigation, and any extra labor, had also to be borne by the landowner while the sharecropper provided only his labor and his expertise.[16] The Syeds grumbled, of course, and it was clear why—they had been impoverished by the greater claims on their capital, labor was valued more highly, and their own lack of technical knowledge about cultivation showed up badly against the seasoned experience of the sharecroppers.

This, combined with a rise in daily wages, meant that there was a knock-on effect for many. The rural proletariat was recognized and rewarded and found a new dignity in work. This, combined with the reduction of chronic debt and hunger—"no one goes hungry anymore"—meant that a dignified existence was made possible, perhaps for the first time ever, for large numbers of West Bengal's rural population.[17] As one sharecropper explained to me, the "relief" provided by previous Congress governments in the past had been welcome, but it always came with the price of needing to swallow the humiliation of having to queue for it, which made their need visible. "But now we can get the just rewards of our hard work that should have always been ours." This newfound sense of entitlement and justice, combined with growing solidarity created through membership of agricultural unions and the availability of more paddy through the introduction of HYV varieties, strengthened a growing self-confidence in daily dealings with the higher castes. As a result, the heads that used to be perpetually bent in labor and humiliation now were literally and metaphorically held perceptibly higher.

Consider the case of a sharecropper called Okho Dom in Madanpur, who was in some ways a poster boy of Operation Barga. He was a low caste Hindu man known to be close to the Comrade who was always impossibly busy, and understandably so as he was the biggest sharecropper across both villages. He worked on Mukhtar's 7 acres (20 bighas), which meant that his share of every harvest was equivalent to 3.5 acres. Mukhtar was a Syed from Tilaboni who had inherited the land from his father-in-law and now lived in Madanpur. He was an unusually upright man who worked hard and also made time for the finer things in life; he had built small retreat by a bamboo grove, where he wrote poetry. When Operation Barga was announced in the late 1970s, Okho's family had already worked on the land for more than five years and so Mukhtar, without much fuss, had accompanied him to the local block office and helped with the paperwork involved in acquiring the certificate.[18] This was an unusually cordial relationship between landlord and sharecropper which, combined with Okho's relatively large share of land and reputation for being a good farmer, gave him a natural place as a leader among the sharecroppers and agricultural workers. Okho's support for the Left Front cause was passionate. He could remember his father's days as a sharecropper, when the family was dependent on the whims of the landowners, who rarely renewed their contract beyond a year. The resulting peripatetic childhood and the constant hunger they experienced as they survived on a Rs. 10 daily wage and the tiny share of the harvest which was dispensed at the whim of the landowner, rather than the need of the share cropper and his family, were recent memories and kept him committed to the communist cause. As he told me one day, when I was finally able to pin him down for a chat out in the fields as he was regulating irrigation water into different fields, "In those days if we wore nice clothes, we were accused of having stolen them; if anyone had the temerity to acquire a bicycle, he had to dismount and walk with his head down if he came across a member of a Syed household; we had to punctuate each of our sentences with the respectful 'ji' while talking to anyone from the landowner's household, including children; my father would be dragged by his ears to do jobs—the humiliation was constant." Okho's anger and outrage were palpable and overwhelming, and it transpired during our chat under the blistering sun that he had been initially reluctant to talk to me because he thought I might look down on them because of my high caste and education. But gratifyingly, having observed me over several visits, he had concluded that I was a true communist as I seemed to be genuinely interested in understanding their lives and comfortable in the modest huts of sharecroppers and agricultural workers and so he had agreed to talk to me. What was striking was that despite his relative stability and prosperity in the present, Okho showed no complacency. The slightest insult by a member of the higher castes or a delay in payment was met with immediate protests to preempt a potential slide back to the past. Crucially, he used the relative security of his own bettered circumstances to ensure that the rights of the agricultural workers who were also drawn from the lower castes, and who still relied solely on the daily wage, were not compromised. His commitment to the Comrade for inspiration about ideas of social justice, and his political work with other sharecroppers, was total because the process of land reforms had made it apparent that collective action was the only way to effect and preserve change. His leadership on behalf of the agricultural workers was of vital importance and could not be left entirely to the Comrade, for as president of the Block Krishak Sabha, he worked for an organization that had a wide membership of agricultural workers but who did not attend their meetings.[19] It was left to sharecroppers such as Okho Dom to represent the interests of the workers at these meetings, which were "dominated by middle peasants and non-peasant middle classes," and he did so more out of caste and neighborly solidarity than because of class (Bhattacharya 2016: 72). As a result, Okho's reputation as a leader among sharecroppers was widely known, as was his prickly temper in the face of the slightest insult. And it was during harvest that the fear of his temper was at its height among the landowners.

*

At the time of harvest and during the days of threshing and winnowing, however, no one rehearsed any of these discussions of the material and social effects of land reform; what was uppermost in everyone's minds was the final yield. Work on this crop had begun many weeks even before the first planting, for just to prepare the saplings themselves took about six weeks.[20] Once planted, weeks of work involved the timing of fertilizer and pesticide application, watching the color and shape of the leaves, checking for stray animals—while always watching the skies for rain. A rain-fed crop was not simply dependent on it, fields of tender saplings could also be destroyed by badly timed rains and hailstorms. Cultivation was therefore a nerve-wracking and back-breaking business involving several factors, many of which were beyond human control.

The harvest itself was made up of a series of tasks—cutting the ripe paddy in the field, gathering them, tying them in bundles, transporting them into the village, threshing the crop on machines, collecting the grain and husk, winnowing it twice to thoroughly separate the grain and husk, and finally storing them into tins, ready to be parboiled and milled. Throughout this period, a large number of people were involved as each task had to be completed quickly and efficiently as work moved from one field to the next. Alongside the sharecroppers, extra labor was also drawn from among the Shekhs, Mughals, and Pathan castes as well as Bagdis and Doms, and sometimes forty to fifty people worked each day on just one plot of land. With such a task force, the crop from 10 bighas could be reaped and tied in one day, and the winnowing took another three days.[21] The terms of contract for this extra labor were finely calibrated; the most usual sort was cash payment at Rs. 80 (about $2), which had to be paid out at the start of the working day, but there were also others.[22] The most commonly seen, especially among servants who worked within the courtyard of a Syed house, was payment in grain for specific jobs of husking or boiling rice. In the past, the amount of grain offered as payment was at the discretion of the landowner, though since the reforms it had become necessary for them to agree on this amount mutually with the recipient at the beginning of the job. A third kind of labor arrangement of the past was that of the *mahinder*, when a small child was attached to a landowner's household and all the child's expenses were met in return for his or her help with small tasks.[23] These kinds of labor arrangements had been increasingly discontinued as more and more families sent children to school, but during the harvest period, older forms of labor, employment, and payment with tins of rice were briefly reintroduced. This ad hoc arrangement worked to the advantage of the workers, because such work brought instant replenishments of rice to their household stocks, which ran at dangerously low levels in the days before each harvest. Children were particularly useful as hired hands at this time as they joined their parents after school, helping with the innumerable but low-skill jobs that needed to be accomplished within a very short space of time. Landowners, too, found it beneficial to be able to tap into instant labor supplies which they could pay for in kind rather than having to regulate their cash flow during the busy season.

All jobs and payments seemed to be coordinated jointly by the landowner and his sharecropper. Decisions about when the crop would be harvested, how much labor was required, where the unhusked paddy stalks would be stored, where the threshing machines would be set up, who would guard the grain through the night, and so on were all made as much by the sharecropper as the landowner, and the two had to work closely together. The sharecropper usually arranged for the extra labor required, drawing on members of his family first and then other close allies among the daily wage labor pool in the villages,[24] and the landowner arranged the payments. One potential source of friction was where the freshly harvested paddy stalks would be stored before the winnowing began. Most landowners did not have enough space in their courtyards to store all of them and were therefore reliant on some of the village's communal spaces to store the paddy and sometimes even set up threshing machines right next to the stockpiles. This made them vulnerable to pilferage and forced the landowners to trust their sharecroppers to personally guard the precious stocks through the night. It was not uncommon for a landowner to visit his stocks several times through the night despite the pitch-black darkness of these un-electrified villages. Whenever possible, therefore, the landowners preferred for the winnowing to take place as close to their homes as possible. They did not seem to mind the fumes, noise, and disruption of the threshing machines as it allowed them to keep a close surveillance of the work. But this arrangement also made the landowner entirely reliant on the *bargadar* to actually transport the harvest from the field to his courtyard. This was hard and back-breaking work and required the physical labor of many people, especially as the use of motorized transport was virtually impossible in the narrow village lanes. Given the landowning Syeds' abhorrence of manual labor, they were entirely dependent on the sharecroppers for such portage. This dependence had been used as a powerful tool of protest and negotiation by the tenants when the reforms were being introduced, and countless stories of the humiliation of a landowner whose harvest had been left to rot in the fields still circulated; even in the present day this threat still hung in the air whenever the harvest had to be brought in from the fields.

After hours of work on a simple motorized threshing machine (or one run by a foot pedal) when threshing was completed, the stock of grain and hay had to be first carefully separated through winnowing. These were then transported in separate sacks to the Syed courtyards for the final stage: the all-important moment of the sharing of the grain heap. But first, on a freshly prepared courtyard floor painted in cow dung, the grain was carefully winnowed one more time by hand to remove all remaining stalks of straw from the grain heap and was collected just as carefully as the grain. Only after this could the *bargadar* and his family finally undertake the delicate task of actually dividing the grain heap, making two identical piles, one for each party. The same was then done for the straw.

The image of the "grain heap" carries enormous resonance in anthropological and wider literature on India.[25] "From the nineteenth-century reports of British administrators in India to the modern literature of anthropology, the enduring symbol of this moneyless institution has been the grain heap divided into shares on the village threshing floor" (Fuller 1989: 33). In his influential piece, the anthropologist Chris Fuller comprehensively, refuted the portrayal of the division of the grain heap as a substitute for monetized transactions in the Indian village economy. By doing so, he challenged Dumont's portrayal of the jajmani system as a "traditional" institution that determined the division of the harvest between different castes according to laws of interdependence and an "orientation to the whole" (of the caste system) outside of monetary exchange. Historical evidence showed that money, the circulation of currency, and the pressures of revenue extraction by various imperial forces have always prevailed in the Indian context and have had enormous bearing on how the grain heap was, in fact, divided. While there had been previous challenges to Dumont's "integrative" model by others who had demonstrated the "exploitative" nature of the system between patrons and clients, Fuller went further to argue that Dumont's model evoked a dichotomy between a modern monetary system and a traditional non-monetized system of dividing the grain on principles of holistic interdependence of castes that was "inseparable from the premise of India's stability and exclusion from history" (Fuller 1989: 54). This debate continues to the present day, including a very recent challenge by the historian Sumit Guha, who argues for caste as an outcome not of a ritual logic but a political and economic one (see Guha 2016).

My own account of the division of the grain heap is set in the context of agricultural production in the twenty-first century in a setting where a period of revolutionary violence had led to land reforms introduced by a democratically elected coalition of communist parties that had created a rebalancing of power between the castes that owned land and those that provided agricultural labor. The context also included a little reformed system of agricultural markets in which the government set the Minimum Selling Price (MSP) of paddy and local mill owners were allowed to exploit the system because of their clout with the Communist leadership (Harriss-White 2005). Thus the division of the grain heap in Madanpur and Chishti was certainly part of a much wider rural economy and agricultural market system whose dynamics had direct bearing on the grain heap. As Mekhala Krishnamurthy points out, "what makes the heap so interesting and insightful . . . is its ability to hold and hide within it both the 'economic/technical' and the 'social' dimensions of commodity exchange and market maintenance" (Krishnamurthy 2018: 50). Within the village, while the production of grain and its division directly and indirectly involved all castes, it was not "integrative" in the Dumontian sense. While Dumont's explanation provided a justification for the status quo of caste hierarchy to endure, this was almost the opposite in the scenario I describe here. Instead, the influence of a number of different factors—communism, currency, kinship, cultivation, constitutional rights, and the state—were variously at work here, alongside those of caste.

Watching the division of the grain heap in Meher Bibi's (the Comrade's first wife's) courtyard, I noticed that she stopped her usual bustling around to watch the process very carefully, while trying not to make her interest too evident. And so did all the other workers, including the playing children and even, it seemed, the chicken and cattle. All eyes were on the grain—the precious treasure for which everyone had worked hard for six long months. The grain heap was a physical manifestation, an object that did not metaphorically stand for but was, in its very material form, the profit of labor. Before the land reforms, miniscule portions of this treasure used to be shared by agricultural workers, but now it would be divided exactly in half. The attendant silence was pregnant with meaning, replete with both the remembrances of angry and humiliating times past, and a

contemporary palpable threat of disorder. For the reforms had been the culmination of nearly two decades of violence, meetings, and demonstrations, in
which Birbhum district (where the villages were located) had been at the center
of much of the agitation. The minister in charge of land reform, Harekrishna
Konar, had urged peasants to fight the landlords with the slogan "Peasant, occupy the land, and then cultivate it."[26] Settlements between owner and tenant
had been far from amicable, though there were such cases too. Thus, during the
harvest, when all able-bodied men were to be found among the ripe stalks in
the field, the memories of days when the Syeds had had to hide in the tall paddy
to avoid being killed re-surfaced. Equally, the sight of them, who until recently
held such disdain for manual work, working shoulder to shoulder with the tenants evoked memories of the crops that had been burnt of those who would not
support the reforms. Every man in the village had his own story, and the scars of
past violence were inscribed on bodies and relationships, and the Syeds who had
been outmaneuvered or punished by the Comrade now dreamed or even plotted
of how to get even. For instance, Akbar, who was now one of the wealthiest Syeds
in Madanpur, had been during the reforms severely beaten and outmaneuvered
by the man who emerged as the Comrade, and the continuing threat of violence
meant that he now chose to keep to himself and give up all aspirations to any
overt political work. His revenge had been to keep all *bargadars* off his land by
discontinuing their tenancy before the reforms were introduced and hiring daily
wage labor instead. He and his sons, who though educated had been unable to
find salaried jobs, worked harder than anyone else on the land, and while they
remained disgruntled through the year about the Comrade and the state of village politics, their enormous harvest brought brief smiles to their faces.

To watch the tense and silent dividing of the crop was thus to grasp how significant and revolutionary the reforms had been, replacing as they did the older
divisions when the grain heap was never really divided but small portions of it
were given away as payments to workers according to the whims of the landowners. At the moment of division, each party therefore shared a history that
had to be contained and accommodated in the present so as to carry out the division peacefully. For the *bargadar*, this division marked the end of the humiliation
their fathers had to suffer when they had to repeatedly "beg" for their rightful
share; for the landowners, it was the harshest reminder that they were no longer
powerful patrons and had to now share according to some rules of equity. Little
wonder, then, that as the workers started filling the two piles of grain into tins,
everyone seemed to breathe again.

After the drama of the division of the grain heap came the anti-climax
of storage. The Syeds could afford to store their grain within their largish
compounds and the two-storied brick houses that they had managed to build.
In fact, most rooms within these homes were used for either tools or grain, and

only two or three rooms were actually lived in. But the tenants continued to live in mud and thatch huts where the lack of space and vulnerability to the elements meant that storing any significant amount of grain was impossible. Just enough grain for daily consumption was kept in sacks (after being twice boiled and husked to increase its weight and to increase its longevity), and any share of the harvest that was required for a future wedding or as insurance had to be kept well away from the hungry mouths of the household. Thus, once the sharecropper transferred his share of the crop into tins, he had to store it in "his" landlord's house instead of carrying it home with pride. For this he remained under obligation, and that rather sullied the triumph of the larger share of harvest.

The Social Imaginaries of Democracy: Cultivation of Solidarity and Cooperation

This study began at a time when West Bengal was the largest rice-producing state of India, paddy cultivation flourished, and the villages were surrounded on all sides by fields covered in lush green crop. But just fifteen years later, when this study concluded in 2013, many fields lay fallow, their drab brown reflecting the state of desperation. This dramatic change in Madanpur and Chishti reflected a wider trend in West Bengal whereby growing paddy had become less and less economically viable with each passing year. The net profit from every acre was a negligible sum of Rs. 1,500, and given that the average landholding was about 5 to 10 acres, the profits did not amount to much. As noted earlier, studies have shown that a combination of institutional reform and technological change had indeed boosted productivity, but the lack of revision in pricing policy meant that the growth in productivity had not translated into greater profit for producers. Thus, while the HYV paddy output was indeed "like winning the lottery" in the early days, the attendant risk of a lottery ticket was also ever present with rising costs and declining prices. "There is too much stress involved" is how farmers put it. As a result, more and more fields were left fallow as farmers could no longer afford to cultivate paddy and looked for other sources of income instead. So while every year they saved stocks of seed (*bichon*) in the hope that circumstances would improve, more and more sold them off at the start of the growing season for a small profit before it was too late to fetch a good price. If they did, they chose to cultivate the rain-fed and less expensive swarna crop instead, which delivered a smaller yield but was enough for household consumption, for both humans and animals.[27]

An important reason for the growing unviability of agriculture was the lack of institutional reform in agricultural markets in West Bengal and the low MSP for paddy set by the Indian government. In her work on agricultural markets,

Barbara Harriss-White argues that the reason for continuing agrarian poverty in West Bengal despite being ranked as India's largest rice-producing state was largely because of the manner in which firms in West Bengal controlled the marketed surplus for staple foods (Harriss-White 2005). Pointing to the Left Front's cynical pragmatism in keeping their electoral base among mill owners satisfied, she points out that "not only have the reforms in production not been matched by any reform in the structure of control in rice markets, but for most of the last quarter century, the Left Front government has been reinforcing the old pattern" (Harriss-White 2005: 2). As a result, despite the results of Operation Barga and the introduction of HYV, which revolutionized agricultural production, there was a de facto protection of the privileges of the agro-commercial elite at the expense of the agro-commercial poor, the producers of paddy. For the gains in agricultural production to have benefited the farmers, what was needed was a coherent policy (linked to but separate from production policy) for the emerging agro-commercial petty bourgeoisie which would have allowed for the gains from trade to be spread more widely so that "the balance of returns to agro-commerce and returns to production might also have been less disadvantageous to production" (Harriss-White 2005: 3). Given that most of the rural population was involved in the production of paddy, by doing so, agricultural labor "could have claimed a higher proportion of the distributive share and the agricultural miracle [which] would have had a manifest impact on rural poverty" (Harriss-White 2005: 3). Unfortunately, this never happened. Instead, by trying to keep the costs of state procurement and trading down and by trying to preserve the electoral support of the agro-commercial elite and the non-landed factions of the business class who owned the large rice mills, the Left Front severely let its agricultural work force of sharecroppers and wage laborers down. Therefore, despite its record rice production, West Bengal remained among the lowest performing Indian states on every human development indicator, with most people in the state still denied basic access to education, health, and employment. The story of West Bengal was not isolated and reflected a larger Indian phenomenon of shortchanging farmers and the producers behind India's self-sufficiency in food production. As the noted agronomist M. S. Swaminathan said while recommending radical proposals in raising the MSP of cereals, "India has done well in production, but not in consumption."[28] While this was a failure of all governments in India, it was a particularly severe failing on the part of a communist government that counted the rural proletariat as its main constituency and whose votes allowed them to remain in power for over three continuous decades.

Over their tenure in government, thus, the Left Front's legitimacy was increasingly called into question. Not only had they failed in implementing market reforms to create some advantage for the producers of paddy, they had also failed to further revise the minimum daily wage such that the initial five-fold increase to Rs. 50 in the 1980s no longer seemed a princely sum twenty-five years later. The tenants experienced their lack of disposable income acutely and could not even afford to improve their thatch-and-mud living premises in over three decades. The lack of credit facilities drove sharecroppers to take out loans against their land certificates, which then took years to pay off if they managed to pay them off at all. The hard-won land rights had thus, in less than a generation, been lost as sharecroppers sold their tenancies back to the original landowners and new forms of indebtedness grew as agricultural work became less viable. Tenants had to therefore increasingly diversify the contexts in which they sold their labor, such as in the sand and brick businesses where the immediate returns were greater and there was less short-term uncertainty of the final outcome than there was in the harvest.[29] Land as capital thus steadily diminished in value and was now only good for growing enough paddy for subsistence but nevertheless relied on their finite capacity for labor. The precarity of agricultural work and the losses it brought increasingly felt like a millstone around the necks of farmers.

To compound the preceding factors further, the worst long-term consequence was the irreversible ecological damage caused by the cultivation of HYV. The dependency on irrigation to grow this thirsty crop had made unsustainable demands on the water table, which dropped annually, and submersible pumps had to be pushed deeper and deeper until they hit arsenic and had to stop. The price of extracting water also rose with the rise of diesel prices, since diesel fuel was required to drive the pumps as electricity was not available for any of the pumps except the Comrade's. The cost of fertilizers also rose annually, the need for them increasing as the soil incrementally lost its nutritional value through double cropping and an additional wheat crop. The natural crop–livestock integration that had allowed for manure to replenish the soil had been thrown out of kilter with the increased need for chemical fertilizers for HYV. Health had also deteriorated as incidents of malaria increased as a result of mosquitoes being driven from the fields sprayed with pesticides into villages. Thus, the Green Revolution that occurred with the introduction of HYV was short-lived, because the high input costs it required and the lack of further policy interventions that were required to make it an "Evergreen Revolution" had simply not come.[30] Every harvest raised these questions and deepened the sense of crisis.

Thus, while the reforms had initially translated into overwhelming electoral support for the Left Government, their failure to design policies to make paddy cultivation profitable for farmers, combined with their inability to create new opportunities for employment, led to a growing disenchantment. The interests of common agricultural workers were increasingly ignored in forums such as the Krishak Sabha and panchayats which had been effectively captured by elite interests. The cynical use of the *gorib* ("poor," as they were patronizingly called by Left Front workers) for building up electoral support while doing little to materially improve their condition was embodied in Madanpur and Chishti in the figure of the Comrade and his eye-catching prosperity. Back in the 1980s he had used his advance knowledge of impending reforms to rid his own landholdings of all his sharecroppers before their tenancy rights could be enforced. Thus, while he had publicly fought the ideological and political agenda of gaining rights for tenant farmers, he had personally not suffered any of the financial losses that his fellow Syeds had as a result of the reforms. Over the years, it emerged that he had taken full advantage of being the mouthpiece of the Party and had made up additional measures that would hurt the Syeds in his village even further. Thus, while they took up manual work to make agriculture viable and looked for means of survival, he himself did not need to, having amassed enough wealth to hire labor from neighboring Dubrajpur during the planting and harvesting seasons. These Santal families came with their own food during the day and returned at night and so posed no added responsibility to the Comrade. And as he did so, he continued to threaten dissenting Syed rivals with additional tenants while winning plaudits with the sharecroppers who saw him as their champion. After many years of skillful maneuverings, therefore, his landholdings were now the largest in the village and through the use of an army of daily wage laborers working under the supervision of his sons, his harvest was of a different order of magnitude than anyone else's. In physical appearance, his torse was plumper and his skin looked paler and less lined than all the others who toiled in the fields. Every harvest therefore reasserted his omnipotence in the local politics, but also laid bare the cynical workings of "vanguard" ideology even to party supporters like Okho and his friends. They understood that they had to tolerate the personal enrichment of the Comrade in order to gain any benefits themselves, for he alone had access to the higher echelons of the Party and state administrative machinery which could bring investment to the village and grants to individuals. The severe loss of electoral credibility of the Left Front (that was to come in subsequent years) can be traced back to the growing disillusionment with the double standards of such Comrades.

In the villages of Madanpur and Chishti, there were no harvest festivals as such, but in the year that I was present, the harvest happened to coincide with Ramzan, the Islamic month of fasting that preceded the festival of Eid, and the routine prayer meetings called *milads* held in the evenings allowed for some post-harvest work sociality.[31] This was also the first Ramzan after the resolution of the scandal discussed in the previous chapter, when the seeds of an opposition to the Comrade had been sown, in collective outrage to his naked manipulation of people, resources, and ethical norms. The harvest and the congregational prayer meetings in the evenings together created an ideal scenario to evaluate the potential for cooperative action and the nature of their shared human project of social life. The collective work of the harvest facilitated such a moral evaluation by creating an altered sociality in which different social groups in the village, otherwise divided by caste, class, and religion, had been united in the common purpose of making every grain count. The harvest, by its very nature, was an activity that could not be accomplished by a single individual and required the coordination of a team in which each member was assigned a specific task that was determined by their capability. It therefore brought about cooperation within a social group based on a division of labor rather than social hierarchy. Within the context of low returns on an increasingly expensive crop to cultivate and the paucity of alternative options of income, the very survival of each member of the village was dependent on this common purpose and this forced older divisions to be suppressed, for the duration of the harvest at least, to accomplish the task at hand. In this, the harvesters were exactly like the sailors of Aristotle's ship, whose common purpose was the navigation of the vessel.[32] This solidarity, though temporary and characteristic only of the few weeks of the harvest, had nevertheless the quality of transcending the everyday nature of transactional life and reinforcing the ideal of a larger collective whole.

During the harvest, as we have seen, the nature of the work required an obfuscating of identities based on caste and class and highlighted instead roles determined by the needs of decision making, knowledge, and organization. Manual work itself served as an equalizer, and the tacit understanding shared by all was that it was in everyone's interests to bring in the harvest efficiently and collectively without conflict—and it was as if people no longer saw each other as a Shekh or as an educated man, but were able to imagine what Maurice Bloch (2008) calls the "invisible halo" of a "role" based on expertise and experience, such that an emaciated but knowledgeable laborer might wear it. Prior hierarchies between the elite, landowning Syeds and the lower castes of sharecropping Shekhs and Doms gave way to the dominance of the latter in decision-making and organization of labor. Now it was the Shekhs who had the superior knowledge about agriculture and so had the edge over the Syeds, who were late entrants. The land reforms had also forced a more equitable distribution of the grain heap that had in turn compelled the Syeds to take up manual work, the eschewal of which up until this point had been the cornerstone of their elite status. While they did not do any manual work other than in their own fields, the very sight of haughty Syed men in hitched-up sarongs and with dusty torsos, indistinguishable from any other castes, working shoulder to shoulder with them, was evidence of this new equity. The Syeds, for their part, their skins burned in the sun and hands cut by the sharp stalks of paddy, looked embarrassed when I visited them in their fields.

This degree of social leveling was unprecedented in the history of this region, and while it was rarely articulated in words, an event such as the harvest created the sight of a low caste tenant looking straight into the eyes of an elite landowner, his body language that of the man in charge with superior knowledge of agricultural know-how discussing arrangements as equals. Given the deep inequities of the caste system, this would have been unimaginable less than a generation ago and had to be, literally, seen to be believed. Similarly, the constant comings and goings from the landlord's house, particularly during the harvest period, was a reminder of how relations had changed over time. Earlier the tenant used to be essentially a household retainer who was expected to spend all his daylight hours at the landlord's house, available at his beck and call. But now the tenant came and went as he needed to, controlling his own time and work, and to that extent farming and the accompanying harvests had become more like paid jobs than the overwhelming life occupation that they had been in the past.[33] This scenario was a radical reversal of what harvests were like less than a generation ago in the same village. But even in this altered scenario, the Syeds attempted to maintain hierarchy in subtle if feeble ways. The constant social interaction during the harvest meant that the rules of hospitality were tested, and matters of who was invited to sit and rest, and who was not, took on immense significance. Thus, while tenants were now offered tea, it was served in china cups that were especially set aside for them, and not in the metal or glass tumblers that the Syeds used themselves. Thus, despite the enhanced social exchanges between tenants and the owner-cultivators, an unambiguous message of relative "purity" and worth was still encoded.[34] In retaliation, some of the Hindu tenant castes of Dom and Bagdis, who like everyone else always looked forward to the gifts of sacrificial meat at Qurbani that had been part of the more paternalistic but also sociable order to distribute the luxury of consuming meat once a year, had lately begun to refuse it, citing a Hindu religious proscription against consuming beef.[35]

There had been, therefore, some rebalancing of prestige and dignity between landowners and members of the rural working class. In the context of India, where ownership of land had always marked upward social mobility and the coveted status of *moddhobitto* (or middle class) was possible only by its distance from manual work, land reforms had gone some way in redefining respectability. The increase in wages and, crucially, the new rule of having to pay the wages at the start of the job rather than being left to the employer's discretion had ended the humiliation that manual work inevitably brought. At the same time, the reforms had also forced all strata of society, including the middle farmers, to do more manual work. Further, because of the growing unviability of farming, share-cropper families who could have moved up the social hierarchy with their new entitlement to land created by the reforms had to now undertake extra manual work in brick kilns and sand mining to provide the income that agriculture no longer provided. Middle-class status for them thus remained permanently out of reach. What they could do, however, was draw satisfaction from the loss of *moddhobitto* status by the arrogant Syeds who had been forced to do agricultural work to make cultivation financially viable for themselves. What was particularly striking was the pity that the erstwhile elites drew from the sharecroppers, despite the injustices of their past behavior. People recognized that even a relatively modest holding of 5 acres by a Syed family could dwindle over a generation into small plots. A Bagdi family pointed out to me that most of the Syeds didn't have much land or salaried jobs and they couldn't sell their labor, either, so they really needed to grow paddy mainly for sustenance rather than for profit. Thus, after the land reforms and their denuded profits, the Syeds had been kept from starvation mainly by the cultivation of higher yielding varieties of rice. The precarity of their existence had also led them to do the unthinkable—namely, sell off their prized assets. For instance, a Syed desperate to raise capital for his daughter's wedding sold his rights to a water tank to Tinkari Dom, who in turn could use the income to buy the land on which his hut stood.

Thus, the roles occupied by the people of Madanpur and Chishti during a post–land reform harvest were defined, if not by a new permanent social equality, at least by a fragile new equilibrium. The equilibrium was brought about by a combination of land reforms that had led to a new and palpable self-respect for the lower laboring castes while instilling sobriety in the erstwhile arrogant Syeds and had led to an intensification of the cooperative effort of the harvest itself. The sweat equity and quantum of work by each individual had been redistributed to make them comparable, creating a more fair and equitable society. This is what economists, in a classic understatement to describe non-material gains, have called the "indirect impact" of the reforms (Gazdar and Sengupta 1997).

Further, the agitational politics and collective action on the basis of which land reforms had been introduced also had an enduring effect. In the first instance "collective action . . . [had been] severely handicapped by the extreme inequality in the distribution of political and economic power within the society" (Banerjee et al. 2002: 258).[36] But their very success in reducing inequality had in turn created better conditions for better collective action in the future. Bardhan, Ghatak, and Karaivanov show how economic data from the macro and micro levels strongly indicate "that the propensity of individuals to join groups, to participate in social activities, to cooperate in various collective action problems, or the provision of public goods and services is negatively related to inequality" (2007: 1843). One example of this could be seen in the continuing agitational politics led by sharecroppers like Okho Dom, who continued to provide leadership to the agricultural workers who had done relatively less well from the reforms. Some of these were from his caste but most were not, and the majority were drawn from the Muslim lower castes of Shekh and Pathan as well as other Doms, but the basis of his solidarity with them went beyond caste identities.

The harvest expressed these features of rural life in West Bengal—a new egalitarianism, greater dignity of labor, class solidarity, the power of collective action—par excellence. It is perhaps for this reason that agrarian societies in many settings mark such moments of collective labor and its triumph through

a variety of harvest festivals. The "beer work parties" held to celebrate and reinforce the cooperative labor of harvest work in east Africa are one example, and
those parties and music celebrated not just the bounty of the harvest but the collective achievement of aggregated labor in Africa (Donham 1999; James 1988).
In Donham's account, the Maale used a special phrase, *wolla soofane* (working
together), to describe such cooperation that was much more than "a simple instrumental relationship" of helping each other out; instead it indicated that
"labour cooperation fused a variety of economic, political, and even religious
concerns into one social form, one symbolic image . . . [and such] cooperation
in the public sphere [was] marked as a key symbol of social solidarity" (Donham
1985: 262). It is this solidarity, created through cooperative labor, that I suggest is
a key social imaginary created during the harvest.

Milads (the Ramzan prayer meetings) started a couple of hours after sunset,
and once the dawn-to-dusk fast had been broken and the evening meal had
been consumed in their homes, people gathered in the roomy courtyards of
Syed homes. Typically, the host invited an orator of repute to sing parts of the
Quran for the audience, who were then provided translations and encouraged
to join in singing the refrain. This lasted for about forty-five minutes, at the
end of which everyone stood for the recitation of the final prayer, including the
non-Muslims present who also stood in respectful silence with hands folded in
prayer. Once this religious aspect was over, sweets were distributed to everyone
and sent out to members of kin and close friends across the two villages. People
attended *milads* largely for the religious entertainment and also as a relaxing di-
version at the end of a hard day's work—and for the rare luxury of sweets. The
Hindu/Dalit tenants particularly enjoyed the egalitarian spirit of these Islamic
gatherings—sitting shoulder to shoulder, irrespective of caste—a convention
that they found sorely lacking in the gatherings of their own religion. In theory,
the *milads* were for everyone, and the hosts always tried to attract as many of
the *gorib* (the poor) to them. A Syed would typically invite his sharecropper, the
sharecropper's family, and a large section of the daily wage agricultural workers
to these events. Attendance at a particular *milad* was also read as a show of political support to the host, so if a particular Syed could attract, through various
techniques, the right people to attend his *milad* he could expand his network of
tacit supporters. If these new links were successful and acceptable, they were reinforced at future *milads* held in the home of the new allies, when the invitations
were returned.[37] This served a number of purposes. It revived, at least for a moment, a vertical, older style patronage between a landowner and his tenant in the
face of growing horizontal ties among tenants and workers. But because the congregation itself was conducted in a spirit of egalitarianism where everyone sat in
an unassigned manner, sang together, and mingled freely with each other during
refreshments at the end, it also generated a new type of horizontal cohesion. That

year, the coincidence of *milads* (which occurred in different months every year as Ramzan was determined by the lunar calendar) with the swarna paddy harvest in December was particularly beneficial to reinforce and renew the solidarity of the daytime harvest work in the evening and also to put on public display the new alliances against the Comrade that had been formed during the resolution of the scandal some months ago. Those fragile new bonds that had challenged the Comrade's authority had been created despite a possible violent backlash from him could now be strengthened further by using them to form the congregation at the prayer meetings. The happy coincidence of Ramzan with the harvest that year meant that the solidarity created through shared labor during the day could be celebrated further through communal worship in the evening. These *milads* also served to isolate the Comrade further and remind him of the ties that he had lost by expelling his own sharecropper; they also showed him that people went to the *milads* of other Syeds voluntarily, rather than out of the fear, as they did to his. During the harvest, therefore, the shared labor and know-how between Syed landowners and lower caste tenants was productive of new solidarities that could surge stronger than even the bonds of party membership. The *milad* gatherings therefore created an altered sociality in village life through which ties of kinship and loyalty could be mobilized to balance the more divisive tensions caused by the land reforms, party politics, or scandals and were thus important in keeping a sense of community intact.

This perhaps explains the unexpected sophisticated political discourse that could sometimes emerge from even the most ordinary of men at this time. Once people had completed their harvesting, in the twilight zone between seasons, when the stumps of harvested paddy still stood in the fields and the village was enveloped in a haze of paddy dust, many of the farm laborers who were otherwise too busy or too shy to talk with me became more forthcoming. It was as if the intense labor of bringing in the harvest, the knowledge that it was more equitably distributed, the respect with which, perforce, those with greater experience had been treated during the daily decisions with the landowners, and the sheer performative power of the shared knowledge of the routine of cutting, tying, and threshing of the paddy had emboldened them to talk. It was as Victor Turner observes about all social dramas: "False friendship is winnowed from true communality of interests; the limits of consensus are reached and realized; real power emerges from behind the façade of authority" (Turner 1980: 151). It was during one of these conversations that I learned that when the grain was first harvested, a rice pudding was made with the newly milled rice and offered at the mosque before any part of the new harvest was consumed. It was in this context that I was told the Story of the Rice Pudding that held profound meaning. In brief the story was: There was once a feast in a village in which everyone was expected to contribute a cup of milk to a common pot for pudding. A miser decided that he would add a cup of water instead of milk, in the hope of free-riding on all the other cups of milk. When the pot was opened at the end of the feast, it was found to be full of water. The moral was: one man may dilute the common good, but in the end, everyone cannot afford to do the same; each has to do their bit and add their cup of milk if they want pudding at the end.[38] It was an interesting story in the context of the harvest, where such sociality and imagination of a common good was on display. We have seen how such an imagination required each actor during a harvest to imagine others not as members of a certain class or caste or gender but as people who were performing a role, and it was by pulling together in their individual parts that the larger drama of the harvest could be performed. This can be characterized as a "whole-sum" game to distinguish it from the "zero-sum" game that characterizes more transactional social life. The key to this altered sociality was a capacity to imagine this larger whole (a vat of pudding) that could be achieved only if each person performed their own individual task (i.e., provided their cup of milk).

It could therefore be argued that as an "event" in village life, the harvest may in fact be comparable to other such significant events in the village—such as Islamic festivals or even Election Day—that stand apart from the ebb and flow of everyday existence. Each of them presents a social drama at the heart of which lies a moment of "communitas"—the brief and ambiguous experience of social leveling experienced during the harvest that was comparable to their experience of queuing at the polling station, where they stood cheek by jowl with others regardless of class or status or at congregational prayers. These moments of egalitarian mixing stood out in a village of deep social divisions, and it provided a brief but palpable glimpse of social equality. And conceptually, the paddy dust that covered everyone during a harvest was not dissimilar to the identical black ink mark on every voter's finger or the prayer caps on every man's head—they each highlighted a common, if transient, identity that was equalizing and shared. Further, each task during a harvest, each vote, each prayer, each cup of milk pointed to the need of individual effort and everyone's participation to create a common good, a whole that would be larger than the sum of its parts—a harvest, an election result, a congregation, a vat of pudding. The fragility and disappointment of the low returns on paddy cultivation was also not unlike the disappointing performance of elected governments or, indeed, not unlike prayers that went unanswered. But, for the duration of the collective activity such as a harvest at least, the collective labor of ordinary people was generative of a different social imagination, one that went beyond the material returns of their labor and created immaterial and desirable values of solidarity and cooperation.

*

5

Sacrifice

Cultivating Faith

In a small clearing in Madanpur, on a chilly morning in March, the stage was set for the festival of Qurbani (lit. sacrifice), as Eid-ul-Adha is popularly known. A small patch of land next to a water tank (*pukur*) and clump of bamboo at the heart of the village, where boys usually played cricket and paddy stalks were stored during the harvest, had been cleared. On this day it was to serve as the arena for the climax of the festival—the cattle sacrifice. The entire village gathered, encircling the space, as families dressed in their best stood together. As the first cattle was led out, a hush of expectation fell on the scene and the only sound was the distinctive rustling of bamboo leaves in the wind.[1] The first one was a large cow which was firmly but gently forced to sit down and then placed on its side on the ground to face Mecca. Several men held down its legs to keep it still as the pesh imam stepped forward to recite verses from the Quran and Mukhtar Ali helped him with naming the people on whose behalf the sacrifice was offered. After this was done, in complete silence, the animal's throat was slit. This was done slowly and carefully with a firm sawing motion. As the big vein was cut, blood spurted out in a huge burst before quickly soaking into the earth below. The big animal continued to kick its legs for a long time after, until all the blood drained away. The men continued to hold on to the beast until the end, and even after it was no longer necessary. The head was not totally severed from the body and once the blood had completely stopped flowing, the entire carcass was removed to a space near the household making the sacrifice, for skinning and carving. Eleven head of cattle were sacrificed that year.

The ritual of sacrifice was a key moment in one of the two Eids celebrated by Muslims globally and was a "moment of exchange between the human and the divine" in the religious life of the village (Hubert and Mauss 1964). Qurbani was an annual event that required the sacrifice of a loved animal, and the structure of the ritual allowed participants throughout the day to experience transcendental truths about what was desirable and what could be, truths that were normally hidden in the everyday life of the transactional social.[2] In this chapter, I will examine the "event" of the ritual of Qurbani in the life of Madanpur and Chishti, for its subjunctive nature, as a practice that is generative of an imagination of the potentiality of human action. As Turner notes, this indeterminate nature of ritual is its most important aspect "since it is that which is not yet settled, concluded and known . . . it is all that may be, might be, could be, perhaps even should be" (Turner 1980: 157). Further, placing the practice of animal sacrifice alongside other Islamic religious rituals provides an opportunity to explore the role of religious rituals in creating values and principles that guide and inform social and political life within and outside of ritual time.

The sacrifice, like the other events discussed in this book—scandal, harvest, and elections—was a social drama that reversed social relations and created new possibilities for the duration of its performance, and in doing so it brought its participants in confrontation with imaginaries that were both fleeting and profound, and helped reorient values toward them. As was evident from the discussion in previous chapters, rivalries of rank, caste, class, age, and gender marked social life in the village, and such everyday pettiness and gossip was evident in religious life too. The men in Chishti and Madanpur had, at any point in time, deep enmities over who would deliver the *azaan* (the call to prayer) over the mosque's tannoy, or who would lead the prayers at the next Eid, or who had been invited to which house to lead the *milad* gathering at the previous Eid. Each Syed considered himself better than the others, and Shekh men tried to outdo each other to secure the extra income that the small jobs of the mosque brought, to prove their religious worth through personal talent if not by caste status. The job of the *peshimam* (also known as *khotim*), for instance, was simply to recite the call for prayers five times a day, but the choice was under constant debate and discussion, with several candidates vying for the job. Women subtly tried to outdo each other in their piety by making their daily religious observances conspicuous in a variety of ways. But each religious festival brought a pause in these quotidian struggles and demanded the participants to behave in better ways and forced them, through the demands of the ritual, to rise above the base instincts of pride, greed, and touchiness and behave instead with restraint, generosity, and gratitude.

These virtues were, of course, not absent in everyday life, but during the religious ritual they were not simply desirable but essential qualities for the proper conduct of the proceedings. For the duration of the ritual itself, prescribed practices intensified these qualities, and virtue could be gained only through their successful performance. Victor Turner evoked the metaphor of a river to successfully capture this relationship of rules and performance, drawing attention to the importance of the latter. While a ritual is indeed about rules, without the performance, he noted, it is nothing. "A river needs banks or it will be a dangerous flood, but banks without a river epitomize aridity" (Turner 1980: 160). The discussion here will therefore present the river—the performance and the ritual *process*—to explore what it creates. With performance came knowledge of how to feel and behave in ways that were extraordinary; for instance, Qurbani required the ability to part with a loved animal, to silently share its physical pain, to watch its slaughter with a prayer, and to be generous in sharing the rare luxury of meat; so the participation in the ritual shaped the participant's disposition regarding some key values. While Qurbani was a quintessentially religious event to mark an individual's sacrifice, its ritual performance required the community to collectively cultivate values for it—inviolate commitment, mutual responsibility, solidarity, and social cohesion—and these continued to inform social conduct afterward, at least in aspiration if not in practice. They emerged as "exemplars" of the ethical ways of individual conduct in all fields of social activity. The sacrifice, like other transcendental events in social life, brought into sharp relief the contours of values that were considered important but were normally diffuse, and in this they generated values that were held dearly but were rarely or imperfectly articulated in everyday life. Joel Robbins has made a persuasive case for rituals, or such transcendental moments, to be considered "the key social form in which exemplary representations of values are made socially available" (Robbins 2016: 18). As anthropologists of ritual have consistently pointed out, imagination is a crucial aspect to such transcendental moments, and sacrifice is an important institution in the creation of a religious imagination. Therefore, I argue, the virtues of generosity and commitment generated during a religious festival were not simply practiced during the festival itself but joined a wider repertoire of social practices that people drew from when acting in a variety of contexts beyond the ritual. Values created and reinforced during Islamic rituals—the giving up of possessions for a wider redistribution, participating in a collective activity, consuming meat while making sure that others also had some to enjoy, giving without expectation of immediate returns—all contributed to the aspiration of being a good Muslim. Later, in more ordinary times and especially at times of rupture and conflict, such as the divisions caused between people during the Scandal or through loyalties of rival political parties, it was these examples of ethical behavior that were remembered and that served as guidance for how to maintain a sense of community despite divisions.

Rural Islam has rarely been in the spotlight in the scholarship on the anthropology of Islam, dominated as it has been by tribes or city dwellers. Instead, as Magnus Marsden notes appropriately his work on a remote community in Pakistan, "the pre-dominantly rural societies in which much of South Asia's and other Muslim populations live continue to be stereotyped as intellectually barren, rendering Muslim villages as places of non-thought" (Marsden 2009: 10). As the discussion in this chapter demonstrates, the lived Islam of the villages of Madanpur and Chishti was fluid, changing, contested, and aspirational all at once and a key source of ideas and values. The analysis of cattle sacrifice explores the values that this particular ritual produced: renunciation (offering a favorite animal for slaughter), redistribution (only a few households could afford to offer the sacrifice but everyone consumed meat), egalitarianism (exemplified in Eid prayers), and the idea of giving without expectation, and these also animated a wide range of Islamic practices and festivals. In the concluding section of this chapter I will return to a discussion of these values to explore their affinity with the democratic/republican spirit of citizenship that required similar sensibilities of the suppression of individual self-interest for a common cause, participation in a community activity, and commitment to wider redistribution.

Religious Ritual in Everyday Life

The animal sacrifice and accompanying Eid celebrations took place within a wider context of Islamic practices of the village, which were in a state of constant evolution. At the start of the research in the first years of this century, most members of the two villages were Barelvis whose practices were syncretic in character and shared a common set of practices of daily prayers; they tended to share many Shia practices, and Eid, Qurbani, and Muharram were the most important festivals.[3] There were also some variations in religious practice across castes. For instance, the number of *rakats* (the set of prescribed gestures and movements that accompany the five daily prayers) required of different castes varied considerably, and this was an important daily marker of both one's identity as a Muslim and one's caste ranking within Islam. These gestures involved ritual ablutions, the reciting of prayers, standing with a head bent low, prostrating oneself and touching the head to the ground, sitting on the feet tucked in, and turning one's head once to the right and once to the left. These gestures are completed in sequence and repeated according to a prescribed number of times on each of the five daily occasions when prayers are offered. So prayers at dawn (Fajr), midday (Zuhr), afternoon (Asr), evening (Maghrib), and night (Isha) were meant to contain two, four, four, three, and four *rakats*, respectively. These *farz*, or compulsory prayers, totaled 17 *rakats* through the day, and all castes were expected to perform them. Syeds, however, believed that only they were required to also perform *sunnat* prayers in addition to the compulsory ones. Hierarchy was thus firmly established in the basic practice of being Muslim, and, unsurprisingly, the performance of daily prayers had the potential to be highly performative.[4]

While most people said their prayers in the privacy of their homes, those who wished to be known for their piety performed their prayers more publicly. So it was common for women to leave a gossip session pointedly in the middle to offer prayers on time or to conduct their ablutions by the most visible water tanks in the village or for Syed men to position their prayer mats conspicuously in the doorways of their homes so as to be visible from the main village lane. These performances, along with all the other practices, gradually aggregated to establish the credentials of individuals and thereby a hierarchy of piety among individuals. This interplay of status and competition amid faith and generosity was a feature of all Islamic rituals, as we will see.

The lunar Islamic calendar regulated ritual life in the villages of Madanpur and Chishti; almanacs were available as cheap publications at shrines and local markets, and most Syed households had a copy.[5] The other Muslim castes simply consulted them for information, and in a small village, dates for forthcoming events spread easily by word of mouth. The almanacs were printed both in Bengali and Urdu, though most adult women who kept track of ritual obligations were unable to read or write either language and so relied on their children or husbands for the information. It was customary for all children to have lessons with a cleric (ideally a *hafiz* who had memorized the whole Quran) in reading the Quran from start to finish over several sittings. These were published in Arabic and the children repeated after the teacher by rote, as it was considered a sign of a good Islamic education to have uttered the words in the Quran. Copies of the Quran in households were kept wrapped up and out of view for the most part; the more widely read and seen were smaller publications of particular sections of the Quran translated into Bengali and accompanied with annotations. At any village fair or at a saint's shrine, stalls selling religious literature in Bengali were ubiquitous, and these were modestly priced so as to make it affordable for most people. They were printed on inexpensive paper and in monochrome, but it was striking that the text, though in Bengali, was printed from right to left, as Arabic would be.[6] It was common to see groups of elderly women sitting together around one of these books and the most fluently literate among them would recite a verse and read aloud the accompanying commentary and the others listened and discussed it afterward. There was other evidence of a more vernacular Islam too (Stadlen 2018). For instance, an elderly Syed woman, Rokiya Bibi, used to own a book called *Phalnama* that could explain the meaning of dreams, and women flocked to her with questions. But when I asked to see it, I was told that the book had just disappeared one day, which was seen as retribution for overuse. Its disappearance, however, was also read as a proof of its potency. The same woman, Rokiya, and her daughter-in-law, Dilera, also were known to perform *jhaad* (a possession ritual) to cure various illnesses. While women came to them with all manner of complaints, they themselves made a distinction between mental illnesses determined by the environment and those caused by physiological issues of the brain and claimed to be able to treat only the former and recommended that the person see a doctor for the latter. Almost as proof of this, Dilera's own daughter, Ruby, suffered bouts of epilepsy and was on a course of Valporin for all the years that I knew her. But, despite their accommodation with bio-medicine, such practices were frowned upon by pious men like Haji Mustafa Master, who reinforced his greater Islamic learning by attending large theological gatherings that were held from time to time across Bengal. These *jolshas* served as a forum where attendees could air doubts and questions that preyed on their minds and could expect answers from learned men. This was intended to help renew their commitment to being better Muslims. People like Mustafa Master attended such *jolshas* and brought back to his kin and neighbors new interpretations and debates that he had learned by interacting with scholars from a much wider circle than the village. His ability to read Arabic and Urdu also gave him access to publications produced elsewhere in India and abroad, and as a result of this wider understanding, someone like him could gain a reputation as a knowledgeable *maulana*.

This nod to Arabic and, by extension, all things from the epicenter of Islam's origins in the Middle East dominated the practice of Islam in the villages. As we have seen before, a not-so-subtle hierarchy was maintained by the Syeds in relation to the other castes by virtue of being descendants from a *pir* from Iran (see Chapter 2). This was often qualified by the slightly defensive assertion that the only reason the Syeds resembled the locals in physical features was because Kamaal Baba's second wife, whose children they were, was a local Bengali woman. The rare green-eyed or pale-skinned Syed provided some proof of their theory. Their ability to speak Urdu was cited as evidence of their western origins, and they used it as a way to maintain boundaries with other castes and also as a mark of distinction. Another recent marker of Islamic distinction was the capacity to go on pilgrimage. While some families had been to Ajmer (located far away at the opposite end of India) by 2013, two couples had been as far as Mecca. On their return, they were treated as nothing less than celebrities, for to complete the Haj is the most coveted obligation of a Muslim identity, and stories of their travels and their experiences of the "Arab lands" were recounted over and over again. The first of the elderly couples played their part perfectly. Rokima Bibi, who had always worn saris like everyone else, was suddenly to be seen only in the all-enveloping black hijab which she advocated as the more appropriately modest clothing for Muslim women instead of what she called "the naked" sari. The two Masters strutted about the village with even greater self-importance than before. That the ability for travel relied foremost on economic capacity, which they both had, owing to their landholdings and schoolteacher salaries, was understood by all but was never stated; the afterglow of the Haj overshadowed all else.

But inevitably, all claims to greater piety or learning or travel were marshaled toward one's reputation within the village and led to frequent clashes of ego between the men. Each Eid, while eagerly anticipated, also brought trepidation about their shenanigans, for as on other important festival days the issue of who would lead the congregational prayers caused no end of drama and intrigue. It was customary for a senior man to do this, but in light of several aspirants to this role, this was always a difficult decision. One year (in the year that the scandal of Shohin and Feroza occurred), two of the Comrade's staunchest supporters (and therefore influential men), Lulu Master and Munsab, refused to join in the Eid prayers because they were going to be led by Mustafa Master. Though the latter was also a close relative of the Comrade, their stated reason for displeasure was his control of all the revenue from the Waqf lands that they had recently tried to wrest away from him.[7] It was not so much a financial benefit they envied (there wasn't any) but the prestige that such a responsibility gave Mustafa Master in the eyes of the village. The unstated reason was more likely to be Mustafa's growing dissent against the Comrade's actions in the arbitration of the scandal.[8] The other possible and less controversial contenders were the two *pesh imams*, Amir Ali and Abu, both of whom were Syeds, but their impoverished circumstances made Mustafa Master consider them too lowly for him to follow in prayer.[9] This led to an impasse which was finally broken by Mustafa Master announcing that he would spend Eid in an altogether different village of his relatives. This in turn had a knock-on effect on others, such as Hanif Master, who was also on the arbitration committee of the scandal, flouncing out of the village on Eid as well, to show he was no less than Mustafa. This kind of drama was not unusual, and each year the rest of the congregation lived in apprehension of such last-minute ruining of the festivities. As a result, the otherwise egalitarian assembly of congregational prayers and celebratory festivals remained threatened by the spirit of petty one-upmanship.

Nowhere was the spirit of competition and contest during an Islamic festival more evident than in the finale of the festival of Muharram in the contest of *lathi khela* (young men displaying stick-fighting skills). This much-anticipated event was held next to the *imambara*,[10] and teams from nearby villages, where the Syed inhabitants of Madanpur and Chishti shared extensive kin and social relations, attended. It was the culmination of the ten-day Muharram festival that was announced by the local mosque official (*khadim*), and it commenced with an offering of *shinni*[11] of rice pulao, cooking oil, and sweets at the mosque which was redistributed to all the children of the village. Over the next four days, households were divided up for each to make a contribution on consecutive days. On the remaining five days everyone made a contribution every day, starting with the *Khuski* offering of rare foods, such as chicken and pulao and *pithe* (flatbread made of rice flour). The seventh day was *Matom* when men mourned the martyrdom of Husayn by beating their chests. The eighth day was a day of rest before the crescendo of the last two days. On the ninth day, a *tazia*, an elaborately decorated bamboo float, was carried by men dressed in fresh clothes followed by a grand procession of several hundred men and children through the villages before being finally brought to the village mosque in Madanpur.[12] From Madanpur the *tazia* was then taken to Chishti, and everyone stayed up much of the night doing *matom* (mourning practices) before the dawn of the tenth and final day of Moharram. On this day, the Deh Majlis book was recited until noon in the presence of a congregation, and at its conclusion everyone went home, had a bath, and then collected again in the open space near the *imambara* in Madanpur. When they emerged, they found the open space cordoned off by rope, decorated with bunting, flags, and strings of marigold and stalls selling fried food, candy floss, and ices doing brisk business with eager children clutching small change. All the *tazias* from the nearby villages of Rengna, Madanpur, Chishti, Turulia, Shimoldi, and Mohammedpur stood lined up on display, and women in their best saris and young girls in jewelry and makeup sat together on mats to one side. Teams of about thirty young men, dressed identically, made a grand entrance down the main village lane, dancing to the beat provided by live drummers to perform the *matom* in the arena in the middle. Each team spent the next half-hour displaying their skills in jousting with long bamboo poles, with some solo and duet drills, ending the display with a giant pyramid involving the entire team. This was repeated with each team and the testosterone, adrenalin, and dust in the air were impressive as each group of young men worked hard to outdo the other teams with their skills, to the growing volume of the music and drumming. The audience was spellbound, and adults looked away only to respond to children asking for money to spend at the stalls. The event drew to a close at sundown, allowing everyone just enough time to rush home for ablutions before the evening prayer with which they would end the day's fast and the long and demanding festival of Muharram.

Over the fifteen years of this study, the nature of Islam and its practices altered in response to new influences. One year, the neighboring village, Rengna, as a result of its adoption of a more pious form of Islam ("they have become Deobandi" is how people put it), stopped participating in the Muharram tazia procession and the stick-fighting contests (*lathi-khela*) as its communal effervescence was considered too excessive for their more austere religion. The alienation was exacerbated by the lack of interaction that used to occur regularly during elections, as the polling booth for all three villages was located in Rengna. Another neighboring link that was broken was with Turulia over the income from a tree that was cut down to make way for a shrine for one of the brothers of their ancestor Kamaal Baba. This would have been an important shrine, but the Comrade's rapacious greed caused him to pocket the money, and plans for the building fell through as did the links between the villages. Within Madanpur and Chishti, too, some families had begun to send their sons to study in faraway madrasas, and these young men came back with different manners and norms as they prayed more conspicuously and dressed differently in white clothes, trousers hitched up at the ankles, beards, and skullcaps, and they did not attend all the Barelvi festivals in their home villages. While these young men could not control the celebrations, they told their mothers off instead for wearing saris, recommending in their place a head-to-toe shapeless garment that covered the entire body. Village women tended to tie their saris high, leaving their ankles free for movement, and the revealing nature of the sari had been discussed by us women on many a lazy afternoon. My shalwar kameez was enviously considered to be the "proper Islamic dress"; it was considered more modest as it covered the body properly, unlike the sari "that left you naked." It was hard to determine when this sense of inferiority had begun to develop, as the shalwar kameez was practically unknown in Bengal generally and in rural Bengal most definitely until the late 1990s. But since then it had been widely adopted by urban Indian women as the more "practical" garment and did not necessarily carry with it an association of being a Muslim garment.[13] However, even though women on television and on urban commutes were increasingly seen wearing it, no married woman in the village wore one. The first person to do so was Feroza when she visited Chishti after her marriage to a man in Uttar Pradesh, and while she had left in a state of disgrace after a scandal (see Chapter 3), her return in a bright pink shalwar kameez had made the women go green with envy. Along with stories of wheat being the primary staple rather than rice and the pleasures of twenty-four-hour electricity, Feroza also told the gathered neighbors about how much more modest the shalwar kameez was, especially if you didn't need to work in paddy fields. Her account of leisure and nutritious food, no manual work, and the cool of ceiling fans set up a subtle hierarchy between the clothing, food, poverty, and lack of modesty of her natal kin and northern India. My own clothing continued these conversations further, and the discussion of dress and fashion led to a discussion of propriety and modesty that inevitably dovetailed to good Islamic behavior. The participants in such discussions were overwhelmingly Syed women whose anxiety stemmed as much from their desire for piety as to mark themselves off from other Muslim castes. But there were few definitive resolutions. Rokima Bibi's post-Haj attire of the all-enveloping hijab initially provided the ideal counterpoint to their "naked" saris, but it was eventually discarded for its utter impracticality in a hot climate, with no electricity, and constant manual work. The unstitched sari offered a flexibility in adapting it to various tasks such as hitching it up in flooded fields or tucking an implement within easy reach into the waistband, that tailored clothing simply did not afford. The hijab's monochrome drabness also prompted women to make aesthetic judgments about its severity compared to the colorful variety of their saris. Thus, each new influence of the madrasa-trained youngsters, the pilgrimage stories of elderly couples, or rumors heard about neighboring villages introduced new debates around the themes of Islamic piety and practice, in the manner that Talal Asad characterizes as Islam's "discursive tradition" (Asad 1986). At no point was the lived Islam in these villages uniform and consensus-based, with clear demarcations between orthodox and heterodox practices, and the concern about "what to wear" and the endeavors of Syeds and Shekhs alike to recite at least the first and last prayer of the day were part of these negotiations. The "event" of the animal sacrifice discussed in this chapter has to be read against such a shifting sense of what it is to be Muslim within such mutability of religious beliefs and practices as well as a wider politics of growing intolerance of minority rights in India.[14]

The Two Eids

Eid-ul-Fitr, preceded by a month (a complete lunar cycle) of fasting and prayer, culminated with the sighting of the new moon. Like with other festivals, the day began with people dressed in fresh or new sets of clothes with men assembling in the mosque for mid-morning congregational prayers. This was followed by feasts of special foods prepared in each home as everyone relished the renewal of normal patterns of consumption suspended during the thirty days of Ramzan. During the month of fasting, each day, a simple meal was consumed at dawn, after which almost everyone went back to sleep to rise again to an altered rhythm. During Ramzan, adults fasted—no substance was meant to pass between the lips between sunrise and sunset—and agrarian work was kept to a minimum. Some people ate during the day so that they could keep going in order to earn a living, but they did so discreetly within their huts. While the smell and sounds of food dispersed quickly through thatched roofs and open doorways in huts, people did not usually comment on it if they detected these transgressions. The shared understanding was that everyone strove to do their best and kept as many fasts (rozas) as they were able. Syeds, on the other hand, and especially their women, most of whom could afford never to have to leave the four walls of their homes, spent much of the day looking after their animals and feeding their children and offering extra prayers. There was great performativity in their religiosity too, as many chose not to swallow even their own saliva as part of their strict fast. Conversations during Ramzan were therefore punctuated by constant spitting by women by turns, and was hard not to alternate between worry that one of these projectiles would land on me and admiration at their aim because it never did! Prayers and food were cooked and offered at the mosque from where it was given away to anyone who needed it. The last few hours of the fast saw a flurry of activity in preparing the evening feast, which was consumed after the fast was broken at the appointed time with dates or fruit. While the fast and cooking and planning meals dominated all household rhythms, the month of Ramzan was also a month of piety and a test of discipline and self-restraint that fasting brought. After the first fifteen days of the month had passed, special prayer meetings called *milads* were held each evening in various Syed homes (see Chapters 3 and 4 for a discussion of *milads*).[15]

Eid-ul-Adha, or the Feast of Sacrifice, celebrated on the twelfth day of the moon, was, however, considered the more important of the two Eids and was celebrated on the tenth day of the last month of the Islamic calendar.[16] The ritual was a re-enactment of the sacrifice that Abraham had offered to God of his son Ibrahim, and one that the Prophet has re-enacted for Allah.[17] For the Muslims of Madanpur and Chishti, as it was for Muslims the world over, offering animal sacrifice was part of their inviolate commitment to the core teaching and practice of Islam and being Muslim. In the village, this Eid began as all festival days with people rising earlier than normal to complete several tasks before the rituals began. In each home, the special food of *shemai-lachcha* pudding (vermicelli, dry roasted and mixed with ghee, sugar, and water), chapatis made of rice flour (rather than the usual wheat flour), and halwa with ground gram flour, coconut, and sugar—were prepared, among other foods. The quantity and variety of these foods depended on the prosperity of each household, as the ingredients of these special foods were rare and expensive. Some households acquired the scarcer items, such as coconut, on their previous visits to the nearby town of Dubrajpur; others sent their children in a panic on the day to scout the local grocers in the village in the hope they would not have sold out. Sugar, the coveted and absent luxury in daily life, made these foods eagerly anticipated by children and adults alike. Everyone aimed to be bathed and dressed in new or best clothes before the festivities began, and men invariably took precedence at the tanks because they had to present themselves punctually for the Eid prayers. Prayers were held in the walled cemetery that lay on a slight hill just outside the village. It was considered auspicious to watch them pray, and women and children gathered in the main village lane to do this, watching the men's heads, covered in clean white caps, appear and disappear from view above the low wall as they bowed and straightened in the *razaks* of prayer. When the men re-entered the village, youngsters touched the feet of their elders three times, and the elders in turn said a small prayer for them over their bent heads; people of the same age greeted each other by touching palms. After this, families returned to their homes for a small snack of the special foods before gathering in the open area inside the village for the sacrifice. This first part of the day could be read as the separation stage in van Gennep's well-known tripartite structure of ritual that prepared participants for the ritual by disconnecting them from normal structures and temporalities. In

Islam such separation was part of *Ibadat*, that is, the ways in which to correctly perform acts of worship and service to God, and it was part of a Muslim's daily routine of ritual ablutions before each prayer.

That year, eight Syed men and their families offered sacrifice in the village of Madanpur. They were: Comrade Maqtool Hussain, his brother Shaqtool Hussain, their father's brother Maqbool Hussain, Mukhtar Ali, his neighbor Akbar Hussain who had the second largest land holdings after the Comrade, Rafiq whose son's wedding was in a few days' time, Ismail who was an "outsider" settled in the village but close to the Comrade, and Shaaker Ali. They were all prosperous Syeds, but each shared complex relations over generations with the others. At the heart of these tensions was the Comrade, who had brought disrepute to Madanpur by abandoning his wife and marrying a young girl from Chishti (he was the only man with two wives), and he used Eid to make amends by offering his sacrifice in Madanpur where his pious first wife lived, rather than across the road where his home now was. During the course of his political career he had outmaneuvered possible contenders and had made several enemies, Akbar and Shaaker among them.[18] Akbar now kept to himself, speaking to very few people and concentrating his energies on farming. His two sons, despite good qualifications, had failed to secure jobs, lacking the patronage of the Comrade.[19] Shaaker had been an avowed Congress supporter and a critic of the Comrade, but the retaliatory tactics of the Comrade had reduced Shaaker to a catatonic silence. Mukhtar was not a supporter of the Comrade either, but he preferred to hold his counsel and cultivated a reputation for poetry, books, religious knowledge, and piety instead. He had built himself a small shed on the edge of the village, near the fields, where he spent a lot of his spare time. Ishmail did not have any kin in the village apart from a brother who lived in Chishti, but again, like almost all other brothers, the two were estranged as a result of the Comrade's tactics. The Syeds who offered cattle in sacrifice that year were therefore a fractious bunch, divided by long-held grudges and deep enmities caused by the Comrade and his politics. But when they formed a circle around the sacred space waiting for the ceremony to begin, dressed in their Eid clothes and unusually accompanied by their wives, children, and dependents, one wouldn't know that they were anything but fellow Muslims joined in prayer.

Each sacrifice was offered in the name of seven people from every family to "make explicit that the victim represents the person sacrificing the animal: its flesh stands for his flesh" (Bowen 1992: 78). Each of these individuals was expected to keep a total fast, going without water or food, from sunrise until the consumption of the sacrificial meat. There were also strict guidelines about the cattle that could be offered for sacrifice. Ideally, they should have been reared from birth by the sacrificer and should have been a favorite member of the herd, to maximize the wrench of losing a loved creature to echo the original Abrahamic sacrifice. The sacrificial cattle also needed to be in their prime and blemish free, and so an elderly or disabled animal did not make for a good candidate. While it was increasingly possible to buy cattle from the markets for sacrifice for the considerable sum of Rs. 5,000 to Rs. 6,000 ($100 to $120), this was frowned upon as such a creature would not be tied through affective bonds to their owners. As a result, it was only wealthy Syed households with enough resources for cattle sheds and fodder who could meet the criteria for the ideal sacrifice.

Immediately after the sacrifice, the Syeds had the cattle skinned just outside their compounds by members of specialist castes from outside the village who were paid a fee to do the job. In turn, they paid the Syeds a price for the hide, which they would sell in the leather market. I decided to watch the next stage of the proceedings at the home of the Comrade's first wife, Mehr, who was a good friend of mine, and I had seen for myself the love and attention she lavished on her herd during the hours I had spent with her. She worked relentlessly and ran the household composed of her teenage daughter, adult son, and mother by herself, and it was her herd of cattle and flock of chickens were her constant companions on whom she lavished care and attention. While her assets were un-doubtedly owned by the Comrade, he played no role in the day-to-day running of affairs, and Mehr made all decisions about agricultural cultivation, livestock, labor arrangements, and cash flow on her own. And although she was utterly competent in her role, the sorrow of being abandoned by the Comrade at the age of twenty-one after just seven years of marriage was constant in her eyes, and one she sublimated in the attention she paid to those in her care. For her, the sacrifice of her favorite cow would have been therefore a significant wrench. Arriving in her courtyard, one could not help but pick up on the sadness in the air accompa-nied by an unusual frisson caused by the Comrade's presence in her courtyard. I had never seen him there before, and Mehr displayed an uncharacteristic coy-ness. He was present with his brother and their sons, smoking a cigarette (thereby violating the fast) and overseeing the skinning of the carcass. I decided to watch from a distance from my usual post next to Mehr's cooking station that looked out to the tank behind the house. There, by the side of the *pukur*, members of the Hindu *chamar* caste who had been hired specially to conduct this task, skinned the large animal quickly and efficiently in less than an hour. The carcass was sold to them for Rs. 3,000, and this money had to be given away to charity.[20] Once the commercial transactions were completed, the Comrade hurried away, leaving the more delicate task of divvying up the meat to Mehr, saying he had to go on to mark the festival in his second wife's household, and, in a nod to my Hindu identity, he invited me to come by and have the (vegetarian) pudding of *shemai-lachcha* later.[21]

The meat itself was carved into small pieces of about 50 grams each, and unlike in some cultures, the different cuts of the meat were not assigned to particular kin groups in any hierarchical order but were instead all mixed together. There were, however, certain parts of the animal that could not be consumed by the sacrifice—the four legs and the intestines, which together weighed about 15 to 20 kg, had to be given away to others in the village, as was the blood to the caste of *majhis*, who ate it fried. The rest of the meat was divided into seven equal parts and had to be given away according to prescribed rules. Four out of the seven parts had to be given to non-kin, such as the non-Syed lower castes in the village—Shekhs, Mughals, and Pathans as well as members of the two Hindu castes who consumed beef. It was these groups that also supplied the agricultural knowledge and labor for paddy cultivation and brick kilns owned by the Syeds, so the Syed household prioritized sending this portion of the meat meant for non-kin to their own sharecropper and his family as well as to the other families who either worked as domestic staff in their household—cleaning, frying mudi, gathering fodder, looking after the animals, and so on. Those who had been paid to take the animals out to pasture every day were, of course, affectively tied to the sacrificed animal, and they were on top of the list. Of the remaining three parts of meat, one part had to be given away to agnatic kin who had been unable to offer a sacrifice that year, the second part had to be sent to the other households that had also offered a sacrifice, and the final portion, one-seventh of the total, was kept by the sacrificer. The amounts exchanged between sacrificing households invariably differed in quality and quantity depending on the cattle sacrificed, but the exchange followed the same rules in each household and was important for future exchanges. All day, covered trays of meat circulated across the village as the sacrificed animals were carved, the meat weighed and divided up and dispatched; in her courtyard, Mehr made a mental note each time a tray arrived. By the end of the day, a significant amount of meat accumulated in the households that had offered a sacrifice (as they received offerings from others who had sacrificed), but so did a significant amount arrive in all the other households in the village, as each one was tied either through kin or through labor arrangements with the eight households offering Qurbani. In Misratan's household, for instance, I saw trotters in a pot on the fire. As a valued bargadar family, they had been no doubt presented with these from Shaqtool's household, and the delicacy was eagerly anticipated by the children, who could barely wait for the dish to be ready.

In a place like Madanpur, the anticipation of consuming the rare luxury of beef was acutely felt across the village as Qurbani was perhaps the only day in the entire year when everyone ate red meat; the more common luxury for weddings and *feasties* was chicken (*polty*), which was cheaper and more easily available.[22] But that too was rare, and an average person in Madanpur and Chishti mostly consumed a vegetarian diet, and beef was eaten just on this one occasion each year.[23] Most Syed households, who were often related to each other either through descent or marriage, received portions from relatives and so the amount of meat that accumulated in their homes was larger than the others and so impossible to consume in one day. The absence of electricity and refrigeration made storing this luxury a challenge, so it was minced by hand, mixed with onions, chilies, ginger, and garlic and deep fried as small patties to prolong its edibility by a day or so. Once these were consumed, everyone returned to the largely vegetarian diet of rice, dal, and a few vegetables. This came almost as a sense of relief for most, because living in a Hindu-majority country, where the consumption of beef attracted strong sentiments, people preferred to return to a "safer" diet.[24]

Interestingly, despite this rare consumption of meat and the anticipation of this treat, the festival of Qurbani Eid was not referred to as a festival of feasting; in fact, food was not mentioned at all. Qurbani was treated as any other eagerly awaited festival that broke up the monotony of quotidian time, and it was only after the sacrifice was carried out and the meat distributed that anyone expressed any excitement about the feast that lay ahead. This "suppression of the idea that cattle were a source of food" is an observation that is widespread across societies where cattle were the source of life and was central to the idea of sacrifice (Hutchinson 1996). Unlike other consumption practices (such as playing a radio on batteries that were expensive or offering guests tea with milk from one's own livestock), offering cattle for sacrifice was not done in the spirit of conspicuous consumption. Instead it was animated by a desire for virtue accrued through sacrifice which the Syeds, in their aspiration to greater piety in all religious matters, wished to fulfill. But there was also a wider community pressure for them to offer a sacrifice so that the whole village could celebrate Qurbani. During the rest of the year, other castes conceded a higher religious status to the Syeds without much contestation and left them to quarrel among themselves about who would get to lead the prayers; they tolerated their boundary maintenance through the use of Urdu among themselves even in a mixed group, and they put up with their constant spitting during the Ramzan fast. But for Qurbani, these accommodations translated into a not-so-subtle expectation that the superior Syeds would offer a sacrifice and share the sacrificial meat with everyone. As Syeds and other castes alike often remarked, Qurbani was about "giving, not keeping," and clearly about charity and a redistribution of scarce resources. The distribution of the meat was a reasonably smooth affair, as each sacrificing household knew exactly who to send the meat to—their sharecropper, their domestic servants—especially those who had been involved in the care for the animals—and their agnatic kin. The delivery of these gifts was enacted without much fanfare as children were recruited to deliver portions to various households swiftly so that by the afternoon all households had received at least a small portion which they could expeditiously start to cook before it went rancid in the heat. Thus, while just eight families could offer Qurbani that particular year, all households in the village joined in the feasting on the day.

Charitable giving was, in fact, the hallmark of all Islamic festivals, as was the tradition of *zakat* for all Muslims, of giving away 2.5 percent of one's income. As we have seen, the schedule of key fasts, festivals, and rituals regulated by the Islamic calendar that marked the key dates following the lunar cycle of twenty-eight days, began with Muharram which was associated with a whole set of small practices of giving over several days, and culminated in the more public, spectacular ones that were known by non-Muslims. Each of the big festivals was associated with various forms of "giving"—every household was required to put aside a certain amount of rice per member of the household to be given away as *fitr* to other Muslims,[25] and wealthier Syed households also regularly gave away four or five sets of new clothes every year. At the start of any festive season, householders put aside a certain amount of grain and clothes and over the next few days, it was habitual to see itinerant beggars and travelers arrive in the village, asking for alms. Turning a beggar away was unheard of, even after the stock for charity had been emptied. During Qurbani, no one was expected to profit from animal sacrifice in any way, and so any profits made from the sale of the slaughtered animal's hide had to be given away in charity. Thus, my informants were keen to emphasize that while festivals were of course about the preparations of special foods and new clothes, their significance lay in the circuits of redistribution they created. It was common within the village for people to use the pretext of the festival season to gift clothes and food to impoverished neighbors and kin to avoid compromising the dignity of the recipient. In the wider context of rural Bengal, too, those in need could look forward to festivals as a redistributive moment when they expected to receive gifts of rations and clothes that would keep them going until the next one.

The social inequality that exists between those who have resources and those who don't is mediated through a moral economy in which Islamic gift-giving is unilateral—that is, the gifts are given without expectation of return. The redistributive function of Islamic festivals has been noted by Pnina Werbner, who argues that such redistribution exists within a "semiotic of inequality" that characterizes "hierarchical gift economies" (Werbner 1998). Werbner notes that these "gifts to God" are directed either "downwards" to the poor in the form of alms or "upwards" as religious tributes to holy men—or then to "communal causes" (Werbner 1998: 104). In Madanpur and Chishti, as indeed across India, it was during festivals that charitable donations to individuals or institutions such as madrasas were collected, and these donations were part of a wider repertoire of virtuous giving, to a greater cause and to those who were less fortunate, and there was no expectation of material return. The sacrifice of a much-loved animal at Qurbani and the distribution of meat described herein has to be read therefore within this context of virtuous giving.[26] The distribution of Qurbani meat in Madanpur and Chishti may have existed on the small scale of a village but it is structurally and analogically similar to the institution of *langar* or a communal feast in a Sufi lodge in Pakistan that Werbner describes. The communal kitchens of the lodge were centers of collection and distribution of food and are, she argues, conceived of as a "perpetual sacrifice." The distribution of the meat at Qurbani, we could argue, is thus just as important as the act of sacrifice itself. While the act of sacrifice marked self-denial of the sacrificer to Allah, the gifting away of the sacrificial meat was an expression of self-denial to the community. This observation is confirmed by John Bowen, who observes that in his Indonesian fieldsite, Isak, the key moment of the festival of Eid was not the sacrifice itself but the ritual congregational meal, *kenduri*, afterward. As in Madanpur and Chishti, each year three or four households offered a sacrifice, but this enabled them to sponsor a village-wide feast which was followed by an all-night recitation session. Bowen notes that the Feast of Sacrifice has been made part of the institution of Kenduri, a generic ritual congregational meal, that provides the "framework for ritual in gayo society." By doing so, the Feast of Sacrifice is "configured . . . as an event of transaction and communication," much like other rituals (Bowen 1992: 84–85).

The "Domestic" Set-Up and Dialogic Transcendence

Whatever the religious virtues gained by the sacrifice of animals, it must also be recognized that practices of violence toward animals have come under severe criticism from animal rights and vegetarian activists alike, and rightly so. Much of the criticism is leveled against the rearing, farming, and killing of animals in the most desperate conditions for the meat industry, causing an enormous amount of pain and distress for the animals. The single motivating factor for this cruelty is the insatiable greed for meat among human populations, as indeed the desire for profits by the owners of the meat industry. It should be recognized, though, that the setting of Madanpur and Chishti where the ritual of Qurbani was conducted was of a radically different kind, termed a "domestic" set-up of human-animal environments, precisely to distinguish them from the large-scale animal farms and abattoirs of the "post-domestic" set up. In these villages, there was little distance between humans and animals and there existed close bonds, verging on the anthropomorphic, between them. Further, very little meat was consumed generally, and it was the combination of these two aspects—of close bonds with their animals and the low everyday consumption of meat—that marked the "domestic" regime. For animal sacrifice to be truly meaningful and generative of the virtues of renunciation and charity, deep bonds (what Prasenjit Duara calls "dialogic transcendence") between animals and humans was, in fact, not just ideal but necessary for a meaningful sacrifice.[27] Where animals are crucial to the survival of humans—as in pastoral, hunting, or mixed economies such as India—animals are considered to have souls.[28] And in Islam, it is believed that animals, by virtue of having souls, can aspire to Paradise after death and so by undergoing the sacrifice the animal is not merely a victim but a being with some agency of its own. Drawing on Tlili's work *Animals in the Quran*, Magfirah Dahlen-Taylor argues that the Quran can therefore serve as a "starting point for recultivating a spiritual understanding of animals" who can earn an eternal life in heaven like humans, and are not mere instruments for human salvation (Dahlen-Taylor 2016: 364).

In Madanpur and Chishti, most domestic spaces were almost equally shared with livestock such that animals were kept within or close to residential spaces; cattle were either tethered inside the courtyard or just outside, but where they could be seen and could themselves see others. Chickens and smaller animals had the run of the house, and it was therefore not unusual to walk into a dwelling where the smell of cattle dung was part of the domestic atmosphere and chickens dodged between my ankles as I sipped my tea. They often tried to steal food, and so most of the time if they were shooed away it was to protect human food rather than to demarcate explicit human space. Women and men communicated with their animals using a different voice than they did with other humans, and the animals seemed to understand when they were being called to be fed or asked to go out to graze and so on. During the day, large cows and goats were often entrusted to the care of others who took them out to pasture, and at sundown when they returned, the cattle found their way back to their individual homes on their own without error. People formed deep bonds with their animals and shared what Radhika Govindarajan calls "animal intimacies" (2018). For instance, the abandoned first wife of the Comrade, Mehr, poured her love and energies into her dependents, and the chickens and cattle in her relatively large yard were equal recipients of these, alongside her children and mother. She rarely left her home to travel, insisting that only she knew how to prepare the fodder for her fussy herd and no one else could be trusted to tend to them as she would. It was customary to see her, and others in the village, painstakingly cutting long stalks of straw into bite-sized fodder for the cattle on the curved blade of a *bonti* exactly as they would chop vegetables for their own food. In another part of India, Govindarajan's informants used the term *mamta* (maternal love) to describe their feelings of "exasperations and annoyances" toward their animals and described their behavior as children, just as Mehr does (Govindarajan 2015: 511). Thus, while materially the animals in one's household were alienable beings that could be bought or sold or given away, the ties of intimacy and care between the carer and animal made these creatures as inalienable as children. The wrench of giving up one's favorite cow for Qurbani was as close as it was possible to get to the original Abrahamic sacrifice. As Govindarajan observes, "It is this painstaking labor, as intense and prolonged as that entailed in rearing children, that is at the heart of the idea that because animals are like children, they can substitute for human children in sacrifice" (2018: 57). And it should be noted that despite the obvious patriarchal ideology underpinning the original sacrifice of son by father, in rituals of sacrifice it was women, through the everyday acts of care, who felt the wrench much more than men. In the example discussed previously, Mehr's sacrifice was of an immeasurably higher order than her husband's.

This human-animal linkage is one of shared emotions, but also that of a shared economy and what Anna Tsing calls "collaborative survival" (2015). Cattle subsist largely on crop residue and grasses and are kept for plowing, milk, and manure, and chickens provide eggs that are a rare source of protein. Sunita Narain, an Indian environmentalist, calls this the practice of "agro-silvo-pastoralism," in which people use the land for crops and trees as well as for livestock. In such an ecosystem, livestock are the most important economic security for the farmers: "It is their insurance system, not the banks" (Narain 2017). Thus, unlike post-domestic economies of Europe, North America, and Latin America that produce the bulk of the 95 million metric tons of beef in the world in which animals are sequestered in large farms, fed a combination of animal and plant-based food, and slaughtered in abattoirs—each stage of which has an enormous environmental impact—in the domestic set-up livestock are not kept in animal farms but within domestic spaces by big, small, marginal, and landless farmers. In this agro-pastoralism, animals have a productive purpose, and they are cared for by those whose livelihoods depend on their well-being. Narain reports a figure calculated by India's expert on animal energy, N. S. Ramaswamy, who reported in the 1980s that the energy capacity of 90 million work animals was equal to the installed capacity of the electric power in the country. In India this subsequently changed with mechanization, though cattle continued to be kept for milk, but in Madanpur and Chishti, where fields were small and tractors rare, the animals continued to plow the land and so had an important productive role to play even in cultivation.

But the maintenance of animals was not cheap; it could cost up to Rs. 70,000 a year (according to estimates that Narain reports), which would explain why only the wealthiest in the village were able to keep them.[29] Given the material poverty that characterized life in Madanpur and Chishti, the question of giving away resources without any expectation did raise the question of whether sacrificing a large animal made economic sense. Could not the equivalent sum of the animal's worth be distributed as alms to those who need it, saving the animal itself, as a more pragmatic solution? Economists Syed Waqar Hussain and Muhammad Muhsin Khan explore precisely this question in an article entitled "Poverty Alleviation: The Redistribution Impact of Eid-ul-Azha Animals' Sacrifice on Rural Economy." Calculations indicate that discontinuing animal sacrifice would add 20 million head of livestock over four years (Hussain and Khan 2009). But this increase, they show, would also cause greater pressure on fodder, and that would cause an increase in price while also having a negative impact on human food or cash crops with the net result that "the standard of living of the rural poor will be adversely affected" (Hussain and Khan 2009: 256). Thus, they conclude that on balance, taking costs and benefits into account, even in purely monetary terms, the practice of animal sacrifice is an arrangement that helps "to stimulate the rural economy and balance the growth of livestock" (Hussain and Khan 2009: 258). Detractors of animal sacrifice have proposed the act barbaric and cruel, but these objections often refer to non-domestic set-ups in which animals are farmed, rather than where they are part of an integrated domestic set-up. Other objections have been raised by those—such as reformist governments in the Indian state of Tamil Nadu led by Tamil Shaivites in the nineteenth and twentieth centuries and then by the Legislative Assembly in 1950—who have tried to carve a new political language that transcended secular and religious sentiments and shared an aesthetic and moral abhorrence for the violence toward animals and the unsightly blood and gore (M. Pandian 2005). But as Pandian notes, the "language of reform planted in notions of culture" is, he claims, "so reductive that it is incapable of comprehending and engaging with these web[s] of sacral significations which are important for communities, families, and individuals," and what they failed to understand was that "animal sacrifice as a mode of worship is saturated with a network of significations ranging from remedying worldly afflictions, to mark[ing] life-cycle transitions, to reproducing community links and hierarchies" (Pandian 2005: 2317).

This network of significations is characteristic of animal sacrifice rituals in all "domestic" set-ups, whether Islamic or not. Among the Nuer in southern Sudan, whose study E. E. Evans-Pritchard made famous and foundational to the discipline of anthropology, we learned that they used to say, "Cattle are not killed just for nothing" to convey that meat is not sacrificed for consumption and the idea of cattle as food is suppressed. In this setting cattle were plenty, but they were also the basis of social relations, and so there was almost a "moral injunction" against killing them simply to consume meat (Hutchinson 1996: 299). Nuer pastoralists practiced transhumance and cattle were not only their most valuable assets but also their exchange currency at the time of marriage or for the settlement of a blood feud that were key to maintaining social relations. The Nuer believed that there was an identification between human and cattle vitality, and cattle were the principal medium through which humans could connect with divinity. Traditionally, cattle were sacrificed in a variety of piacular and collective rites, either to appease the divinity to stand in for a human victim of illness or misfortune or to mark rites of passage "by making God and the ghosts, who are directly concerned with the change taking place, witnesses of it" (Evans Pritchard

1956: 199). Cattle were therefore "objects of spiritual dedication" whose sacrifice allowed the Nuer to strengthen the bonds of human blood to be negotiated and affirmed. It was for this reason, Evans-Pritchard notes, that there was almost a "moral injunction" against killing them simply to consume meat, and he conveyed the seriousness of this claim by stating that the Nuer "must not only kill for sacrifice but that they must sacrifice to kill" (Evans-Pritchard 1956: 269). Thus, sacrifice was at the heart of killing and "sacrificial flesh at the very centre of the idea of feasting" (Evans-Pritchard 1956: 269), and to disobey this injunction was to invite the ghostly vengeance of the ox.[30]

In Islamic contexts, where all meat consumed is not strictly sacrificial meat (as it is with the Nuer), nevertheless "killing an animal for food must make it clear that the killing is done in the name of God" (Bowen 1992: 78). As Werbner clarifies, it is important to "conceptualize the difference between Islamic ritual slaughter (halal) and ritual sacrifice, since nominally in Islam every animal slaughtered is a sacrifice (Werbner 1998: 101). Werbner makes the distinction between these two kinds of slaughter by making the first part of a cash economy, in which meat is sold for regular consumption, and the latter a part of a moral economy of ritual and sacrifice. The latter is distinct from the former because the slaughter in a sacrificial ritual had to be of an animal that was freely given, rather than bought in a market, and the animal itself had to be further sacralized by the reading of prayers recited before the slaughter, as also the congregational prayers before it. In the former, although the prayer renders animals clean for consumption (*halal*), the sacrificial dedication "is deliberately abbreviated so as not to imply that God condones the suffering inflicted on the animals during their sacrifice" (Werbner 1998: 936) when the principal purpose of killing is cash and consumption. But in the moral economy of Qurbani it is through making the idea of killing an animal inextricably bound with the idea of sacrifice, the process of sacrificing a much loved animal is made possible. By offering it as a symbol of one's commitment to the Divine, inalienable ties to the animal are made alienable. .

In the very different context of Hindu societies in the Himalayas, Govindarajan reported a similar connection between humans and animals. In such a context, "ritual sacrifice acquires power and meaning through its grounding in precisely this world of kinship between human and animal" (Govindarajan 2015: 508). In Uttarakhand, unlike in Bengal, most of the sacrificial meat is consumed by the immediate family and relatives who provide the animal. But, as in Bengal, the Uttarakhand example also reiterates the importance of offering for sacrifice something precious. Explaining why substitution as a principle doesn't really work—that is, substituting animal for coconut or cucumber—Neema explains, "Coconuts aren't precious . . . there's no loss when you give Devi-devta coconuts. But giving an animal is like giving a person. A life is given in place of a life" (Govindarajan 2015: 508). Although in Bengal cattle aren't included as kindred subjects—as they are in Uttarakhand in what Govindarajan calls "kindred mutuality"—the emphasis on giving up something precious is common to both contexts. When asked on the day of sacrifice what made for a "real sacrifice," a young woman said, "I'll feel terrible tomorrow. . . . The cowshed will be so empty. But this is real sacrifice" (Govindarajan 2015: 515). Thus, the violence of sacrifice is inextricably linked to its "companion constituents—love, guilt, grief, devotion" (Govindarajan 2015: 516) and must be considered germane to the practice of animal sacrifice across contexts, among the Nuer, Himalayan Hindus, or Muslim societies anywhere.

As a result, in preparation of the sacrifice, the animal itself was given special care and attention and at the moment of the sacrifice, Bowen notes that "Muslim commentators have emphasized the importance of sparing the victim undue anguish, and that the sacrificer must keep the knife out of the animal's sight and speak to it in a calming way" (Bowen 1992: 78). For that reason, "ome Muslims emphasize whenever an animal is killed, it must be aware of the act itself, and that the person killing the animal must recite a blessing and quickly cut the conscious animal's throat" (Bowen 1992: 78). By taking part in the killing of the animal the sacrificer thus bears moral responsibility and suffers a bereavement, and the animal submits willingly to its fate, as did Abraham and his son. In the Feast of Sacrifice the animal offered for sacrifice is viewed as "a vehicle for the afterlife" (Bowen 1992: 84–85). As noted in the account of Qurbani presented at the start of this chapter, the men who held the animal down continued to keep their hands on the beast long after it was strictly necessary. It was as if they wished to continue to share the pain directly, and to comfort to the animal viscerally, even after its body stopped twitching.

Several weeks after the festival, I asked Mehr, as she painstakingly and lovingly chopped fodder by hand into bite-sized stalks for her fussy herd, if she missed her favorite animal, the one she had given up for Qurbani. Her smile belied the sadness in her eyes. "I try to be a good Muslim, Didi," she said, "and a good Muslim performs their duty. Sincerity of intention is very important," she added. It is this struggle, this bundle of ethical reflection and practice to do "the right thing," to suppress self-interest for a larger purpose, to be sincere in what ones does, and to force oneself to recognize the justice of redistribution, that I turn to next, to examine its implications for the democratic project.

Sacrifice and Social Imaginaries of Democracy

In classic anthropological terms, Qurbani displays a ritual's classic tripartite structure proposed by van Gennep as rites of separation, threshold rites, and rites of aggregation, or "preliminal," "liminal," and "postliminal" stages. These define what Turner proposed as the banks of the river, through which the ritual process flowed. The sequencing of these stages is an important aspect of the ritual, as they mark "a transition from one situation to another and from one cosmic or social situation to another" (van Gennep 1903: 13). In the case of animal sacrifice, the animal is made a transcendent subject through various mechanisms, first by being separated from its owner, who voluntarily offers it for sacrifice, then through prayers, and finally, through the solemnity of the act of sacrifice itself. As noted, the prescription is for the voluntary surrender of an animal with whom one is inalienably and intimately connected, to reinforce the pain of the separation. The basic meaning of the word "sacrifice" (*zabiha*) communicates a giving up or "sublimation of an item or interest for a higher value or principle," and it is this self-denial that is the basis of a true spiritual offering to God or Divinity (Hedley 2011). Rearing cattle, as we have seen, was a labor- and capital-intensive process, and so giving up one that had been tended with care caused a great wrench and took enormous self-restraint. This was possible because the act of sacrifice existed within a wider repertoire of religious giving and charity that prepared its adherents for the act of giving away what was theirs. As Werbner notes, "in Islam voluntary labour, sacrifice, donations, offering and charity merge. All these acts are vehicles mediating the relationship between person and God. In all, moral space is extended, objectified and personified, while the identification between person and community is revitalized" (Werbner 1998: 113). And the practice of animal sacrifice turned on the idea that their cattle were a link between the human and the holy, and they served in a sacrifice as the link between the perceptible and the transcendent (Evans-Pritchard 1956).

The second phase of Qurbani was dominated by the act of killing, which was accompanied by an extraordinary silence mentioned in the opening vignette of this chapter. It was in this moment that a relationship with the sacred was established through the elimination of the vitality of everyday life and its substitution by the transcendent. The violence inherent in the sacrifice held deep significance, as Maurice Bloch argued, for the violence of the slaughter pointed to the violence that pervaded human and animal universes. The killing of the animal symbolically displaced the violence from the community onto the scapegoat and was thereby conquered in the ritual violence. The gathering of the Syed families around the sacrificial arena was a visual clue of this displacement. While each of them shared deep antagonistic relations in everyday life, for the duration of the sacred ritual, at least, they put aside these differences for a higher common purpose as they stood shoulder to shoulder in shared silence. As the philosopher Douglas Hedley puts it: "The idea of sacrifice exhibits the natural and legitimate human sense of the sacred dimension of life" (Hedley 2011: 267).

In the third stage, the sharing and consumption of the sacrificial meat in the community allowed for the transcendent to be reintroduced into quotidian life. In Bloch's reading, the vitality of this meat was taken from external sources, from the transcendent, and this new vitality is literally ingested through the consumption of the transcendent subject—namely, the meat of the sacrificed animal. The re-entry of the transcendent into the quotidian is what he calls "rebounding violence," and the re-entry of ritual participants into everyday life was a "conquering return" whereby the original vitality of life (before the ritual) is replaced by a different vitality that has been touched by the transcendent. The vitality of the everyday that is re-established in the third phase of the ritual is thereby altered from before as it now is a combination of the both the profane (of the everyday) and the sacred (of the transcendent). "The third stage is not a return to the condition of the first but an aggressive consumption of a vitality which is different in origin from that which has been originally lost" (Bloch 1992: 15). As we have seen already, the rules regarding the sharing and redistribution of the sacrificial meat by everyone were emphasized over individual consumption. While the sacrifice created a sudden abundance of coveted meat, very little—only one seventh of it—was actually consumed by the sacrificer. Further injunctions against keeping particular parts of the animal by the sacrificer and giving them away to others reinforced the suppression of individual desire or appetite. On the whole, the consumption of meat was generally seen to be a secondary, and rather unmentionable, aspect of the festival.[31] No pleasure was expressed at the time of consumption or discussed afterward, and the lack of refrigeration made the meat last only for a fleeting few meals. The significance of Eid-ul-Adha was instead on offering the best creature one possessed, and one that was valued and loved, to Allah—and whose meat kin and dependents could share. Further, as we have seen, the sacrifice by a few families resulted in a feast in every home in the village, thus establishing a connection between sacrifice and a moral responsibility to share with those who were willing to receive, thereby creating a moral community.

Each Qurbani ritual and each congregation of Eid prayer was therefore a ritual process that replenished each participant and the community with desirable values after every performance. As we have seen, each festival demanded enormous self-restraint and discipline from participants. Fasting for any length of time is always a demanding activity, and to do it without even a sip of water passing the lips for over twelve hours in an Indian summer, without fan-cooled interiors, exacted astonishing discipline. Similarly, the Islamic practice of giving (*zakat*) that required giving away 2.5 percent of one's income as a sacred duty also inculcated a certain detachment from one's possessions. As these gifts were made to a wider economy of circulation—to kin, neighbors, itinerant ascetics, and religious seminaries—they helped connect individual acts of giving with a wider moral economy of giving. This also allowed an individual even when they lived in a small village, to imagine a much wider society they did not know personally but were a part of. These rituals and their accompanying virtues therefore re-committed people to the goals of egalitarian participation, abstinence, shared suffering, redistribution of resources, restraint, and accommodation—and these values formed the basis of ethical behavior that people utilized to guide social life in a community, during and beyond ritual time. In the final chapter of this book, we will examine how it is precisely these values—the imagination of collective good, suppression of individual interest, and discipline—that are vital for the creation of democratic citizenship.

Coda

The effects of the ritual process extended even to those in the community who were not direct participants. In the religiously mixed population of Madanpur and Chishti, the egalitarianism practiced during the Islamic festivals had an afterlife in the non-Muslim groups of the village too. The reader may recall that the two Hindu communities of Doms and Bagdis joined their Muslim neighbors in watching the Muslim men at prayer during the Eid and Qurbani festivals. It was believed that the act of even watching this performance of piety brought merit to the observer. Muslim women routinely did this as a result, but so did their low caste Hindu neighbors. Standing with them one Eid, as we watched the heads bent in prayer, a Dom woman remarked wistfully, "Isn't it wonderful that their religion makes them stand shoulder to shoulder with others, regardless of caste? All the Syeds, Shekhs, Mughals, and Pathans are standing next to each other randomly, as a single congregation." The remark was a poignant one as it came from a member of a low-caste group who had spent her life in the knowledge that her caste identity had made her an "untouchable" until recently and her community was of such low status within their religion, that even in the present, that found it hard to persuade a Brahmin to conduct a community *puja* for them. After years of watching their Muslim neighbors celebrate their festivals, the Doms and Bagdis were inspired to start their own celebrations by collecting small donations toward a communal fund. As noted in the previous chapter, land reforms had had a significant effect in rebalancing social hierarchies, and the newfound dignity in sharecroppers and agricultural workers emboldened them to freely ask for donations from everyone, including the Syeds. Eschewing Durga Puja, which required a Brahmin to conduct it, they chose instead to worship the goddess Saraswati for whom, it was believed, anyone could conduct the ritual. By choosing the goddess of learning as their object of worship, the Doms and Bagdis also chose education as the truly liberating force that would allow for both material and ritual social mobility. And though Saraswati was tradition-ally worshipped on one day (unlike Durga, who required five), the idol of the goddess was installed for five days mainly to make the most of the investment. Following the worship itself, traditional vegetarian food was cooked in giant communal utensils specially rented for the occasion, and everyone was invited to share in it. This was followed late in the evening by a series of music programs and "video evenings." It was a modest affair, but clearly the biggest religious ritual in their calendar and respectable in its ambition to complement the Qurbani and Eid festivities of their Muslim neighbors. These celebrations also inaugu-rated a repertoire of village-level sociality around a new deity, which was manip-ulated effectively by the BJP in the run-up to the 2019 elections, through their strategy of campaigning under the cover of Hanuman puja described at the start of this book. It is to such electoral dynamics that we turn our attention in the next chapter.

*

6

Election

Cultivating Citizenship

One July morning, as I arrived at Dilera's thatched hut, I found her in a flap, perched on a rickety stool, frantically searching among items in the rafters. She looked among boxes and plastic bags, bundles of old clothes, and rolled-up quilts, examining their contents with growing frustration. Finally, she clambered down and, noticing me, gave me a smile but seemed exasperated. "I can't imagine where she might have kept it," she said, indicating with her head the house next door. Her husband's sister lived there, and the young daughter-in-law had not been able to find her voter card on the morning of the election and everyone was now looking for it in their usual safe-keeping nooks. Dilera opened a plastic box to extract her own EPIC (Electoral Photo Identity Card) and checked through it once again to see if the young woman's was among them.[1] I noted that despite the early hour, Dilera was not only bathed and dressed but was also draped in her special handloom sari that she saved for weddings and festivals, and the crisp folds billowed on her slight frame. Usually women bathed late in the day after completing household chores, after which they changed into a fresh sari and said their afternoon prayers before lunch. But Election Day was clearly different, and the usual rhythms changed as everyone rose early and got ready to vote before doing anything else. Having failed to locate the missing card and clutching her own, Dilera looked at me. "How can she not know where her Voter ID is?" she expostulated. "It is such an important thing! If she can't find it, how will she vote?" She then added with a growing hysteria, "And how can she not vote?!" For an otherwise phlegmatic woman who did not say much, this was a remarkable outburst.

It was this sense of inviolate commitment to voting that had sparked my academic interest in studying Indian democracy as I aimed to understand what shaped the political subjectivity of the electorate that voted in high numbers. Over the following fifteen years, I witnessed nine elections in the villages of Madanpur and Chishti—three each at the national (1999, 2004, 2009), regional state (2001, 2006, 2011), and local panchayat level (2003, 2008, 2013)—and this commitment to voting remained unchanged with turnout figures recorded above 85 percent.

In this chapter, I present the event of an election in the life of a village community and, as with the other events discussed in preceding chapters, the aim is to "pick out the threads that link the event to be explained to different areas of the context" (Turner 1980: 144). Election Day is thereby conceptually placed alongside other events—the scandal, the harvest, and the sacrifice—discussed earlier, to explore the family resemblance they share and investigate how the logics of the explicitly political activity of voting interacted with other social actions of agrarian rural life. In Chapter 3 we met some of these actors during the events of the scandal that catalyzed the formation of a political opposition against the Comrade around the young Majhi for the first time. In its resolution we witnessed the work of "the political" as a space of potentiality, in which new horizontal alliances emerged, overturning standard vertical ties of class and caste to create new solidarities that challenged the status quo. We now turn to the election itself as the arena where these new formations were put to the test in a contest. The new formation had taken the identity of a rival political party, and the drama of the election itself was "a ritual idiom within which people [could] express their visions of a moral community and moral order" (Spencer 2007: 79). It is this aspect of elections as a moral and social drama that makes them similar to the other events discussed previously and one that we will be consider here.

The analysis in this chapter will move between the state (and sometimes national) levels and the very micro level of the individual voter in a village, to place the analysis of the event of an election within a wider context. Changes at the macro level of West Bengal affected and shaped elections in Madanpur and Chishti, as alliances and electoral strategies formed in the headquarters of political parties in the capital of Kolkata percolated through districts and small towns to the rural hinterland. In turn, the small and significant changes that took place from one election to the next in villages like Madanpur and Chishti shaped the wider arc of startling political change in West Bengal during which an invincible Left Front was routed by a young political party. Each election was an event when entrenched power was either re-established or challenged by new actors emerging at every stage and it is these shifts, when plotted cumulatively, that explain the arc of change. A meaningful account of any story of electoral change thus needs to move between the micro and macro levels of electoral politics, as the analysis here will attempt to do.

The election of July 2013 was especially significant as it was to elect the panchayat, the most local tier of government in Indian democracy. "National and state level elections are only dress rehearsals for the real election of the panchayat," Majhi told me, when we finally found a few minutes to talk in the middle of his frenetic campaigning. And as people confirmed, this was indeed the election they most cared about because the candidates were people they often knew personally and whose governance decisions and budget disbursements would determine whether everyday concerns such as a paved road, a primary health center, or help with housing materials would come through. In July 2013, there was added frisson as it was an election that Trinamool Congress wanted to win at all costs, having won the state-level elections in 2011. "Winning this election will give us real power (*khomota*) and capacity to bring change; without power in the Panchayats we will not get anywhere," Majhi added. Consolidating power at the local level was therefore vital for Trinamool to feel that they truly had control over West Bengal politics.

Majhi's theatrical metaphor was apposite here as the stage seemed set for the grand performance, the drama of a panchayat election. A social drama, Turner argued, was agonistic and resulted from conflict over norms and through opposed interests. "Social dramas are in large measure political processes, that is, they involve competition for scarce ends—power, dignity, prestige, honor, purity—by particular means and by the utilization of resources that are also scarce" (Turner 1980: 153). But the agonism was only part of the plot and the theatrical effect of the social drama was achieved not just through naked rivalry, but rather through the transformative potential of the performance itself. This Turner calls the "subjunctive" nature of ritual—the realm of the possible, the imagining of what can be. The account of the election that follows should be viewed through such a subjunctive lens, for the possibility of "anything can happen" was the essence of an election. Each actor in this social drama—the officials conducting the election, the voters, and campaigners for political parties—is alive to this potential, and the anticipation of the unknowable outcome is what drives the action. The officials are in constant dread of the procedures of voting going wrong ("an election is both an exam and a wedding," one said); the voters look forward to the altered sociality of a polling booth, and campaigners are always open to the possibility of a win or a loss. "There is no room for complacency," even seasoned workers of a winning party told me. Thus, the social drama of an election is subjunctive in the extreme, allowing for each actor's imagination of the possible at every scene, and the only way to find out how the drama will end is to undergo the performance for anything can happen between the first scene and the curtain call.

The path to this particular election had been a long and arduous one for Trinamool Congress and its local representatives such as Majhi. In 2011 they had finally ended the Left Front's unbroken winning streak of thirty-four years, which was a record for any communist party in any democracy in the world. These thirty years or so of Left Front government in the state of West Bengal can be seen to have had three distinct phases (Bhattacharya 2016). In the first "revolutionary" phase, lasting roughly into the 1980s, land redistribution and Operation Barga were implemented and the daily wage was raised. Cadres and leaders were created during this period to represent the interests of the sharecroppers and landless agricultural workers against the entrenched dominance of the landowning classes. The resulting re-distribution of land, raised wages, and most importantly the newfound self-confidence generated through challenging the status quo and redressing old power equations brought the Communists their first wave of support.[2] This was also the phase of lived communism, when ideas about social redistribution, egalitarian practices, and dignity for labor were widely discussed and began to set the new norm. In the second phase, during the 1990s, this support was consolidated and saw the establishment of the complete hegemonic capture of all social institutions by the Communist Party, leading to the establishment of a "party-society" (Bhattacharya 2016). This was achieved by gaining further support among "the poor," that is, sharecroppers and agricultural workers, through a system of incentives and punishments, and local "Comrades" marshalled the resources of the Party, state, and government such as the machinery of police, developmental grants, and employment opportunities, to support this capture. This second phase was also the most brutal of all, especially in the rural hinterland, as the dominance of the Party also required silencing the activities of any rival political formations and establishing each local Comrade as the sole and indispensable arbitrator in all village disputes. Any opposition, whether through organized political parties or through individuals standing up to the writ of the local Comrades, was summarily crushed through the use of violence, humiliation, inflicting personal tragedies on the families of the detractors, withholding all benefits from them, and, in extreme cases, killings. There was a pervasive sense of terror (*shontrash*) in rural Bengal during these years. After the 2001 elections, a newer phase can be said to have emerged under a new chief minister, Buddhadeb Bhattacharya, when a sixth consecutive victory was won by the Left Front despite the vociferous opposition led by Mamata Banerjee's newly formed Trinamool Congress in 1998. In 2006 the Left Front won their biggest-ever victory, despite greater scrutiny of the election process by the Election Commission of India, thereby allowing them to put to rest the charges of "scientific rigging" of elections by the opposition parties. But despite victory, an urgent need for new policies to generate growth and development was evident—most crucially, an industrial policy that would create the employment opportunities the electorate wanted above all. Their performance in the panchayat elections in 2008 and the national elections in 2009 declined, confirming this, and led to the government's desperate measure of forcibly acquiring land from farmers to set up new industrial plants in Singur and Nandigram. This caused outrage among their traditional support base in rural Bengal and provided the perfect opportunity for the opposition to gather unstoppable momentum. The stranglehold of the local Comrades in villages relied even more on terror tactics than before as nascent opposition to their politics began to re-emerge more openly.

In Madanpur and Chishti, when I began research in 1998, two decades into a Left Front government, all politics was dominated by a single man, Maqtool Hussain, universally known as "Comrade," the local representative of the Communist Party of India (Marxist) or CPI(M)-led government. There was also a man called Nathu Dom who was the elected representative of the local panchayat government (each panchayat covered 10 villages) and was officially responsible for disbursement of funds and representing the village's interests. But for all intents and purposes it was the Comrade who was the local boss. He had been a Party worker for over twenty-five years and served as the gatekeeper to the villages, controlling access to news, information, and opportunities to the villagers. His house commanded access to both villages and also enjoyed the easiest access to the main road for his motorcycle, the first privately owned motorized transport in the villages. Both villages were full of men who were his erstwhile comrades and whom he had outmaneuvered to become the sole party boss.

Such a figure was fairly typical of Bengal. The CPI(M), realizing the fragility of vanguard political movements such as the Naxalites that mobilized the urban intelligentsia to revolutionize peasants, had over the years built up an intricate network of such Comrades across the State who were Party members, and who belonged to the area in which they worked and where they often owned land and businesses that sustained their political activities. They took their orders from the Party and organized political activities in their area, and were the conduit for the disbursement of funds, loans, and benefits for much of the rural population. The Party headquarters in the state capital, Kolkata, utilized this capillary network of Comrades and cadres to exercise control in the furthest corners of the state. The most visible evidence of the efficiency of this machinery was available during elections when voters were mobilized to turn up, resulting in consistently high voter turnouts in West Bengal. Elections were frequent with three tiers of elected government, and each election campaign and its conduct was dominated by the activities of the Comrades and Party cadres. "An election is like an exam," the local Comrade said to me. "We work hard for two months to get good results." He also added that it was less onerous than working in any other political party, because so much good work continued the rest of the time that elections were merely the opportunity to cash in on this work. In between elections, political activity did in fact continue and was conducted through meetings of various labor unions of the Party who passed decisions that were in turn implemented by the cadres. In these meetings, agricultural and housing loans were awarded, budgets were allocated for various developmental activities, and strategies for inducting new members into the Party organization were discussed. Through the allocation of their shares among the villages in which they lived, the cadres built their allegiances which, when aggregated at the state level, gave the Communist Party its power base among the rural population. The success of the Communists in West Bengal thus relied heavily on the success of the tireless efforts of its Party cadres (see Bhattacharya 2016; Chatterjee 1997; Ruud 2003, 2016).

The Comrade's "political work" was hard to define and relied on a curious mix of omniscience and invisibility. He dominated politics but was seldom actually seen around the village; the occasional roar of his motorcycle announced his arrivals and departures, but he did not stay still for long. Even when he was around, one never saw him actually doing anything in particular. Although he had the largest landholdings, he was never seen to be farming, or mending a tube well, or carrying diesel fuel—the sorts of jobs that able-bodied men, including the elite Syeds, of the village routinely did. Occasionally, he could be spotted at the tea stall with a group of laborers and supporters, although one never saw him eating or drinking; an occasional cigarette or bidi was all he consumed in public. His figure was unmistakable, well-built and fit (though padded with more fat than your average farmer), a complexion just a shade lighter than those burnt by the sun in the fields and brick kilns every day of the year. And while he dressed like everyone else, his sarong was less faded and frayed, he wore slippers when everyone else walked barefoot, and he wore a gold chain around his neck. These differences made him stand out, but only just, so people would know that he was one of them but also that he was someone important. Thus, much like the gods of India, he ate and drank in private, rested in private, was better looking than his devotees, and his public appearances were just that—"appearances." To glimpse him therefore was almost akin to divine *darsan* (an auspicious sight). Despite the lack of evidence, he enjoyed a reputation for working hard from dawn to dusk and at all hours of day and night when he would be sometimes called away from the comfort of his bed to attend to matters. People said that he was well connected to a wide network of Party workers throughout the state, with whom he met, consulted, and negotiated funds and facilities for his villages, and he was widely considered to be the most important asset of the villages' life. When he was elected to the president's post of the Block Kisan Sabha (a farmer's union), this fact was noted with awe by all, and interpreted as a reward for his political talents, his deft maneuverings, and his ability to stand out within a large Party network. That the new post might bring him even more power to wrest resources for the village was acknowledged but not overtly stated. Instead, people called attention to the fact that it was *their* Comrade who was frequently called upon to firefight when there was trouble elsewhere or when urgent help was required in the Party's business, and these facts were cited as further evidence of his personal abilities. It was therefore assumed by most people that the large measure of his political work was conducted beyond the village, at the nearby town, or district headquarters, or the various Party offices dotted around the countryside. The mobility afforded him by his coveted motorcycle was seen to be a fitting symbol of this ability to bridge the vast distances between the life of the village and that of far-off official spaces. This was an important aspect of the "work" he did. His political work thus did not include any of the obvious activities that one may assume to be the stuff of a villager's life, at least not at the village level.

Among hard-working farmers, the Comrade was clearly of an elite man, a *bhadralok*, a status whose minimum requirement was the eschewing of any manual work (see Broomfield 1968 and Ruud 2003: 72–75). In this, he was representative of a broader trend according to which upper caste dominance in leadership positions was the norm (Bhattacharya 2016; Chandra, Heierstad, Nielsen, 2016). The work that the Comrade did was manifestly not like the work done by the rest of the people of the village, who conducted hard physical labor. Their labor, in their jobs, and at home, was mostly physical, covered their bodies in dirt and dung, aged their complexions, and used every ounce of energy that they had. Even when paid work was completed for the day, the domestic chores of a village life demanded the time and energy of those who lived in it, and so even "leisure" time was dominated by a multitude of tasks, big and small. And the work was relentless, especially given the lack of basic amenities such as running water and electricity. So there was always another chore to be completed before darkness fell, animals to be tended, another meal to be cooked, and a yard to be swept. Even the other *bhadralok* of the village, the schoolteachers, who spent their working days in white-collar work, returned home to carry out similar sorts of tasks to others. Almost all of them continued to have modest landholdings and therefore spent the daylight hours outside their working day tending to their fields and crops with their own hands, mending fences, fetching diesel on their cycles, and tying up cattle. Thus, everyone apart from the Comrade did physical work that placed an enormous demand on their bodies and time.

The Comrade's political work, on the other hand, while obscured from view, was manifest in very different ways. Over a period while this study was conducted, the physical changes undergone by the villages themselves were noteworthy. Each visit revealed new roofs, submersible pumps, freshly installed electric wires, mobile phones—all of which were evidence that someone somewhere was doing something to make this all happen. There were also non-material signs—members of lower castes assumed an air of self-respect vis-à-vis the elite, landowners lived in nervousness of the sharecropper's whims, women formed cooperatives, rival political groups waxed and waned, people could explain the virtues of democracy in a language of citizenship and rights, the ideal of social equality was regularly discussed—these were all also signs of some work being done somewhere by someone. Arild Ruud, who studied two villages in the neighboring Bardhaman district in the early 1990s and returned to his fieldsite nearly twenty years later, confirmed changes there too, noting that "in terms of visible material change in everyday life, the contrast between 1993 and 2011 is striking…" (Ruud 2016: 203).

Rather bizarrely, the Comrade's actual physical absence from the village led to his omnipresence in conversations and decisions among people. No disputes could be considered resolved until the Comrade's opinion had been considered, and all decisions, big or small, whether about new businesses or village festivals and even private events such as weddings, were finalized only after his final approval. After years of living among them, when I could say that I had a fairly astute sense of most of the people in the villages and their personalities, I began to appreciate just how well the Comrade knew his constituency. Conversations with the Comrade himself revealed his thorough knowledge of the goings on in each and every household, of what people described as *haandir khobor* (knowing the contents of the cooking pot). This allowed him to anticipate where trouble was brewing and the reasons behind it, and spent considerable time in planning and plotting his moves. On more than one occasion, his inexplicable decision made sense only once the full set of events that his action had triggered had unfolded. But in my occasional chats with him, he did not discuss these manoeuvres with me. What he presented to the anthropologist instead was the face of the local leader who knew his constituency well but also had a good grasp of Communist ideology and its critique of American neo-imperialism. After 9/11 he demonstrated to me with some deft arguments how the incidents in New York and the subsequent war on terror by NATO had serious implications for India and its Muslims, Muslims like him and his fellow villagers. His understanding of international politics was characterized by an ideological hatred of capitalist America and its allies, a line that was held resolutely from the headquarters of the CPI(M) to workers like him. In fact, on any given day, by noon, he usually knew what the "Party line" on any current issue was. This was achieved through remarkable discipline whereby cadres read the official Communist paper *Ganashakti* every morning and went prepared to discuss its articles with other cadres whom they met during the course of the day in the local Party office and elsewhere. By the evening the Comrade was able to slip some of the ideas he had picked up into conversations with the circle of men at the village tea stall. Their ideas about communism, empowerment, and the place of their struggle on a larger stage were all filtered through his prism. His main asset, therefore, was his connectedness, that is, his ability to bring some of the outside world into the village. In choosing to discuss the economy or international politics with me, the Comrade was thus keen to give off the impression that his work was mainly ideological, or at least driven by ideology, rather than about the petty machinations he knew I was hearing about from the rest of the village. While we were both aware of how much of his work in fact was more humdrum and even "dirty," he chose never to mention this aspect of it.

One incident that exemplifies the Comrade's tactics to maintain his preeminence occurred early in my fieldwork when he was said to have slapped a young man across the face in full view of several people. The news spread like wildfire— such a public humiliation was extremely rare, and it was evident to everyone that the slap was more than a punishment for troubling a girl as the Comrade attested, but really a warning to the man's political ambitions. At that stage, I had filed it away as yet another example of the Comrade's terror tactics and noted that the irony of the Comrade, a twice-married and insatiable womanizer reprimanding a young, single man's interest in a woman, was not lost on anyone. But this small incident gained greater salience a few years later when the event of the scandal occurred (see Chapter 3) and the same young man emerged as the magnet around which a coalition of interests aligned against the Comrade. This young man was none other than Majhi, who we met at the start of this chapter, who in the 2013 elections was trying to ensure victory for Trinamool Congress, to end the electoral stranglehold of the Left Front. Majhi had all the qualities required to mount this challenge—he had time because he had failed to gain employment, he was an upper caste Syed with a good education, and the family had income from land and his brother's salary. His young age was initially a problem, as the other Syed men who remained in a state of permanent but silent disgruntlement with the Comrade were much older than him and did not take him seriously. Many of them were also related to the Comrade through marriage or descent and shared political history with him and used these to leverage personal advantages at the cost of any group loyalty. But the slap had caused them to pause, and while they were too cowed to publicly support Majhi, public opinion imperceptibly began to turn in his favor. People across the two villages talked about the incident and discussed the reasons for the Comrade's fury. These discussions allowed people to air their opinions about the Comrade's actions that were otherwise left unarticulated for fear of retribution, but confirmed that resentment toward him was very much present. Majhi wished to channel these anti Comrade sentiments but needed the backing of an established political party that he could officially join and represent in the village.

At that stage, his only option had been the Congress. This old party still enjoyed plenty of silent support in West Bengal generally (polling about 40 percent of the vote share throughout the Left Front years), and in Madanpur and Chishti, several Syed families were known to be Congress voters. But the Comrade had managed to keep those voters divided between themselves and silenced in village affairs. Their only expression of dissent was at the ballot box at elections. At the state level, despite its loyal supporters, the Congress itself had grown increasingly moribund and ineffective in opposition to the Left Front. And then, in 1998, there was a real opportunity as, impatient to challenge the hegemony of the Left Front, Mamata Banerjee broke away from the Congress and launched Trinamool (grassroots) Congress to break away from the stranglehold of lofty male politicians. Echoing her ambitions at the village level, a young man like Majhi hoped to achieve the same breakaway. By expressing his ambition to ally with the Trinamool, he could effectively distance himself from the older Congress voters in the village (mainly composed of those elderly Syeds who had been outmaneuvered by the Comrade) whose politics amounted to a sullen, aggrieved, and ultimately silent opposition to the Comrade. By slapping him in public, the Comrade had presented the young man with an opportunity of bringing out into the open his intolerance for any challenges to his preeminence from fellow Syeds. As the local Trinamool worker, Majhi's selling point while trying to build support for his group was to appeal to the deprivation of the Muslim community for whom there had been no reservations in jobs, and Mamata had promised them a 15 percent quota. Majhi's criticisms of current politics began to be framed in terms of the rights of Muslims, especially when compared to the Scheduled Castes (SC). My notes report him to be saying:

> Muslims should get the same privileges as the SC. In name we could write we are Syeds but it doesn't mean anything. There is no economic infrastructure in this state. Jawhar Rozgar Yojana and Indira Rozgar Yojana [welfare schemes], none of them come to us. In Dubrajpur Block we are 25 percent Muslim, in the PC we are 18 percent Muslim. About the same as SC. But the candidates at every level are always Brahmins because their economic situation is better. In every party, we Muslims are always the foot soldiers, we have no influence anywhere.

By focusing on the lack of opportunity for Muslims, Majhi hoped to achieve two things in particular. First, he hoped to unite all the Muslims in the village under one banner, de-emphasizing in the process the caste divisions that existed between them. By doing do, he was able to underplay his own Syed identity and hoped to win over the support of Shekhs, Mughals, and Pathans who formed the bulk of the support for the Comrade and the Communist parties but who had always been kept in the penumbra around the Comrade. By appealing to their Muslim identity he of course ran the risk of alienating the Hindus in the village, but their numbers were smaller and they were also led by members who belonged to the inner circle of the Comrade's influence and so were unlikely to be easily swayed to the other side. It was a calculated risk, but Majhi seemed confident it was worth taking. In the national elections in 1999, Trinamool Congress did not field any candidates in the Bolpur Parliamentary Constituency where these villages lay, so he could not really marshal votes for a rival candidate, but the election itself allowed for the airing of discussions about political alternatives that the Comrade would not otherwise have tolerated.

The scandal caused by the Comrade some years later presented a real opportunity. His arbitrary ruling of forcing a marriage between two young people who were matrikin and from different generations had caused moral outrage in the village across castes, who considered this as totally taboo (*haram*). It was privately acknowledged by all, including the Hindus, that the Comrade had crossed an ethical red line here and in evaluating this particular transgression, his other corrupt practices were also evaluated and discussed, at first only quietly within families, but increasingly more volubly. This process allowed people to critically assess and test their shared understandings about standards of moral and ethical behavior and the limits of these. Majhi's fledgling efforts so far at forming a political opposition now provided an ideological place for this disaffection to gather, and his house became the focal point for those who wished to challenge the Comrade. Then came the 2001 elections, and Mamata Banerjee announced an alliance between her party—Trinamool Congress—and the Hindu chauvinist BJP party. It was said that she did this mainly for the latter's financial resources, but she suffered a severe loss of credibility for aligning with an ideology of Hindu chauvinism, which until that stage had had no electoral presence in West Bengal. At the local level, the consequence of this alliance with BJP was devastating for Majhi's efforts, as it effectively demolished his well-laid plans, and despite his best efforts it was impossible for him to sustain an argument for Muslim empowerment by joining a party that had just entered into an electoral alliance with a party whose political ideology of Hindutva was committed to reducing Indian Muslims to second-class citizenship. Trinamool Congress did not do well in the 2001 elections, and many commentators at the time blamed it on her alliance with the BJP. In the villages of Chishti and Madanpur, as with the rest of West Bengal, the Comrade's and the Left Front's writ returned further emboldened.

As the account in Chapter 3 demonstrates, the resolution of the scandal took several years, and in the twists and turns of that event two key things emerged. First, a shared awareness that there a distrust of the Comrade and the politics he represented, was widely shared. Second, building political alliances with people with whom one differed on other matters, involved the art of compromise and accommodation that had to be cultivated. As John Pocock, drawing on Machiavelli, points out in his discussion of active citizenship, while freedom brings social conflict, if that conflict is well-managed through compromise it can be a source of strength and bring "liveliness to political life" (Pocock 2006). The social imaginaries that contributed to a lively and pluralist politics of the democratic project—the need for political competition, the dangers of capture of power by a single party or politician, and the need to suppress individual egos to create a group—were gradually but successfully practiced by this new group in Madanpur and Chishti. Most of the Syeds began to put their differences to one side and came out openly as belonging to Majhi's group, and for the first time since I had begun my research there, people began to openly acknowledge that there were two parties in the village, a statement that was unthinkable in the past, so strong had been the Comrade's hold on village politics until then.[3]

The Comrade had his own core following among whom the most important, as previously mentioned, was a man called Nathu Dom, the pradhan (president) of the local panchayat committee. As an elected candidate, Nathu occupied his position of importance on the basis of a popular mandate for him as an individual, as panchayat elections were fought on non-party lines. His personality was perfectly suited to the job. He was soft-spoken and sober, and the characteristic bend of his head slightly to one side gave the impression of him being always willing to lend an ear to any demands or problems. He was seen around the village, strolling in the lanes around dusk for his daily constitutional, but also tending to his fields industriously like others. He had a good reputation for even-handedness in disbursing benefits channeled through his office and its allocated budget. His visibility, accessibility, and personal integrity made him an excellent candidate for a popular politician. But it was also widely accepted, implicitly even by Nathu himself, that he could not make any decision without prior consultation with the Comrade. They strove for consensus, but overall the Comrade had the last word. It was Nathu's job to announce the formal decisions, and his judicious personality lent credibility to them, but they were not his to make. In fact, their roles were entirely complementary; the Comrade spoke on behalf of the Party to the village, and Nathu spoke on behalf of the village to the Party. Thus, when people had a problem or a request, they approached Nathu for help, not only because they knew that it would reach the Comrade, but also because of their faith in the panchayat as representative of their interests. This village-level faith in the institutions of the panchayat is true for most of the state of West Bengal where the panchayat enjoyed an "intensive and extensive" appeal over all other rural institutions and people preferred "institutionalized problem solving . . . (such as a Panchayat) rather than individuals when in need" (Bhattacharya 2016: 335–336). Research also revealed, perhaps surprisingly, that the appeal of the institution of the panchayat cut across party loyalties, such that Congress supporters were slightly more likely to approach the panchayat with a problem. The sharing of responsibilities between Nathu and the Comrade that was a crucial aspect of their political work, also helped them achieve a wide appeal. Though the Comrade was unambiguously a Party man, by keeping his distance from him, Nathu could project the panchayat as a non-partisan body to the village. This division of labor between the two most prominent village politicians reflected what was a widely recognized phenomenon in West Bengal, namely that all policy decisions were made by the Left Front and the civil service and other elected bodies were seen to be "mere rubber stamps" and executors of these policies (Bhattacharya 2016).

The Comrade was surrounded by an inner circle of staunch and vociferous supporters and an outer penumbra of those who, while pledging their support, also kept their options discretely open. The sharecropper Okho Dom was in the inner circle, and for him the party program, the agitational activities for reform, and the need for solidarity among the landless were central pillars of his existence. It was through these that he had been able to reverse the experiences of acute inequity of his childhood. His success and association with the Party had given him enormous self-confidence, he was taken seriously by everyone, and could stand tall even among the Syeds. His place among the political workers in the village who formed the coterie around the omnipotent "Comrade," and his fierce protectiveness toward other sharecroppers, was at all times a thinly veiled threat that the slightest insult to his honor or that of his friends' would be met with retribution. He was rewarded for his loyalty with a loan from the government for a tube well and irrigation pump, which he could rent out profitably to others who needed it.[4]

Majhi's challenge was to build a similar group around him, and the election itself was the perfect excuse to do so. Several prominent Syeds who had been supporters of the Comrade had to be gradually weaned away, and Enayat Master was his first prominent win. He used to be a heavyweight among the Comrade's supporters, but then a combination of events whereby his son Raju was beaten up by the brothers Munsab and Mansur and the Comrade's attempt at ruining Raju's wedding by ordering his supporters not to participate in the celebration turned Enayat against the Comrade. Each Syed had such a story, and the challenge was to sustain their interest in the new Trinamool Congress formation and their support for Majhi, without being able to offer any material benefits in return for their loyalty. To Majhi, it also became evident that in order to form any substantial political opposition to the Comrade and to register a significant number of votes in an election, it was essential for him to gain the support of the agricultural workers and sharecroppers who formed the majority of the population in the village. The Syeds were capricious and even when united, their numbers were too small. By the 2008 panchayat elections, Enayat Master's family was rewarded for being the first to throw their hat into Trinamool's ring, and Raju was rewarded with a ticket to contest a seat, although he did not win. In the meanwhile, an interesting churn began to take place among the agricultural working class, composed of the Shekhs, Mughal, Dom, and Bagdi castes who had formed a consistent support base behind the Comrade through all the years of Left Front dominance. After the Scandal, cracks began to show, and stories of people being held back from new opportunities because of the Comrade began to circulate. The man who drove the Comrade's truck that was used for his various enterprises found a better-paying job in the neighboring village, but he was forced to stick with the Comrade who paid him much less. He was Ismail's nephew. Bishwa Dom was another case. He had been a daily wage worker all his life and was an articulate participant in the vision of rural communism and had a fierce loyalty to the Comrade for having been the agent of change in Chishti and Madanpur. But he had never been allowed into the Comrade's inner circle because of an old enmity between his father, Tinkari, and the Comrade. Tinkari had been the Comrade's political guru in the 1970s but, sensing serious competition from the charismatic and well-informed low caste Hindu, Comrade had used all his upper caste resources of land and connections to sideline him. Tinkari remained well informed through his travels across villages selling poultry products but kept largely to himself in village affairs. His wife, Memdasi, took a keen interest in the news that he brought home while keeping him informed of village affairs in turn. A visit to their home, where I spent many happy hours, was always lively, full of news and discussion about issues, policies, and the state of wider politics in general. Bishwa had grown up in this atmosphere, and despite his father's firmly held grouse against the Comrade, he had pledged his own loyalty to the agenda of rural communism. But the Comrade's guilty conscience about Tinkari resulted in keeping Bishwa firmly on the fringes despite his clear talent for politics while simultaneously, in a now familiar tactic, rewarding and supporting Tinkari's brother, Otul Dom. Otul was therefore a reliable supporter of the Comrade and thus even at the height of the scandal, when many had begun to revise their opinion of the Comrade, he held firm. Memdasi, on the other hand, despite not being Muslim herself, was outraged by the Comrade's transgression of the Islamic taboo against marriage across inter-generational maternal relatives and quietly but firmly expressed her deep distrust of the Comrade to me. It was thus no surprise to hear Bishwa say one day during the 2006 elections that he had heard that Mamata Banerjee was coming to address a political rally not far away and asked if I was going. While I had planned to go, I asked him whether he wanted to, and to my surprise he said yes. "I just like her," he said. "I like the way she speaks, the way she dresses. Simple. Just like us. Not with the airs and graces of our big Left Front leaders." Several years later, in 2008, when Trinamool fielded candidates in the local panchayat elections, I learned that the candidate who stood from the neighboring village of Rengna was Tinkari's older brother's wife's sister's son[5]. But the pressure from peers on a low caste poor daily wage laborer was immense as the Left Front continued to be considered the only party for the poor while any other was seen to threaten their rights. He was thus weaned away from Trinamool, being told that a poor Dom ought not to join a party of the rich.

In the meanwhile, as the star of the current Comrade waned following the events of the Scandal, his replacement was being groomed. Just prior to the 2006 Assembly elections, a visit to Madanpur and Chishti revealed that a young man, Shontosh Dom, had been identified as the ideal heir to the mantle, and his biography seemed well suited to the job. A young man, in his early twenties, he had just completed an undergraduate degree from the local college. Like his contemporaries in the region, he was unlikely to find a white-collar job and so had returned to working on his family's modest lands and as a *bargadar* on someone else's. He came from a small, close-knit family of two brothers and a sister who shared the farming responsibilities with the father and a mother who helped out during the harvest. The atmosphere within their dark and ramshackle hut was one of easy harmony, dominated equally by the mother's good humor and pride in her children and the father's ethic of hard work and honesty. They seemed to take collective pride in Shontosh's new role as a Comrade and took it in turns to outline for me how he spent his day. The sister, who was visiting from the home of her in-laws, conveyed genuine enthusiasm and possibly a touch of wistfulness, for the political work her brother now did. She too had decided to make the most of her own education by running a little school for the children in the village where she now lived. Shontosh spent most of the time listening to them with a shy smile on his lips and added a quiet word from time to time. But this demeanor clearly belied a fiery disposition for politics. At college, he had gotten involved in student politics, and it was his role in the student wing of the CPI(M)-led agitations against the Congress-led union that had gotten him noticed by the Party. As part of the induction into his new job he had been entrusted with the responsibility of helping people get their voter identification cards made for the forthcoming elections. This involved accompanying them to the local Block Development Office's office, filling out forms, checking their accuracy, and generally helping them deal with paperwork in a literate world. In his opinion, this had been a personally worthwhile experience as it enabled him to meet people and learn about their insecurities, demands, and desires, and helping had allowed him to develop a bond of trust with them. He was also expected to travel widely to the surrounding villages, making a note for the Party what the government was doing on the ground and not managing to achieve in his area. In this, the two monthly meetings with more senior Comrades had been invaluable. From them he had started to learn the art of rhetoric, the interpretation of the Party's ideology, and techniques for its dissemination and was given basic lessons in "how to behave with people." In the grooming process of this new "Comrade," elements of political work discussed earlier could be observed clearly.

By the national elections of 2009, he was already more confident in himself, though a bit defensive on behalf of his party whose star had begun to fall. The rival political faction had now taken root in the village, and for the first time since the

1960s Congress supporters openly expressed their preference for Trinamool and volubly campaigned in the Lok Sabha elections. The secret resentment against the Comrade's interference in their lives had begun to be publicly expressed once the Left Front itself had been held accountable on the national stage for its actions against those involved in the Singur and Nandigram protests. As a result, one of the Comrade's own penumbra had stood against the Left Front candidate in the 2008 panchayat elections, and had registered a respectable defeat. The young Majhi, whom the Comrade had humiliated in front of others many years ago, had persisted in his political ambitions and now had a strong and visible following and they actively campaigned for the forthcoming elections. Initial forecasts had projected a drubbing for the Left Front in 2009. The scenario for the budding Comrade was not, therefore, entirely dissimilar to the one that the older Comrade had had to face at the start of his political career. But, unlike his predecessor, Majhi did not have the luxury of a strong and ascendant political party behind him. The results of the national elections confirmed a severe loss of Left Front seats in the national parliament from West Bengal and the Left Front candidate from the parliamentary constituency containing Madanpur and Chishti also lost to the Trinamool Congress candidate. The dress rehearsals had therefore progressed well, albeit with some hitches, and the stage was set for the drama of the panchayat elections of 2013.

Election Day

I tried to reassure Dilera with limited success and trailed behind her as she went next door. There her sister-in-law stood waiting for her, similarly dressed in a crisp sari, her normally bare feet thrust into flipflops and clutching her ID card. She looked different, a bit nervous and excited. The special saris, the footwear, and the unusual outing all marked the day as a special one. They were going to vote. Time was moving on, so the two older women decided they were going to have to go without Gainda who sat shamefacedly to one side doodling on one of her son's notebooks. I knew her well, having helped her with her exam preparations some years ago, and could see how humiliating it was for this otherwise educated young woman to be temporarily disenfranchised thus and admonished by older illiterate relatives. She would have to wait for her husband to return home to check if he had put aside her Electoral Photo Identity card for safekeeping. Promising to return later, I accompanied Dilera and Naseeba out of the house. As we stepped into the main village lane, the women pulled their saris further over their heads, which they kept down as they hurried, although hampered by their uncustomary footwear through the familiar paths. Their village, Madanpur, now had its own polling station that also served the voters from the village Chishti across the road. The two villages were already intimately connected through ties of kinship, marriage, festivals, and work, and sharing a polling station had cemented that bond further. The local primary school that served both villages had been converted into a polling booth for the election and they approached it using a shortcut that the children from Madanpur did to avoid going past the highway on which it stood. The path was muddy from recent rains, but the adjoining tank (*pukur*) was full of fresh water. This was a welcome sight as there was no piped water in the villages and everyone had to rely on the many rain-fed tanks for their household needs. As they neared the booth, they looked up anxiously to check the length of the queue. The search for Gainda's card had delayed them and, like everyone else, they didn't want to have to wait too long. But the damage was done, and even though polling had started only ten minutes earlier, at least thirty women were already ahead of them in the line. It was hard to tell if they were disappointed, as they had pulled their saris even more protectively down on their heads as they entered the school compound. Men from both villages stood in an adjoining queue to the women, and there were a couple of security guards and some visiting officials who had just alighted from their car to check on arrangements. It was a much more public setting with a wider mix of people than they were accustomed to within their village, for as elite Syed women they tended to stay within the confines of their compounds or those of their neighbors. As they took their place in the line, the woman ahead of them turned to look, and she turned out to be from Chishti, a newly arrived bride. Though Dilera rarely left her home she kept herself well informed of news and gossip and could guess immediately which family the new bride was from. The young woman's sister-in-law and mother-in-law stood ahead of her, and they confirmed Dilera's guess. Pleasantries were exchanged and it was noted that though she was clearly "modern," she was also dutiful in having come to vote with her new in-laws. There were warm smiles of welcome and recognition all around before they lapsed back into solemn silence. Soon after, a couple of women walked past on their way out of the booth. They were daily wageworkers who needed to get to work at the brick kiln that was nearing completion and for which work was not going to be stopped for the public holiday of the election. They held their newly inked fingers, marked to avoid repeat voting, slightly aloft so as not to stain their saris with the wet ink but also perhaps to show off their efficiency in having completed their duty early. Their self-satisfied air was in marked contrast to their caste status as they both were Pathans, who, along with the Mughals, was held below the Syed and Shekhs. Women from the queue turned to throw admiring glances at them and then settled back to wait silently and patiently, occasionally craning their necks to see how close to the door they had gotten. Not being a voter myself, I could afford to walk up and down the queue chatting and catching up with everyone. It was odd to see all the people

I knew suddenly gathered in one place and to realize that after fifteen years of regular visits, everyone was familiar to me. Though the women knew each other quite well there wasn't much chatter, although they did answer my questions. It was an ideal opportunity to catch up on news, admire recent babies and newly acquired "best" saris, complement the old ones, and note the changing trends of prints and materials of those worn by the younger women, while catching up on goings-on since my last visit. Everyone had clearly made an effort to make themselves presentable even though they had only traveled within the village, and they looked quite transformed from how I was used to seeing them. Many men wore shirts or tunics either over their sarongs or with trousers which, like the women's "best" saris, were usually reserved for trips out or for festival days.

Guards managed the queues as men and women were let in to the booth by turns, one at a time. No one seemed to make eye contact and kept to themselves, occasionally fanning themselves in the oppressive humid heat. I went up the steps to the schoolroom where voting was being conducted, and stopped where women were taking off their shoes before entering the voting booth, as I was not allowed to go any further. I turned therefore to explore the men's queue to see who was there. Like the women, they too stood in somber silence and, seeing me, seemed unusually shy and self-conscious of being seen in formal attire within the village; the sudden proximity to so many women may also have been a factor. As I talked with them, a couple of giggling young women swept past, just emerging from having voted. I asked them how it had gone, and one of them said, "I feel fabulous!" (*khub bhalo lagchey*). "I have been waiting for this day for so long and now finally I am a grown-up," she said, holding up her inked finger as proof. I had known her since she was a toddler, so it came as a surprise to me to see she had turned eighteen. But she had to rush off to be at home as her sister, who had been married some months ago, was returning to her natal village to vote and was expected soon. By this time Dilera and Naseeba were halfway up the queue, but before I could get back to them, I spotted the two officials leaving and hurried after them to ask them a few questions. They were talking to the paramilitary guards when I caught up with them, and they were surprised to see me. They told me off roundly, for as a stranger I had no business to be anywhere within hundred meters of the polling station. It was only when I called out to several passing voters by their names to attest for me, and they laughingly did, that the officials relaxed. I invited them to a cup of tea, but they declined, saying they had to cover a dozen other polling stations to check if things were running smoothly. They were on "monitoring" duty and had to make rounds of about ten or so polling stations all day. I had to use all my powers of persuasion to be allowed to accompany them so as to visit some of the other polling booths which would have been impossible for me to locate by myself. Only after they established that I would follow at a respectable distance and not ask to be let into any of the booths, did they agree, and I spent the next couple of hours with them. At each booth, the scene from Madanpur was repeated. Neatly dressed village folk, standing silently in long queues waiting in blazing sunshine, and others emerging with newly inked fingers. At one booth where there was a lull in polling, the officials invited me in and introduced me to the presiding officers who rather proudly explained the procedure of voting to me. I had witnessed this in other parts of the country many times, but I was always struck by the obvious pride they took in what they did and their extraordinary diligence in handling the process. The physical discomfort of heat and mosquitoes, working with strangers in a team in the unfamiliar location away from their own districts, and the bewildering array of forms in their safekeeping didn't seem to affect the diligence with which they approached the job at hand or the courtesy with which they dealt with voters.[6]

On my return to the village, I noted that polling was proceeding briskly. I returned to Dilera's house to find an even more morose Gainda, now dressed and ready in her "going out" sari but still waiting for her husband. After a cup of tea with her, I went around other households in both of the villages; like with so many other Election Days that I had spent in the village and elsewhere in India, the atmosphere was much the same. The children were at home from school due to the holiday, people were more relaxed as their normal routines had been disrupted as all activity had been arranged around going to vote, and many seemed to prefer to continue in this mode, catching up with neighbors and relatives who had traveled back to the village to vote, asking others if they had voted and swapping stories about what they had made of the polling experience this time and what the likely outcome was to be. At regular periods during the day news rippled through the village from the main road where young men on motorcycles stopped by to deliver news they had gathered from other parts of the constituency. For weeks there had been reports of incidents of violence as workers from rival political parties had clashed and men had been killed. We had seen trucks crammed with troops from all over the country trundle by, destined for "sensitive booths" on Election Day. There was much at stake at this election for the Trinamool Congress, who were desperate to win the local panchayat elections to consolidate their power in West Bengal. This anxiety was evident in the Trinamool party workers in Madanpur and Chishti who gathered together periodically in the newly opened tailor's shop stall by the roadside. They pored over voters lists to tick off those who had showed up to vote before dispatching volunteers to chivvy along those who hadn't. This was a close election and much was at stake, so every vote was seen to be valuable.

Election Day was an event that was marked off from everyday life.[7] As with public festivals, the day of voting was a public holiday, and children stayed from school and schoolmasters did not go to work. But agricultural work had its own rhythms, and in the months when elections were often held, the swarna paddy crop was usually in the fragile green shoots stage, requiring vigilance against the first signs of insects and stray animals. So going to vote for men had to be scheduled before or after work in the fields, and they tended to vote early. Women, on the other hand, scheduled all household tasks around having an unusually early bath so as to make themselves presentable at the polling booth. In their preparatory routines, men and women alike made an exception for the activity of voting, changing their otherwise unchanging routines, dressing in their most formal clothes, and approaching the trip to the polling booth with a mixture of eager anticipation and a sense of duty. Many grumbled about the extra bother but would not countenance the possibility of skipping the task. Everyone, and especially members of the lower castes in the village, were keen for me to understand that being able to vote without fear was an important indication that they were indeed equal to the upper caste Syeds and that the act of voting consolidated that sense of citizenship.

In July 2013, however, the confidence of the importance of voting was disturbed by the otherwise regular pattern of voting choices. For the past thirty or so years, agricultural laborers and many of the lower castes had tended to vote for the Left Front candidate as the most reliable champion of the dignity of labor and the poor, while the Syeds tended to continue to support the Congress, more as a protest vote against their impoverishment brought by land reforms than support for a moribund Congress. By 2013, however, the contours of this contest had been shifted with the emergence of Trinamool Congress, and this time Majhi and the core group of his supporters put to good use the lessons learned from growing up with Left Front election tactics. They had planned for the campaign to be carried out in two phases. In the first round they gave out handbills to each household with the logo of their party prominently displayed, and then closer to the election, when they knew the order in which names would be listed on the machine, they returned with dummy ballot papers and sometimes with replica models of Electronic Voting Machines to tell them which button to press. In the past I had accompanied Communist Party workers as they canvassed door to door, and people asked them questions—about Hindu-Muslim tensions, electricity and health centres. "We can tell by looking at a house who they vote for," the party workers told me, but they insisted that they took on board the requests of all, regardless of their party loyalties. In their organization such complaints would have been gathered once a month when zonal committees met and then fed back to the main Communist Party office. Given that a large number of such complaints were about domestic problems, such as harassment from a persistent but unsuitable suitor for the daughter, in the first instance, the Party attempted to solve the problem at hand, but appealed to the police next if they were unable to. "In West Bengal at least, the police listen to us because of Party pressure," they used to say candidly. But Majhi did not have this clout with the local administration—at least not yet, which is why winning the panchayat elections was so critical for him and the Trinamool Congress. He nevertheless had the legacy of the Left Front grassroots work to build on, and could take advantage of their initiatives to empower women, for instance. For years, the women's wing of the communist parties had worked to empower poorer women to take a stand on issues, become trained and eligible for the increasing quotas for women on local panchayat Committees. Their growing sense of self-respect and their increased personal security, which was missing in the early 1970s, had been growing. They had held meetings at regular intervals at various levels of organization, and they had continued to campaign for equal wages for women laborers, maternity leave, and medical expenses, which made their situation better than women in other states. In 2013 Enayat Master's daughter-in-law, an educated woman with an undergraduate college degree (whose husband had registered a respectable defeat five years prior to this), was the Trinamool candidate and she campaigned on similar progressive messages that won the loyalty of more women. Ideologically, therefore, in that early election of their tenure, Trinamool simply adopted much of Left Front's agenda, as also some of its modus operandi, as we shall see later in the chapter.

The Left Front election machine was a formidable one and hard to replicate easily. It required an army of willing volunteers, complete commitment, and some astute strategic planning, but workers insisted that it also brought excitement. The message they took to the voters was clear, unambiguous, and reflected the Party like to a T. For instance, when faced by some women in a completely dark slum in the middle of Bolpur city who demanded electricity so that their children could do their homework, their response was, "How did you even learn to ask for this much? If we hadn't improved your lives already, you would not even have known about electricity, which of course is now the next step." This kind of paternalism was the hallmark of the Communist parties and this particular message was one that I heard repeated at every level of the Party organization: the Minister's office, the Party headquarters in Kolkata's Alimuddin Street, the district-level office, down to the Block, and to every Comrade who lived in the villages of West Bengal. This itself was good evidence of a well-organized campaign—the message was undiluted, there was a clear chain of command, and every soldier was totally loyal to the Party. Before each election every constituency was "mapped" by Left Front political workers to identify "undecided" voters and to estimate not just their chances of winning but the number of votes they would get. For instance, in 2006, they reckoned that the local Member of Parliament (MP) in Bolpur constituency would improve his vote share from 10,000 to 15,000, taking his final tally to about 275,000 votes. This estimate was based on the fact that 35,000 out of 41,5000 families had made a donation to their

Party and the Re. 1 donation, while an extremely modest amount, was an excellent indication of their loyalty.

In 2013 Trinamool Congress had neither this discipline nor organization, nor indeed the funds that came with public subscriptions of loyal supporters that the communist parties had painstakingly built over three decades. Majhi's conversations in every household, therefore, focused more on the injustices of the Comrade in the village, the injustices of the party he represented toward agricultural workers and farmers in Singur and Nandigram, and most of all on the charismatic leader of Trinamool Congress, Mamata Banerjee. I had studied Mamata myself, shadowing her for a month in November 1999 soon after her party had been formed and won nine Lok Sabha seats, to observe her as she set about establishing herself as a potential contender for the Chief Minister's role. In those months she had captured something in the public imagination by her personality, earthiness, and fearlessness of the seemingly invincible Communists. I had been keen to understand why people voted for her, especially as, unlike other women politicians in India, she had not inherited a support base and lacked a male patron or mentor and had built her career entirely on her own steam.[8] She presented herself as the sole woman in a man's world. "I have no *shongshar* (family/household) of my own; the *jonogon* (public) are all I have," she said to her audiences. In turn, everyone referred to her as "Didi," an older sister who would look out for those who depended on her. But I was keen to understand how she was seen in the villages of West Bengal, away from metropolitan Kolkata that was her initial base. Among the women workers of the CPI(M) who sweated it out in the dimly lit streets of Bolpur on humid evenings, one might have expected a secret admiration for a politician like Mamata, who came from a modest background similar to theirs and who spoke their language. Instead what one heard was apoplectic anger, similar to that expressed by their upper caste *bhadralok* leaders in the CPI(M) party office; *Bisronkhola* (disorderly, out of control) was a word used to describe Mamata. When pushed to consider whether having a woman as a head of a political party had some innate value in itself, they were quick to note their Communist politics, which practiced training and empowering women and implemented the policy of reservation of seats for women in local panchayat governments, as infinitely more desirable. They felt, in fact, that she had let the side down by her unwomanly manners that were not suitable to inspire trust among men. Her biggest failing in the eyes of these disciplined female foot soldiers was her unpredictability and the extraordinary nature of her political opposition. "Jumping on a minister's car, lying down on the street outside Writers Building! Is this politics?!" they said dismissively. "She may dress like us but her behavior is anything but ordinary. If we had anyone like her in our party she would have been thrown out." And therein, in a nutshell, lay the difference between the Left Front parties and their arriviste opponent, who by her unconventional behavior had questioned not simply what was politically possible but also what was "socially possible" (Spencer 2007: 176).

This view, like so many other Communist messages, might have been held in Madanpur and Chishti too, though I never heard them but only because no one dared mention any opposition to the Left Front for fear of the Comrade's retributions. But in 2011 the tide had turned, Mamata and Trinamool capitalized on their victories in Singur and Nandigram, where their agitations had humiliated the Left Front government into giving up building the car factory, to win the state assembly elections. Thus, when Bishwa Dom, a loyal communist, expressed his wish to hear Mamata live at a public rally, I suggested going to one together. Mamata Banerjee was particularly renowned for her oratory and her ability to connect with each individual in a gathering of thousands, and this made attending her rallies a rich experience. The meeting we went to was held in a large, open space (*maidan*) which held a crowd of about thirty thousand. Public meetings and political rallies such as this one were essentially a huge fiesta in India. Like village fairs, they were always held in open grounds near main roads, aiming to be accessible to as many as possible. Thousands of people traveled to them using all sorts of means of transport, some walking several kilometers, and even camping overnight with bedding and food. Vendors selling tea, trinkets, toys, and political memorabilia kept people occupied through the wait on a long and hot afternoon when, two hours after the announced time, the restless crowd was rewarded with the roar of a helicopter as it appeared as a tiny speck in the cloudless sky. As the speck grew larger, so did the welcoming roar of the crowd. A small figure descended the steps and swiftly made her way to the stage and greeted the audience with folded hands.

After the customary welcomes from local party organizers, when Mamata finally came to the microphone, the noise rose to a crescendo. With her nondescript saris and plain looks, Mamata's visual impact was always to underscore her ordinariness, her ability to be like her supporters in contrast to the elitist leadership of other parties. When she finally spoke, she did not disappoint, and one could hear the audience listening. She punctuated her fiery speech criticizing the performance of the Left Front government and its patrician leaders for having lost touch with the common man by cossetting themselves in air-conditioned rooms, with witty couplets that she had written herself. These had been reproduced on campaign posters and recited at public rallies by her party workers and had already become part of the electoral popular culture along with cartoons, limericks, and murals. At the rally, though, Mamata did not merely repeat these couplets, she got the audience to join in with her. So, she would recite the first line and fall silent and encourage the audience to reply with the second. Then she would repeat the couplet again so those who hadn't gotten it the first time could join in the second time. To my utter surprise, Bishwa Dom, who had been a resolute solider of the Left Front in the previous eight elections I had witnessed, joined in gustily. This collective performance of the crowd brought home Mamata's extraordinary ability to connect with ordinary people. In a world of erudite politicians, this unglamorous woman with not much formal education had enough wit and literary skill to lampoon her opponents. By inviting her audience to participate in the recitation, she recognized their support for her, which they expressed through their familiarity with her writings. And the effect of this collective chanting of words penned by her had an effect not dissimilar to collective hymn singing by a religious congregation. The gathered crowds fizzed with the effervescence of their concerted efforts and the atmosphere was noisy, rambunctious, and electric. On our long bus ride home that evening, as we excitedly swapped observations about the event, Bishwa's face betrayed his confusion between his loyalty to the Comrade and the politics of the Left, on the one hand, and his newfound admiration for Mamata that he could not but help feel.

I recalled another, very different, public meeting that a group of us from Chishti had attended some years earlier. I had personally been keen to go as the speaker was the erudite Somnath Chatterjee, who was the incumbent MP of Bolpur. Chatterjee had been immaculately dressed in starched white kurta and pajamas, and he arrived as the sun was at its hottest. Addressing a crowd of about three-and-a-half thousand under the blistering sun, he spoke in strident tones, listing the various accomplishments of the Party. Some of these, such as the vaccination programs or the child welfare program, were funded by the central government rather than the Left Front, but he glossed over that detail and instead in somewhat schoolmasterly tones told the audience that they needed to be patient. He pointed out with a smug laugh that while people's demands were valid, it was only because the Left Front government had done so much already that people had "learned" that they could ask for more. My friends from Chishti looked back blankly. The following day, when I tracked Chatterjee down for a chat, he put it more bluntly, dismissing their demands for better governance with "We invited them to sit down, now they ask if they can lie down! (*Bostey diley shutey chai*)." Somnath Chatterjee was a lawyer by profession and a veteran of many campaigns, and he was bidding for his sixth win from Bolpur when I met him. His main opponent was from the newly formed Trinamool Congress, also a lawyer called Suniti Chattoraj, whom he dismissed as a mofussil *bot tola* advocate; Chatterjee had studied at Cambridge and Middle Temple in the UK.[9] Such name-calling was symptomatic of the campaign in general. Chattoraj had been put up as a *bhumiputra* (son of the soil) as he was originally from Birbhum, unlike the more metropolitan Chatterjee. Chattoraj had, like many Trinamool leaders, served as a Congress candidate in the past and had joined Mamata's new party, having given up on Congress's inability to mount a suitable campaign. Trinamool had estimated that winning seats was an unrealistic aspiration but hoped at least to win significant share of the votes and make their presence felt to the Left Front. But in Bolpur at least, their tactics had been crude and had started by nicknaming the incumbent a *shaand* (a bull), ostensibly to describe Somnath Chatterjee's large frame and dark complexion.

Chatterjee was to be found on the outskirts of the town, camping for the duration of the campaign in a hired property, which he called his "election bungalow." As Chairman of the Development Corporation he had access to residences meant for officers on tours, which provided him with comfortable lodgings on his campaign travels. He was no ordinary MP. He had been voted Parliamentarian of the Year and was a veteran of several battles since 1977 who had subsequently become the Speaker of the Indian Parliament in 2004. But even on the eve of his sixth election contest from the Bolpur seat, he seemed to continue to relish the coming battle as though it was his first night playing *Hamlet*. His prospects looked good enough for him to relax and ruminate on his career. He was originally from Hooghly district, but in 1977 two prominent leaders of the CPI(M), Jyoti Basu (Chief Minister from 1977 to 2000) and Benoy Choudhury (chief architect of the radical Operation Bargadar), had personally visited him at home, inviting him to contest the difficult Jadavpur seat. He won in both the 1977 and 1981 elections but then lost to the Congress candidate in 1984, which he attributed to the effect of Mrs. Gandhi's assassination. In 1985, there was a vacancy in the safe Bolpur seat, and he was rewarded with it and won the by-election. Since then, he had seen his constituency grow from a relatively poor rural area with very little infrastructure to one where there was a brand-new highway. A large part of the constituency was tribal, and he seemed keen to target their welfare above others. He was struck most by the escalation of popular demands: small villages wanted more telephone exchanges, spurred by the increasing proliferation of long-distance call booths, areas which had no schools for girls fifteen years ago demanded higher secondary education, and where there had been no roads, constituents now demanded all-weather ones. As their representative, he was proud that very few asked for jobs directly; instead, the demand was always for better resources. But then he repeated what he had said in the public meeting, this time with greater acerbity, that people had learned to demand more only because his government had started to give them something in the first place. He attributed the high levels of turnout at the polls entirely to the "consciousness raising" by the cadres, and while candid about the growing opposition he was dismissive of Mamata Banerjee. Later, watching him on the campaign trail while he spoke at meetings on the edge of newly harvested paddy fields, or at a dimly lit street-corner meeting late in the evening in Bolpur town, his rhetorical ability to spin out these simple messages into hour-long speeches was in evidence. Like many Communist leaders, his language of erudition, his spotless white clothes, and his display of total familiarity with the political world in faraway

Delhi won him the awe and admiration of paddy farmers and local journalists alike. Earlier, while speaking in his rented bungalow, in the middle of elocuting a well-rehearsed litany of his Party's achievements in his constituency, the telephone had rung with news of the elections in Maharashtra where polling was in progress, and his excitement on hearing the gossip about fellow parliamentarians had been immediate. It was this ability to switch registers—from street-corner meetings, to conversing with a visitor, to sharing gossip with fellow MPs—that was his hallmark as a parliamentarian. But serving as an MP of a party such as the CPI(M) also demanded another sort of juggling act. While he was the candidate and star campaigner, his public appearances, the length of his speeches, the list of the Party's achievements and promises, and the mention of special issues local to where he was speaking were all strictly prescribed by the local Party organization. He had to be loquacious without giving too much away, reassuring without being smug, proud of his Party's achievements without taking any personal credit—for the understanding he shared with his party colleagues was that, in the end, they were cogs in a giant Juggernaut. The Trinamool in those early days was no match for such Communist machine politics. Instead, when they began fighting elections, their candidate against Chatterjee had to design his own campaign and was supported by some young enthusiastic workers who worked out of hastily rented rooms, equipped only by their hatred of the Comrades rather than a clear ideological agenda.

By July 2013, however, Trinamool was in an altogether stronger position. A few days before Election Day, I heard that Majhi had been looking for me, but I could not find him in his home. His taciturn mother told me with a mixture of resignation and a little pride that he was barely eating and sleeping. He and other party workers had been tirelessly going from one home to the other, talking to people, listening to their concerns, writing down their demands, arguing about the track record of the incumbent panchayat Pradhan, and using a mixture of promise and threat to garner people's support. I tracked him down eventually in Enayat Master's roomy courtyard, where I found a group of them huddled over some sheets of paper. My arrival was welcomed with enthusiastic shouts, and I was beckoned over to look at what I discovered to be a voters list. They were carefully going down the list, one name at a time, marking those who were most likely to vote for them, those who could still be persuaded, and those whom they could not hope to win. They had watched Communist Party workers do this in previous years and understood how important this process of "scrutiny" (everyone used the English word) was for a positive result. It allowed the campaigners to "map" the area and devise a campaign strategy accordingly.

The Left Front had indeed mastered this art to perfection. In an attempt to understand the Communist modus operandi at the start of my research, I had visited the CPI(M) headquarters in Alimuddin Street in Kolkata where the main campaign strategy was designed. In stark contrast to government offices, these offices exuded an air of calm efficiency and were clean and well maintained. Portraits of Communist leaders (that included Lenin, Stalin, and Mao) looked down on a computer, four telephones, a telephone directory entitled "A Ready Reckoner" compiled by their official daily "Ganashakti," and freshly labeled files containing, among other things, a detailed itinerary of the fifty to sixty guest speakers who would address campaign rallies across the state. The overall state-level operation was managed by twelve coordinators who delegated work to various regiments of district and zonal offices where the actual battle was waged. I started with them, for it was these generals who kept sight of the big picture, who "mapped" the state according to estimated levels of "safe" and "troubled" seats; they made decisions regarding the pacing of the campaign, determining which areas needed extra inputs, where the guest speakers should be sent, and how their movements could be orchestrated.

Following the trail from the capital to the provinces, I had visited the local party office in nearby Bolpur[10] where I found a group of men sitting in an open-fronted office on the main street in the bazaar. This office served as the coordinating center for the activities of their workers and cadres in each village and ward of the towns. In the Bolpur constituency there were 157 Gramanchals, 18 Wards in Bolpur town, and 5 in the Vishwa Bharati university area of Shantiniketan. There were 199 polling booths in all and 149,700 registered voters. To effectively cover this vast area, booth committees had been formed, and seventy offices had been set up such that each ward had located within it two or three offices. Nearly 15,000 party workers covered the 199 polling booths—thereby, effectively, one worker was assigned for ten voters. In this, the Party workers were also supported by teachers' councils and student bodies. All processions, street corner meetings, and distribution of campaign material was coordinated by them. At the office several party members squatted on the rented rugs on the floor of this specially rented space underneath their permanent office on the floor above. The air was one of calm confidence, as workers relaxed and chatted, surrounded by bundles of pamphlets and flyers ready for distribution. After two months of frantic activity following the announcement of elections, this rest was well deserved. It was this team of volunteers and workers who had coordinated a myriad different activities: they had identified walls suitable for painting murals of political leaders and messages, they had made sure that the commissioned cartoons lampooning the opposition and verses which explained their ideas to the general public were painted, stuck, and imprinted on every available space across the West Bengal countryside. This involved coordinating artists, painters, handbill stickers, printers, and transport. As they sat around on a hot afternoon, they were not expecting visitors; in fact, this makeshift office was meant to serve a number of purposes other than hospitality. It was a resting camp for the workers of the party who dropped in once a day during the campaign to gather news from other parts of their constituency and to report on how their own efforts were going. They passed the time by swapping anecdotes from their respective beats, and by quizzing each other on the exact number of votes in their party's victory margins at past elections, not unlike men of the same age who showed off their knowledge of cricket scores of past matches. The office also served as an entrepot for supplies of campaign material, pamphlets, posters, and schedules of future meetings and itineraries.

The pacing of a campaign was clearly crucial. The momentum had to build up gradually leading to the day of polling. In the first phase, as soon as elections were announced, a detailed "scrutiny" of the constituency was done. Specific local factors were identified, such as a concentration of Muslims in a particular ward for whom a particular message would be tailor-made. In 1999, for instance, the opposition's political alliance with the Hindu right-wing BJP provided an argument for the Muslims to vote against them. Accordingly, the required intensity of door-to-door campaigns was agreed to, and these were kept up throughout the campaign. This also revealed which voters did not have the requisite papers and voter identification cards, which the Election Commission had begun to make mandatory since the 1990s. Cadre members helped illiterate voters in particular by accompanying them to the local block or municipal office, filling out the forms for them and generally providing much-needed moral support to have their voter IDs made. In this crucial phase of "scrutiny" and planning, the Party cadres found that their year-round involvement in the affairs of their local beats is what equipped them with an excellent understanding of the particular nature of the area. As two car mechanics observed to me, "We don't know how they know, but the party workers always seem to know if we have voted for them. They know from the way we talk, hold ourselves, our general mood, what we are thinking." Even among their detractors, they were aware of the reasons why people did not vote for them which varied considerably between classes and between men and women. In the second phase, the more visible aspect of the campaigns came to light—the posters, "walling" with political murals, buntings, and flags. Toward the end of the second phase, handbills and party manifestoes would be distributed at the doorsteps and on street corners and public meetings scheduled. In the final phase of the last two weeks before Election Day, dummy ballot papers or electronic voting machines (EVMs), and voter identification numbers would be distributed during the door-to-door campaigns, which now took place three times a day. During this period the local MP would, over a typical two-day period, be required to: attend a big public meeting in a village adjacent to the brand new highway providing the perfect setting of their development work and where people from surrounding villages could be easily brought; flag off a cycle rally organized by the youth wing; address another rally in the vast Bolpur Maidan; meet with local intellectuals and journalists in the library located in the town hall; and, at the end of the second day, address a meeting which would be the culmination of four processions from different parts of Bolpur which would converge in the main market center. This packed schedule was determined almost entirely by the Party organization; the individual contestant merely followed the program he was given.

It was no wonder, then, that the CPI(M) alone won nearly three fourths of the votes in some constituencies. In 1998, for instance, it won 70,000 of the 103,000 votes cast in Bolpur. But while other parties may have rested on accolades, this Party also conducted post-election analyses to take stock of which plan worked better than others, which strategies needed revising, and the follow-up actions required for promises made. Each ward and village conducted their scrutiny of the poll results, informally and booth-wise, and the findings were later aggregated to reconstitute this pixilated picture into overall trends. The percentage of all votes were added up, and any incremental losses and gains were calculated. Individual MPs and speakers were analyzed, and those who had made rash promises of schools and electricity without clearing it with the Party were reprimanded. That the workers of the Party returned to the doorstep after a campaign was over and won was perhaps what won them the loyalty of their supporters. While, in the Indian electoral system of first past the post, vote shares mattered less than the overall seat share, the Party continued to aspire to win larger and larger sections of the votes. And this fact gave away their real game—not simply to win elections but to win every vote for a total "party-society."

Such formidable organization was nowhere to be found in 2013 by either party, but that was also because the campaign planning for panchayat elections was done in a more delegated fashion. The cluster of ten villages making up a panchayat worked as a unit, and a local level worker such as Majhi rarely strayed beyond this ambit. Resources were also limited, but the win in the state assembly two years prior had meant that the landscape of Bengal had been covered by the tricolor of Trinamool, replacing the ubiquitous red of the Communists. Flags and bunting were strung across villages, the party symbol of wildflowers painted on every roadside building, and even some giant billboards had been erected on highways.

As the day dawned and the village rose earlier than usual, getting into the rhythm reserved for special events, Majhi was to be found, sleepless and high-strung on the patio of the roadside tailor's shop that had opened the year before. He was clutching the voters lists, now a well-thumbed bundle, but was restless that there was not much more to do other than ensuring that people turned up to vote. Campaigning had to stop twenty-four hours before Election Day, and so no more persuasion of voters to vote for his party was possible. But what could still be done was to ensure that everyone who could vote, especially those who seemed likely to vote Trinamool, showed up at the polling station. So Majhi and his supporters spent the day watching people as they walked into the school compound to enter the polling booth set up in the building, and checked them off the list. Every couple of hours the group would take stock and dispatch themselves to the households from where voters hadn't shown up to chivvy them along. In the past, the Left Front was famous for what was called "scientific rigging" by their opponents whereby not only did they ensure that their voters definitely cast their votes, but they also had various mechanisms by which to stop others from voting. These included extreme measures such as faking identity and proxy voting or simply populating the queues at the polling booth with their volunteers such that voters would be turned off by the long queues. While these tactics had been possible in urban areas, they had always been less successful in rural ones. And with the increased use of security forces and stricter checking of electoral identity cards even before one could join a queue, they were no longer possible, and anyone who wanted to vote could vote, as long as they had the correct papers. As the day wore on, the ticks on the list grew, and by the afternoon Majhi could finally begin to relax. Occasionally, young men would arrive on noisy motorcycles and would pull up by the tailor's shop and, without dismounting, narrate how voting was progressing in other villages. Every such arrival saw Majhi and the Trinamool scramble to their feet and huddle around the visitors, eager for updates, and by the early evening, their smiles got wider as they began to sense victory. I asked Majhi what this victory meant to him. "It is our turn now," was his prompt reply. "Turn to do what?" I asked, and he hesitated slightly before replying, "to teach them a lesson," by which he implied the Comrade and his supporters. I asked him if he could not contemplate doing politics on different terms, one that was not predicated on violence, punishments, and revenge, but one which built on the solidarities he had created. He looked at me with disbelief. As members of an insurgent party they had almost entirely mimicked the modus operandi of the immensely successful Left Front in their attempts to win an election. And having grown up in their long regime, it seemed that Majhi and his contemporaries could imagine political work only as it has been defined by them. This too was the legacy of communism in West Bengal.

Elections and the Social Imaginaries of Democracy

Every evening during the campaign period, a small procession would pass through Madanpur and Chishti, led by Majhi and Enayat Master, whose daughter-in-law was the candidate. The group included the Comrade's old enemies, each of them unrecognizable from their former selves; Shaaker who had retreated into silence for years now shouted slogans, Mukhtar who kept to himself in his little shed by the fields handed out handbills, Hanif looked less conspiratorial and Mustafa less haughty. Others whom they had reached out to in seeking support during the scandal or had sent special invitations to during the *milads* during Ramzan that coincided with the harvest, also now joined them in the march without fear. The procession was a symbolic gesture that was important to perform, and they charted a route to ensure that every single household caught a glimpse of them. Sensing their elation at being able to display their solidarity in the open, excited children tagged along with them, shouting slogans, trailing kites, and kicking balls. This small parade in a tiny corner of India held a special significance for democracy, for it marked the resumption of regulated political competition after years of overwhelming dominance by one party. The case of West Bengal politics had shown that even while multi-party competition existed formally as part of the procedures of Indian democracy, this was not enough to ensure that it existed in reality. For democracy was not simply about a large number of people turning out to vote but also a punctilious observance of rules which reassured opponents that if they lost an election, they would not be faced with extinction—political, or possibly, even physical extinction. This required public confidence that rivals could co-exist in peace, using elections on a level playing field as the principal arena of battle. These features of democracy had been severely threatened during the Left Front years, and so the visible aggregation of individuals who now marked their challenge to the Comrade and his party with a flag and procession was both astonishing and reassuring. My initial anxiety of their public display was assuaged by noting that the procession was not jeered at by their opponents, marking an unprecedented accommodation of difference in the public space of the village.

By outing themselves, these men made it clear that they would no longer grumble about the Comrade's ways only in whispers within the privacy of their homes but that they were confident of making the challenge public. It is therefore important to note the significance of the small parade as it traversed the villages, for it was symbolic of a return of democratic principles in which allegiance to different political parties could be asserted without fear. Such fidelity to political parties is relatively less explored in writings on politics, often represented by the blandness of terms such as "party identification." As we have seen so far, in the context of Madanpur and Chishti, the formation of a political party to rival the communists was the result of a long process of careful cultivation of solidarities that required the participants to form not just a rival party but the values that would define their moral universe. In her critique of this neglect of the importance of political parties in writings on democracy, Nancy Rosenblum remarks that doing so ignores the "historical innovation of regular party rivalry, and the conceptual breakthroughs required to imagine and accept the political work parties do. Above all, we miss the creativity of party politics and the moral distinctiveness of partisanship" (Rosenblum 2008: 7). As the preceding chapters have demonstrated, this moral distinctiveness came to be defined in Madanpur and Chishti through a series of events and maneuvers that drew on political and non-political sources of social life that helped refine it. The collection of people who marched together every day on those July evenings were a visible manifestation of their ability to overcome their own rivalries to work together for a shared vision.

In the privacy people's homes, too, the scenario registered a shift and inevitably, all conversations turned to the coming elections as people deliberated over their electoral choices. The women, in particular, wanted to discuss the candidate herself—who was young and had a college degree. They recognized what a remarkable achievement that was for a young Muslim woman given the number of their own girls who had been married off as soon as they finished school for fear of social criticism. Nazima had come from another village, and she not only wore her sari the "modern" way, but she also had stories from her own village, not so far away, where it was possible for girls to go to college, where homes had taps with running water, and where all the lanes inside the village were paved and did not turn into a mush as they did during the monsoon in Madanpur and Chishti. Now that she was the candidate in the election, people wondered if she could make their village more like her natal one. But Shekhs, Mughal, Bagdis, and Doms were also genuinely worried whether their hard-won respectability in the eyes of the upper castes would be squandered by voting for Nazima who was, after all, a Syed. And her party's name, Trinamool Congress, carried the dreaded name of the Congress that was associated with rich people and humiliation of lower castes and agricultural workers. The stories of hunger and humiliation before the Left Front swept the polls in 1977 and introduced radical change in their lives, were still very much in circulation. At the same time, it was also true that while their lives had indeed gotten better in the 1980s, their daily wages were no longer enough to meet rising prices, and the basic public goods of electricity, water, and roads still remained out of reach. It was evident, they acknowledged, that even those who owned the land were struggling with the low returns from paddy cultivation and shared, with the rest of the village, the inconvenience of the lack of basic amenities. Only the Comrade seemed to have a better quality of life with running water and electric bulbs in every room and his sprawling house right by the metaled highway, suffering none of the daily indignities that everyone else had to suffer. The few people who had managed to do better than everyone else—Majhi, Mustafa, Enayat, Hanif—seemed to have done so by rejecting the politics of the Comrade and exposing themselves to his potential retributions. But they were all Syed men, and doubts about their potential to subjugate other castes again as they had done before the communists, remained. The more these cogitations continued, the more the Comrade's political work also came to be examined. And the unimaginable spectacle of people they knew, from their own Madanpur and Chishti, marching through the village, urging people to support a rival party through their silent persistence of showing up every day, shook their resolve of voting for no-one-else-but-the-Comrade's-candidate even further.

Thus, over a fifteen-year period, the nature of the anticipation of the election had transformed. At the start of my research, the presence of the "party-society" ensured that no discussion about political competition was tolerated, and it therefore did not take place. It was assumed that the Left Front would win, and everyone's participation was mandatory. If voters stayed at home, they were harangued by the Comrade and his workers to go and vote, to exercise their freedom to vote, discharge their duty as citizens, to avail of their right as voters. They were told that it was important to uphold the mass participation that universal franchise allowed and the implicit (and complacent) assumption was those who voted would do so for the "right" party—and many did indeed. Their opponents, silenced in their opposition, knew their party was unlikely to win but used the secret ballot to register their opposition. But over thirty years of voting thus, each election added to their capacity for effectiveness as citizens. Their votes, when aggregated, demonstrated the result they expected but also the significant number of votes for the opposition that each individual vote contributed to. It was their cup of milk that they had added to the vat of rice pudding.[11] Experientially, the election brought its own rewards, for like with other important events in the village, the collective participation of everyone made it meaningful. The space of the polling booth offered an altered sociality, marked civility from officials who treated voters with respect, and people looked forward to it. The orderliness and reversals of hierarchy that the queue facilitated, Syeds standing behind Bagdis, workers standing in front of landowners, older men having to take their place behind first-time voters—were empowering. It reiterated their identity as citizens above all and by everyone's willing participation brought dignity to everyone, a collective dignity. The identical ink mark on each voter's finger was a coveted stigmata of their willing participation in this collective carnival. The repetitive nature of elections—nine elections in fifteen years— recharged their civic batteries periodically, renewing the demos every time. The elections were social dramas that revealed the competitive and corrosive aspect of politics, but in July 2013, the genuine choice on offer made it different. For the first time in living memory for many, voting for an opposition candidate was no longer simply a protest vote but promised a definite change in the outcome. This momentous change had come about through incremental moves of a more constructive politics. In learning to deal with the Comrade's excesses, people had learned the art of active citizenship which required not just the airing of grievances but also the ability to find solutions. Acting thus, they had learned to build alliances even with those they did not like, make compromises with those whose views diverged from their own, ignore irritations for the sake of the ultimate goal, and to do this with a sense of purpose that went beyond merely individual glory. This was the realm of what Jonathan Spencer calls the "counter-politics"—namely, the reparative potential of political activity that could counter "dirty" and agonistic politics. In observing these two impulses within the realm of the political in the setting of Madanpur and Chishti, we are able to identify the twin workings of the democracy and republic. It is to an examination of these themes that we turn in the final chapter.

*

Coda

In April 2019, ahead of the national elections, campaigning in the village was low key, though everyone talked about them. Members of the Trinamool Congress group, which I had seen at their moment of triumph after the panchayat elections in 2013, were now nowhere. Majhi, the hero of the hour, was "away" from the village I was told, as were all of his closest associates, each of whom I asked after by name. The group that had coalesced around Majhi to challenge the Comrade's hegemony seemed to have simply melted away. Their families continued to live in the village, but their identity as a political group had simply evaporated. To say this was curious would be an understatement. The Left Front was just as rudderless as the Comrade had passed away and no one had quite managed to fill his shoes since then. Piecing the story together over the next few days, much as I had done all those years ago after Mansur's bus trip, I discovered the story of a final master stroke played by the Comrade before his death.

On June 30, 2014, just over a month after the national elections were over and the new government had taken office in New Delhi and the election fever had subsided, a grenade went off on the highway that runs between Madanpur and Chishti. The grenade was allegedly thrown at a police van that had appeared within minutes after an altercation between some Trinamool workers (mostly from Chishti) and members of Madanpur village over the issue of work allocation under Mahatma Gandhi National Rural Employment Guarantee Act (MNREGA). The grenade injured a police officer and in the ensuing commotion several men ran toward their two villages to escape trouble, followed by the police who set off in hot pursuit. It was about 9:00 pm, and in the confusion of the darkness, the group of men scattered into homes and fields and the police immediately enforced Section 144 that forbade people to gather in groups larger than four people. This move was widely understood as the police having carte blanche to arrest anyone on sight, and the men who had been present at the meeting and their families fled in terror into the fields surrounding the villages. The women, children, and cattle of their households also accompanied them, and several of them later told stories of how they had managed to survive the night with no food or water among the mosquitoes in the fields. The men who had not been at the meeting mistakenly assumed that they had no cause for worry and stayed in their homes, but they were rounded up and arrested by the desperate police constables who had to produce culprits to explain the grenade and the injury to their officer. It was said that the policemen already had an arrest warrant with a list of names, but unable to find any of those men, they had made do with the ones they did find and had them jailed.

Majhi's name was on the list the police had, as were those of his closest political allies. They had all fled into the fields and did not return at daybreak for fear of being arrested. The following day, the police went into the fields with megaphones, telling people it was safe to return to the village, but no one came. Then local leaders from both Trinamool and the Left Front came to the village along with the police to reassure everyone that they had no reason to be afraid. Over the next few days, most people returned, but not Majhi or his allies. The Comrade's name had also been on the list, and he went willingly to the police station but was quick to move the courts and managed to get bail. The other sixteen innocent men who had been arrested had none of the Comrade's wiliness or political capital, and so they stayed locked up while Majhi and others stayed in hiding. To exacerbate matters further, the police officer who had been injured by the grenade succumbed to his injuries and died. This made the release of the arrested men impossible and the absconding men continued to remain in exile.

As the rest of the village slowly returned to normality, its political landscape changed dramatically. The ascendant Trinamool Congress and its everyday presence disappeared with its leadership eliminated, and the Comrade was back in charge. But this time, with no government to back him, his political influence was limited although his personal connections built over three decades allowed his sons to grow their own hatcheries business enormously. The Comrade died two years after the grenade event, of a stroke, in his home. With him, the stranglehold of Left Front politics disappeared completely—although before going, he had ensured that no one could take his place.

The innocent men continued to languish in jail and were released just before the elections in 2019, having lost five years of their lives. One of them died just days before his release. Majhi and the Trinamool leaders continued to remain in hiding, unable to do any politics in the run-up to the election. As a result, for the first time since I began this study, there was no overt election campaigning in Madanpur and Chishti. It was as if the Comrade had killed all politics with his own death. I spoke to Majhi on the telephone, and he confirmed my reading of the Comrade's last stand. He was convinced that the whole "grenade incident" had been engineered by the Comrade to decimate the opposition in which the innocent men who lost their lives and their families were mere collateral damage. He had therefore ensured that he did not have to suffer the humiliation of his own opponents using their power against him—as Majhi had indeed planned to do after the panchayat elections win of Trinamool Congress in 2013. Recall Majhi's remark to me, "It is our turn now," on the day of the July 2013 election.

So, will politics return to the villages of Madanpur and Chishti? The jury is out on that question, but the whole episode seemed to have contributed to Majhi's political education. He had spent his exile in a town far away from his own village, where he was meeting different kinds of people, interacting with Trinamool workers from elsewhere, and building his own political capital for the future. "I will go back to Chishti after the election," he said, "and you will find me there the next time you visit, Didi," he promised.

So the Comrade died, but he left behind a political legacy. All new political leaders were called "Comrade" regardless of party affiliation, and the legacy of lived communism honoring the dignity of labor was irreversible. But exhaustion with the tensions between the Left Front and Trinamool also created an opportunity for the fresh new right-wing politics of Hindutva who no doubt also felt that "it was their turn now." Democracy in Madanpur and Chishti would be saved only if its citizens continued to cultivate the counter-politics of active citizenship that they were capable of.

*

7

Cultivating Democracy

On January 26th every year, Akhtar Master organized a picnic for the children of Madanpur and Chishti. It was India's Republic Day; schools were closed, there were no family-oriented activities planned for the day as they were on religious festivals, and so the children missed nothing by way of festivities by being away from the village. Akhtar knew most of the children in Chishti and Madanpur either as students in his school or as their private tutor. The quality of his tuitions was considered very good, as was his generosity in providing them gratis to those who could not afford them. At the start of the day on January 26th, he rounded them all up for a small flag-hoisting ceremony in the village school. The national flag was unfurled, the children sang the national anthem, and sweets were distributed. Then he took them on a picnic (*feastie*) to a little copse of trees, about a mile or so from the village, not far from the edge of the highway. It was a lovely spot, with some unusual trees, the ruins of an old colonial-era inspection bungalow, and a dried-up river bed. Akhtar read out the Preamble of the Indian Constitution, which begins with the words "We, the People of India, having solemnly resolved to constitute India into a sovereign, socialist, secular, democratic republic. . . ." These words were first recited on the same date in 1950 when India was formally constituted as a republic.[1] He explained the meaning of the words, provided a brief commentary, and moved on to organized games for the children, giving away small prizes of stationery and books, after which everyone enjoyed a modest picnic of *mudi*, salted peanuts, and fruit. By late afternoon the children were back in the village.

As we have seen in this book, demotic village life is regularly marked by events, big and small, sometimes involving everyone, and sometimes just a few. The event just described involved the children of the two villages and their teacher. Akhtar kept it low-key, but his choice of Republic Day to mark his ritual calendar was, of course, heavy with symbolism. He tended to stay aloof from Eid and other religious festivals, and chose instead to invest his personal money and time in Republic Day celebrations, making his preference for a "modern" and "secular" ritual evident. This day marked the anniversary of the inauguration of India's journey as a republic, and it was one of only two national holidays,[2] which was an indication of its importance in the national imagination. For Indians with television, the day was dominated by watching the grand Republic Day Parade in the nation's capital, but for my friends in Madanpur and Chishti, who had unreliable electricity and few TVs, it was simply a day when schools, offices, and shops remained shut all day.[3] It was a busy time for adults in the agricultural calendar, so an activity for the children was welcomed by them. At the picnic, the children recited the Preamble to the Constitution, which they did by rote, much as they would multiplication tables, after which Akhtar made a short speech. He took care to explain the meaning of the words they had recited and what it meant to be an independent nation, to have one's own constitution and why it was important to remember, each year on this day, the commitment that the people of India had made to the ideals of justice, liberty, and equality and the need for fraternity to achieve these. He used the example of elections that were always held in the village school and so was familiar to the children, as an opportunity for people to make their voices heard against the "rulers" and how it was important to always hold politicians, however influential, to account. "You will have this power when you turn eighteen and get a voter ID," he told them. "Always use it."

Akhtar himself stayed away from any overt political activity in the village, neither supporting nor opposing any side. During the events of the Scandal and its resolution, Akhtar did not once get involved in any of the deliberations. His absence was notable because he was the most highly educated man in the villages, with a master's degree in English, and his intellect might have been useful. He did not provide any overt support to his younger brother Majhi, around whom the anti-Comrade alliance had begun to take shape, and who went on to emerge as the "new" Comrade after Trinamool Party's victory in the elections in 2011. Instead, Akhtar had chosen to consistently stay away from *real politik* and had concentrated instead on doing his job as a head teacher during the day and providing excellent tuitions in the evenings to children in the village, even to those who could not afford to pay. Republic Day was the only moment when any ideological commitment he may have had to India's democratic culture was evident. He included children from every household, regardless of caste and religion, treated them with kindness, and talked to them about the more abstract ideas of the republican values and citizenship on which the country had been founded. His gesture was seen as affectionate and progressive, if a bit eccentric, but not mired in the usual petty rivalries of Syed one-upmanship. In a context where very few activities outside schools were arranged purely for children, it also seemed a radical sort of investment in the future. For the children, it was a rare experience of genuine fraternity when they were treated in an impartial way regardless of the prosperity of their household or their caste, skin color, age, or gender. And that the event was organized by their highly educated upper-caste and much-loved teacher made it even more memorable.

Akhtar's investment in future citizens was significant given that at every point in its history, India's democratic credentials have seemed precarious. At its inception, none other than the chair of the drafting committee of the constitution himself announced India's new identity with an equal measure of commitment and pessimism. "Democracy in India is only a top-dressing on an Indian soil which is essentially undemocratic," was the way he put it. Ambedkar's warning was to point out that India's democratic project would be incomplete if it only achieved "political" democracy of institutions and elections but failed to achieve economic and social democracy that would require the "annihilation of caste" and the removal of obstacles to social equality. Drawing on Dewey's writings (whose lectures he had attended while studying at Columbia University), Ambedkar reminded his audience that democracy required not simply constitutional arrangements but also a "culture of democracy." A democratic culture required a set of dispositions and values and the ability to imagine futures that shaped the way in which citizens are able to engage with the institutional framework of democracy, and for this India's very soil, characterized as "undemocratic" by Ambedkar, needed to be altered. With his insistence on the word *republic* in addition to *democratic* in 1949, there is "no doubt [that] . . . Ambedkar was trying to redirect India into a very different trajectory" (Rodrigues 2020). The words originally chosen to describe India were *independent, sovereign, republic*, but the change to include both democratic *and* republic indicated that the two were not coterminous (as had been originally supposed by Nehru in 1946). Instead, the two words had different meanings and there was a need for both democracy and the republican spirit to realize the constitutional vision of India.[4] Originally, the term *republic* was intended to describe India's newfound ability to choose her own leaders through democratic means, rather than be ruled by the Crown via the colonial government. Democracy was therefore subsumed within the term *republic*, which indicated both its anti-monarchical stance and a political form of representation. But Ambedkar's understanding of republicanism was deeper and indicated a notion of citizenship that existed not so much between state and citizens but between citizens, which, as Rodrigues argues, was inspired by the writings of the social reformer Jyotirao Phule: "Ambedkar was the inheritor of an idea of republicanism with the stress on the citizen, citizen agency and public spiritedness arising therefrom, and citizens bonding themselves into a community of equals, and enabling it in turn" (Rodrigues 2020: 1). Phule had argued, and Ambedkar was in agreement with him, that "the masses could rediscover their initiative as citizens only through the overthrow of servility that the caste order, revamped by colonialism, subjected them to" (Rodrigues 2020: 1). The constitutional aspiration for fraternity and dignity was germane to the newly imagined citizenship, and the word *republic* was a reminder that fraternity could not be achieved without energetic engagement by ordinary people who needed to reclaim agency and become active citizens. Akhtar Master explained the word *fraternity* to the children through the example of their little picnic and said that it was the feeling one shared when children from different households (by which he meant different castes) could go for an outing together, play some games by following certain rules, acknowledge winners and losers, and share food with everyone in a spirit of conviviality. It was a simple but powerful illustration because, as the ethnographic evidence from the villages presented in this book makes clear, such cordiality was not an everyday aspect of village life, riven as it was by social hierarchies, egos, and competitiveness. Thus, Akhtar made the point that fraternity could not be assumed, nor was it socially determined or inherited, but that it had to be created and cultivated. As Charles Tilly noted in his essay "Democracy Is a Lake," people "actually *construct* a democracy" in which an important aspect of the construction is the "shared understandings, the culture, that people create for themselves" (Tilly 1995: 368). Democratic culture was therefore reliant on a republican spirit among citizens.

The preceding chapters, describing four events—a scandal, a harvest, a sacrifice, and an election—from village life show us how these shared understandings could be created when citizens found the capacity to act in their own right in coordination with others. These social dramas, as we have seen, had the potential to fire the imagination to take their participants beyond the transactional and divided nature of the everyday into an altered mode of social engagement and behavior, an "anti-structure," as Victor Turner called it. The nature of the everyday, as Ambedkar rightly noted was non-democratic and deeply prejudiced and therefore, according to him, unsuitable for democratic citizenship to prosper in it. This, as Pratap Bhanu Mehta reminded us, was India's "burden of democracy" (Mehta 2003). But, as I have shown, these periodic social dramas forced the players to act in ways that were different from the everyday and based on the more decent values of accommodation, mutual recognition, cooperation, and generosity and thereby created an altered sociality. While the communitas of these dramas was fleeting and liminal, to be replaced by agonistic social relations of the demotic, the periodic occurrence of these events replenished a familiarity with these higher values which continued to inflect social life after the event. These events also served to re-commit actors of the dramas to these values and reinforced the importance of their own participation in them. The transformation of India's anti-democratic soil is achieved through such events in social life that assert the pivotal role of citizens in the active cultivation of the altered sociality of "anti-structure."

In the remainder of this chapter, I will explore in greater detail the implications of the insertion of the word *republic* and the associated values of republicanism and active citizenship in creating a social democracy in India and the ways in which an anthropological engagement with these ideas may be productive. I will do so having presented a portrait of the agrarian setting of Madanpur and Chishti to explore how an agrarian ontology is generative of such citizenship, despite the burdens of social hierarchy and violence.

The Agrarian Citizen in a Democracy

The radical nature of the Indian constitution lay in reimagining the individual, rather than society, as the unit of freedom and stability (Khosla 2020). The new constitution of independent India promised that the state would protect a new grammar of rights and liberties of the individual and, by doing so, "a person would be unshackled from extant forms of reasoning and association. It was this liberation which made self-rule possible. Without it—without speaking a new language or being under a new kind of authority or remaining under the pressure of existing groups—one could not truly rule oneself" (Khosla 2020a: 3). The tension between the freedom-seeking individual and the quicksand of Indian society that was "essentially undemocratic" was therefore recognized. The only way to extricate oneself from slipping further into this soil was to begin by reimagining society itself and actively seeking to change it. Further, it required a reimagination of the relationship between citizen and those who ruled over them. As Khosla notes, "to be part of a democracy thus meant being part of a new way of relating both to every other person and to the state. It was an egalitarian promise that extended far beyond the casting of the vote" (Khosla 2020a: 3). This promise encapsulated several tensions. The tension between the individual and her community was a tension between inequality and hierarchy of Indian social life and the freedom that an individual was formally guaranteed as a citizen. Second was the strain in the relationship between the individual and the state, in which the latter was required by law to enable individual freedoms but the individual needed to be vigilant to lay claims to those freedoms. That is to say, the voter in a democracy had the right to choose the government, but the citizen of the republic had the additional duty of remaining vigilant of those they had elected. Thirdly, the nature of the relationship that would exist between citizens would alter as a result of the earlier two tensions. These various tensions have been formulated as the tension between formal and substantive citizenship and that between political and social democracy. Such a formulation also indicates a tension between the "negative" liberty sanctioned by the state and a more active citizenship exercised by the individual citizen. Elections and electoral participation rested on the idea of a negative liberty in which voters are citizens with the right to vote, but safeguarding those rights required a more positive engagement by citizens. While the Indian Constitution may have been more than a "rulebook" and was instead a "textbook" in teaching the new India how to create a democratic society sui generis, as Khosla argues, it is equally true that the role of society in creating the capacity for active citizenship remains key. The citizen, even when constitutionally unshackled from the community, continued to live within it and therefore the capacity of the social in nourishing this new citizenship remains critical.

As we have learned from recent research, at the time of India's constitution making, village life as a source of such reimaginings landed on the losing side in the debate between the pluralists and the statists in the constitution of independent India.[5] Gandhi, alongside economists Radha Kamal Mukherjee and Shriman Narayan Agarwal, argued for the village to be the locus of power in a federated distribution of power in the new republic as they believed that the practices of participation and cooperation at this widely distributed local level would act as a bulwark against a rapacious and exploitative state. "Instead of a state, they offered a landscape of group networks that could make possible the practice of individual self-discipline" (Khosla 2020: 90). Recent work by the intellectual historian Tejas Parasher on India's federalist historians such as Radhakumud Mookerji, Brajendranath Seal, Radhakamal Mukerjee, and Beni Prasad explores their critique of representative democracy and their move to "resurrect sites of lawmaking beyond the state
. . . to find arrangements of sovereignty more participatory than representative institutions could ever be" (Parasher 2021: 3). But, as history is witness to, this pluralist view was rejected by others, led by Nehru and Ambedkar, who had much greater faith in the transformative power of a radical new state based on democratic principles than on the capacity of rural society to transform itself. For Ambedkar, the raison d'etre of village life was caste-based violence and exploitation and "local particularism . . . [that] left no room for larger civic spirit" (Khosla 2020: 96).[6] To address the need for an economic transformation of an impoverished nation and for the social transformation of a deeply divided society, a centralized state with a national judicial system emerged as the better location of power to serve the interests of the country as a whole.[7] Both Ambedkar's demand for social justice and Nehru's desire to create a new nation called India required them to distance themselves from the divided localisms of Indian communities to create a new imaginary of a single sovereign state with the individual as its basic political unit. The evidence in this book confirms their misgivings, especially if we pay attention to social relations as they existed before land reforms

and communist ideas of the dignity of work were introduced, and before the cumulative experience of political sovereignty achieved through voting in successive elections. There was indeed pernicious social inequality and, perhaps more importantly, a deep disregard for the life of those at the bottom of the social hierarchy, which made the fashioning of a common purpose inconceivable. "Village studies" by anthropologists in the 1950s and 1960s reinforced this portrayal of the village, through their accounts of bitter factions and "Sanskritization" as the primary mode of social mobility.

Proponents of political pluralism, on the other hand—which had Harold Laski, G. H. H. Cole, Gandhi, and Mukherjee among them—in their advocacy of limiting state power were willing to give the local unit, such as a village, a new future.[8] Theirs was not so much a utopian model of Indian villages as isolated village republics (as is often rehearsed) but of a "bottom up constitutionalism" in which "village communities would enable citizen participation, and cooperative agriculture and industry would prevent economic exploitation" (Khosla 2020: 89). A good empirical example of this is Robert Wade's study, *Village Republics*, in which he investigates how "some peasant villagers in one part of India act collectively to provide goods and services which they all need and cannot provide for themselves individually" (Wade 1998: 1). The resulting study explores the factors that create the conditions for cooperative organization and also provides contrasting cases of villages where such cooperative action does not take place. It is a fascinating study and reveals some critical conclusions about our understanding of village India. First, any generalization about "the village" is foolhardy simply because similar villages, in the same part of the country, can organize social action very differently. Second, and this is the substantial contribution of this study, factors of scarcity and risk are critical in determining whether collective action is arranged or not. What is valuable for the purposes of my argument is Wade's attempt to identify the village as a suitable site for the cultivation of civic spirit and citizenship, rather than a preserve only of agonistic politics of factionalism and hierarchy, as others have done. The attention to scarcity and risk indicate that the state and a legal framework has a role to play in mitigating these by creating a supporting framework which could enable such collective action to flourish.

The study of village life in contemporary India, when some of the social injustices, while far from erased, show at least signs of change, poses the question whether Ambedkar and Nehru's definitive choice of centralized federalism over Gandhi and Mukherjee's pluralism, may have thrown the baby out with the bathwater. That is to ask if the rejection of the village as the location of power, owing to its characteristics "as a den of vice" and lacking in "civic spirit," betrayed an underestimation of the capacity of the agrarian setting for generating the very values that were required for a new politics.[9] Can one argue for a transformation of the anti-democratic soil of India without considering the capacity of the majority of what constitutes the social in India, to generate this change? To understand the cultivation of democracy in a village in contemporary India it is therefore important to be mindful of these intellectual and historical trajectories of the institutional arrangements of democracy. While the pluralists may have lost out in according primacy to the village as the basic political unit, the potential of village life to create republican values should be dismissed with caution.

We have seen so far that an agrarian setting in India and the activities described in such a setting, such as harvest, brick kiln work, religious rituals, and so on, take place in a domestic human-animal setup that have a distinct orientation about nature, work, and community. Such an ethic could be associated with some core ideas about the nature of work, labor, and reward, as also the relationship between individual effort and a common good. An agrarian ethic rests on an agrarian ontology in which the principal economic activity is agriculture, but it is also animated by a set of dispositions toward natural resources, the relationship of human life to non-human life (including plants, animals, and spirits) governing not just agriculture but social life itself. The process of cultivation of crops therefore requires, alongside it, the cultivation of certain forms of civility, vigilance and norms.[10] As we have seen throughout this book, the agrarian social is characterized by events and moments that not only regulate community life and mark temporality, but also create values of cooperation, the suppression of individual interest, and mutuality. The Scandal demonstrated the capacity of citizens for accommodation and ability to build alliances even with erstwhile enemies to create an opposition to a hegemonic political party. The Harvest showed that, in a society in which labor and capital were sharply divided according to caste hierarchies, institutional changes of land reform brought in by a communist government served to rebalance these divisions and the harvest itself was a material manifestation of a collective good borne of hard work and vigilance that persuaded everyone, regardless of differences, to work together for a common purpose. The Sacrifice demonstrated the virtues of self-restraint and discipline that were required for the practices of Islam, such as fasting and regular prayers, and the institution of animal sacrifice reinforced ideas of redistribution and self-denial over consumption. In this setting, each election brought a reacquaintance with the idea of popular sovereignty and the ideals of political equality that were missing from everyday life. Together such events introduced "he performance of a non-discursive human essence, the kernel of autonomy and freedom, that defined the self-controlled and desiring individual as the theoretical bed rock of the 'people's sovereignty'" (Gilmartin 2015: 381). We can, as a consequence, propose a sort of elective affinity between the values of an agrarian life and republican democracy.

The Sources of *Virtù*

A crucial ingredient in the cultivation of democracy is the exercise of what the philosopher Quentin Skinner calls *virtù*. In such a reading, democracy cannot be brought about merely with an introduction of political institutions; rather, it relies on the actions of each citizen, their *virtù* in creating a democratic culture. An active exercise of *virtù*[11] delineates the relationship between an individual citizen and the community in a democracy and ensures the freedom of the citizen. *Virtù* involves the active participation in public affairs "to cultivate the qualities required for effective participation" that would guard against the dominance by any one individual or group (Skinner 2010: 258).[12] Such a notion of "active citizenship" serves as a reminder that to realize the promise of democracy required much more than the mere casting of a vote. While voting was the necessary first step, it only ensured the political democracy guaranteed by institutions. This was, however, no guarantee of the instantiation of a more expansive democracy that included social and economic democracy, that required the cultivation of *virtù*. As Ambedkar reminded his audience in 1950, political democracy was merely the first step that could be guaranteed by law, but social democracy would require much harder work by citizens as there was "the need for the body of people to cultivate the civic virtues" (Skinner 2010: 260). The achievement of true democratic freedom was therefore reliant as much on the people and their capacity to act as citizens in their own right as it was on the democratic state to guarantee these freedoms.[13] The discussion of *virtù* draws attention to the agentive capacity of citizens to be vigilant in political life to ensure their own freedoms and limit that of the state. To not do this, with the introduction of representative government, citizens would simply defer all political activity to their representatives so that "they remain free-men, they are assured, because the House of Commons 'is' (by the alchemy of representation) the body of the people, so that people may still be said to rule" (Skinner 2010: 260). This, in Skinner's view, leads to the danger of an "oxymoronic concept of representative democracy" whereby democracy comes to be characterized by a lack of active citizenship in which popular sovereignty has been deferred to the will of their elected representatives.

Thus, political participation is required not just to ward off the depredations of the state and as a way to maintain negative liberty but as an end in itself, as a way to be and what Hannah Arendt considers the essence of "the human condition" (Arendt 1958).[14] While Skinner's discussion is taken from the context of the republican theorists of the Renaissance and the freedom demanded by the early opponents of the Crown in England, in the Indian context the transition from slavery to citizenship is marked by the transition from colonial rule into independence and the newly imagined citizenship of Indians as articulated in the Indian Constitution. For Indians, this independence *simultaneously* marked the transition from being colonized by the British to being a sovereign nation *as well as* the transition of being subject to someone else's dominion (as was the case for lower castes and non-landowning groups in India) to becoming a *civis* or genuinely free citizen who was capable of acting in their own right.

Further, and crucially, *virtù* denoted here is not simply the political *virtù* of an individual but a more collective *virtù* of the citizen body. This draws attention to the particular nature of active citizenship that required citizens to imagine the freedom and security not just of individuals but of the republic as a whole, above all else. Constitutional histories are of limited help for an examination of how such a notion of collective active citizenship is brought about, for while they draw our attention to the "founding moment" of the state, an understanding of active citizenship can only be derived from the study of the everyday social practices of new constitutional identities. As John Pocock reminds us, "the history of political thought . . . has from the beginning, and for good reasons, been conceived as an interplay between the languages of philosophy, theology and jurisprudence, and the intensely rhetorical, historical and Roman language of republican citizenship does not fit easily into this framework" (Pocock 2010: 44). The language of republican citizenship is an intensely *social* concept and therefore requires a study of not simply the conceptual but the ethnographic. One way, therefore, to address this "uneasy fit" is, I suggest, to explore, by utilizing the concept of social imaginaries, how a variety of institutions in social life incubate ideas of republican citizenship. Anthropology has the capacity to accomplish this task, for, among all the social sciences, it pays greater attention to the relationships between people, to their life-projects, and to people's modes of ethical living, alongside more formal modes of political action. And, as ethical action is a socially shared set of norms as much it is of individual judgment, it helps us delineate modes of both political *virtù* of an individual and a more collective *virtù* of the citizen body. Such ethical action is an ongoing project, it is processual, it requires vigilance, and it is rooted in society—and, as I have shown in previous chapters, its sources are in the projects of everyday and ritual life. By examining significant events of political democratic life (e.g., election) and those of religion or the economy (e.g., animal sacrifice or harvest) alongside each other, it is possible to see how such virtues of political democracy and social democracy are mutually constituted. The evidence in this book is a contribution to taking the notion of *virtù* and active citizenship of the republican tradition further by highlighting the social foundations of citizenship.

A key aspect of any shared collective citizenship is the need to create a sense of "we-ness" for which imagination is key. As previously noted, the Indian Constitution begins with the words "We, the People of India," but the "we" was not a pre-formed community that existed prior to the first Republic Day. In fact, part of the expectation from democracy was to also create the solidary "we-ness" of citizenship from a disparate aggregate of erstwhile subjects of colonial and monarchical rule.[15] This citizenship was brought into force through a constitutional proclamation in the first instance, but then had to be forged through practice, through the creation of new social alliances that made the existing world comprehensible and a future world possible. Creating a community of sovereign citizens, or any community through new political alliances, rather than existing alliances through kinship or religion—that is, through shared politics and ethical stances rather than shared substance or shared faith—required imagination that could be made real. The new imaginary had to be therefore rooted in the social, and social movements through their membership created the momentum for action. In India, this kind of political creativity was provided in West Bengal by the Communist Party of India (Marxist) who, immediately on assuming power in government in 1977, set about implementing economic reforms that had existed on paper but had been hitherto blocked by the agricultural elite on the ground. The Communists were successful because they found political solutions that anticipated and thwarted the loopholes in the law that had been exploited to stop changes before. But in order to get the mass of sharecroppers behind these innovations, unprecedented self-belief and the imagination of a new social order had to be created afresh. The massive capillary nature of the Communist organization, stretching from the headquarters in the capital to each and every village such that every farmer and agricultural worker knew a local comrade, at least by name, disseminated the language of entitlements, rights, and equality to every corner of the agrarian order. This new imaginary social, in the villages where it was realized, led not only to fairer terms for those who worked on the land, but the new equity was also reflected in better figures of production of crop. As with the Alliance of Farmers in nineteenth-century America, new ways of organizing, working, and thinking to fight—that is, a new way of doing politics against the pernicious methods of creating permanent destitution and despair among farmers—was created. Like the agricultural workers of Madanpur and Chishti, the farm workers of Kansas and Texas and other southern states in America too lived in a political democracy but one that did not bring a social or economic democracy. In America a combination of factors was at work: the crop lien system that caused permanent indebtedness, an unfair two-price credit system that severely disadvantaged farmers, tools and livestock having to be bought at forbidding rates of interest, secret agreements between agricultural middlemen and trunk line railroads, and prices for crop being fixed by terminal grain elevator companies that depressed commodity prices at harvest time all created conditions of de facto slavery and abject poverty. Those who worked the hardest on the land lived in the worst conditions, in sod houses made of mud and straw and with only rags on their feet in the winter. These conditions are not dissimilar to West Bengal before land reforms were introduced in the late 1970s and 1980s when insecurity of tenure, pernicious social inequality, persistent hunger, disadvantageous agricultural markets, and precarity of existence marked the lifeworld of the rural population.[16] In America, from this very context, astonishingly, arose the "most elaborate example of mass insurgency we have in American history," led by the Alliance of Farmers (Goodwyn 1978: xvii).[17]

In his study *The Populist Moment*, Goodwyn provides both an account of how this extraordinary movement came to be, outlining the rise of exceptional individuals and the forging of a new imagination of politics, and also how masses of farmers were able to organize themselves in radically new ways to create a protest against their conditions and against the economic premises of American democracy that clearly worked against them. What these movements achieved was the introduction of a movement culture, of reimagining self-belief in the fight for justice, learning how to "do politics," and creating a recognition for the need of an active citizenry to achieve it. In such a movement, the first stage was to create the social group, a public, that did not already exist as it was divided between castes and classes, and so the very possibility of new alliances has to be imagined. Thus, such a project "rested on the creative shaping of the social world through public action—a project of political poiesis" (Calhoun and McQuarrie 2012: 160). The farmers of twentieth-century India, like those in nineteenth-century America, lived in a democratic republic in which the ideals of equality, universal citizenship, and popular sovereignty were enshrined in progressive founding charters written by visionary thinkers. But their own lived experience of destitution, indebtedness, and deep social inequality fell severely short of these ideals. Further, existing conditions made even imagining the democratic ideals of equality and justice impossible in the face of the disparity between the prosperity of the elite and the hardship of the workers. Every non-Syed member of Madanpur and Chishti had memories of the humiliation of having to deferentially dismount from their cycles when passing an upper caste Syed, being beaten mercilessly for the slightest transgression, or being made to wait weeks or months for wages that were rightfully theirs while their children cried themselves to sleep with hunger—and this "den of vice," as Ambedkar put it, was the norm rather than the exception. It was this forced mass deference for existing norms that illuminated the limits of democratic forms, and so to imagine or effect any change in this scenario was thus a severe challenge.

Goodwyn's central argument is that any protest against social conditions therefore could not be born out of "inherited habits of conduct" of ridicule that farmers had gotten used to and the deference they needed to show for their very survival. Instead, farmers had to locate sources of individual dignity for a new democratic political sensibility to demand justice that could build "insulation for themselves against received hierarchical culture" (Goodwyn 1978: 303). In post-Napoleonic England, the radical politics of Wooler and others who challenged the way in which political representation sought to exclude some classes, Calhoun and McQuarrie point out, was popular constitutionalism itself; as with the idea of representation, it could provide an important source for the radical social imaginary in shaping solidarity. For the Indian context, the Indian Constitution provoked an alternative vision to be formed and marked a rupture with the past, and "it's from this rupture or distancing from history that sovereignty and the political as an expression of a capacious political will comes to be formed" (Mehta 2003: 26).

In 1950, as the constitution was written and released, its authors warned that in order for India to truly realize its potential as a genuine democracy, it needed to build on the constitutional provisions of universal adult franchise and the principles of liberty, equality, and fraternity[18] . Guaranteeing individual liberty, B. R. Ambedkar reminded his audience, was a necessary but not a sufficient condition of democracy, for the three values had to be realized as a whole. For Ambedkar, political democracy was therefore merely the first stage in the achievement of a true social democracy. As we have seen in the context of the politics of Madanpur and Chishti, and the wider agrarian context, it was inculcating the belief in the very possibility of a more egalitarian and just world that was the hardest challenge that democratic politics faced in India. These two ingredients - of individual self-respect and collective self-confidence - were essential components of the foundation on which a new mass democratic politics could be built in India as it was in agrarian America. While individual and collective freedoms were granted on paper by the constitution, Goodwyn's account shows how these values of individual self-respect and collective self-confidence had to be crafted during the agrarian movement through cooperation across classes. The work of creating a new "civic culture" required the participants to work hard to educate themselves, stay informed of developments, and learn to interact with others in new ways—rather than "passively participating in various hierarchical modes bequeathed by the received culture" (Goodwyn 1978: xvi, xix). In the communist movement in India, the impetus for a new civic culture was provided by educated middle-class activists who chose to mix and mingle with ordinary people to initiate radical discussions about the lack of social justice and the dignity of labor. That these ideas were practiced even by high caste and educated leaders who did not stand on ceremony and did not expect hierarchical deference, who dressed simply and shared meals with everyone, ignoring the strict rules of hierarchical caste commensality, and who "shed their middle classness," created contexts of egalitarian participation and was critical in making a social movement possible (Ruud 2003: 9). In a society that is sharply ranked according to an individual's distance from performing manual labor, the dignity of labor that the communist movement brought was foundational, in turn, in creating a new self-respect which was then the basis of cooperation across social groups to ultimately create a "collective self-confidence." This new group "did Party," as it is said in Bengali—*party kora*. It was in "doing Party" and doing "political work" that the "political poiesis" of a new collective whose contours the constitution had imagined, came to be. This required an active engagement with constitutional values and the need to cultivate what Ambedkar called a "constitutional morality" through public action. In England, Wooler had claimed the political high ground for the poor and defined "*the active people* [as] the only legitimate public" (quoted in Calhoun and McQuarrie 2012: 171; emphasis added). This was radical because as Calhoun and McQuarrie propose, it was not a "claim for legitimacy within a preexisting bourgeois public sphere and it is not an argument for establishing an autonomous counter-public. It was a claim that grounded political poiesis in the very group ['the mob'] that had been most consistently assumed to be incapable of such activity" (Calhoun and McQuarrie: 171). Wooler claimed that it was this public that had political knowledge and "insisted that people who work with their hands for a wage could also be world-makers with their minds and public speech" (Calhoun and McQuarrie: 171). The elevation of agricultural worker to "world-maker" was exactly the transformation that the Communist movement attempted to effect in West Bengal. Godwin's summation of what the Populist movement achieved in America reflects the changes in agrarian politics in West Bengal perfectly. It was:

[A] movement that imparted a sense of self-worth to individuals and provided them with the instruments of self-education about the world they lived in. The movement taught them to believe that they could perform specific political acts of self-determination. The Alliance demands seemed bold to many other Americans who had been intimidated as to their proper status in the society, and the same demands sounded downright presumptuous to the cultural elites engaged in the process of intimidation. But to the men and women of the agrarian movement, encouraged by the sheer drama and power of their massive parades, their huge summer encampments, their far flung lecturing system, their sub alliance rituals, their trade committees and warehouses, their dreams of the new day of the cooperative commonwealth it was all possible because America was a democratic society and people in a democracy had a right to do whatever they had the ethical courage and self-respect to try to do. Unveiled in Kansas in 1890, then, was the new democratic culture, one created by the cooperative movement of the Alliance. (Goodwyn 1978: 135–136)

*

Conclusion

In *Freedom and Culture* John Dewey, whose lectures had so inspired Ambedkar, argued that the survival of democracy depended on culture, perhaps even more than institutions. This emphasis on democratic culture rather than the processes and institutions of democracy urges us to examine the nature of society and the values that we are willing to create and imagine the "kind of people we want to be and what kind of society we long to create" (Rogers 2018). In India, the Constitution introduced the vision of a new kind of society that would be populated by sovereign citizens who would be tied through bonds of fraternity and who would be able to elect their leaders for accountable governance. The first step to the creation of such a democratic culture thus required the capacity to imagine a more just and equal society. But to turn the anti-democratic soil of India into such a democratic society required much more than constitutional declarations. It required sustained cultivation by which proclamations could be grounded through the coming together of individuals in common social purpose, wherein each re-fashioned individual was a bearer of rights and responsibilities, not merely on paper and passport, but as a sovereign member of a citizenry. This "newly emerging concept. . . the enchanted individual . . . defined by an ineffable essence transcending his or her social existence, gained increasing significance" (Gilmartin 2015: 381).

Through an account of the politics in West Bengal presented in this book it is possible to assess the imperfect efforts to create such a society. The legacy of the communist movement here was a limited and brief period of economic prosperity but perhaps a more lasting respect for manual labor in agrarian society. Arild Ruud's work shows how communist ideas of dignity and self-worth were popularized through cultural mobilization by communist groups through Bengali poetry recitals and theater. These artistic forms, new rituals, and symbolism of the communist struggle in India were key to capturing the imagination of its participants, in ways that evoke the Populists in America or Peterloo.

The communist parties did "political work" that involved the discussion of political ideas, articulating an ideology, sharing them with a larger group of people, and the constant seeking of new allies and debate. This kind of activity is at the heart of Skinner's description of active citizenship whereby such activity is an end in itself and one does political work because that is what an engaged and committed citizen does. The sharecropper Okho Dom, who we encountered earlier in the book, was an exemplar of this success. His experience of participating in the struggles for land redistribution in the early years of the Left Front government had left him with an ever-present vigilance of the hard-won freedoms for lower caste members of sharecroppers and agricultural workers of which the most significant was a newfound dignity of labor. He was aware that their self-confidence, better wages, and living conditions were watchfully noted by the upper caste landowning Syeds who constantly sought to better their own newly impoverished standards. These often came at the expense of the workers or common resources like tanks or common lands within the village, and so his political work was therefore a continual activity in which every move made by others was carefully noted and measures to deal with it had to be endlessly invented. The reward for such vigilance was that it became unthinkable anymore for a Syed to arbitrarily beat up a low caste poor laborer or to keep a worker waiting for wages. If he did so, he would be confronted with not just an individual who was weaker than him but a collective body of people emboldened with the knowledge of constitutional rights, communist ideas of dignity of work, and republican ideas of egalitarianism.

But we have also seen how, in the end, the land reforms program in West Bengal remained incomplete because it failed to extend the reforms to agricultural markets and the increase in production never brought the corresponding returns in prosperity for the ordinary sharecropper.[19] It was therefore jarring to note that Okho, and others like him, was unable to criticize or ward off was the Comrade himself. As we have seen throughout this book, the Comrade was the most rapacious individual in the village, who served his self-interest over any commitment to the collective good or the rights of others. But in every machination of the Comrade, Okho and others stood firmly with him as long as their own interests were not harmed, thereby providing the Comrade with much-needed support. By far, this was the worst legacy of Communism in West Bengal as it fought for economic justice and dignity of labor in the early years but then shifted its priority to simply winning the next election, at all costs. This led them to leave the reforms of rice mills and agricultural markets untouched in order to secure funds and support for the party, even though this stymied any economic benefits that agricultural workers could have had from the increased rice production (Harriss-White 2008).

As the discussion in Chapter 6 showed, electoral support from the core base of rural voters was secured instead through a vast network of authoritarian islands ruled by a comrade. These figures were ideologically committed to the Communist agenda, attended Party meetings, and made sure "the party-line" on all issues was disseminated to their supporters on a daily basis, but the modus operandi of their political work within the village was one of unbridled selfishness, violence, and a complete disregard for norms of a rural civility. As Edward Shils notes in his work *The Virtue of Civility*, deep ideological commitment of any kind invariably leads to a downfall of civility, and the comrades were an exemplar of this tendency. In their political work, dissent or questions about the Party were stamped out, and no one other than the local comrade was ever allowed any significance. Supporters of the Comrade had to thereby tirelessly further his agenda, campaign during elections, and deliver electoral victories for over three decades, but they rarely went beyond being the cogs in the Communist electoral machine. This authoritarianism came to represent the essence of the Communist movement where the common cause—of justice and dignity for labor—was progressively superseded by naked self-interest of the comrades and their political party, culminating in the hubris of Singur and Nandigram.[20] In this, the comrades were no different from the political "bosses" presented in Michelutti's recent volume, *Mafia Raj*. Like the "bosses," the comrade's capacity to rule over the affairs of Madanpur and Chishti was "not necessarily based on brutality or benevolent charismatic acts à la Robin Hood but rather on opportunistic partnerships" (Michelutti et al. 2018: 265). As a result, he, like other such comrades, could create islands of authoritarianism across rural West Bengal during the years of Left Front rule.

So, what conclusions can we draw for the fate of democracy through the practice of communism in a growing electoral authoritarianism? In the wider context of Indian democracy, the "democratic upsurge" in electoral politics in India led to a wider caste-based mobilization of political parties without a widening of the base from which political leadership was drawn. There were therefore two contradictory trends, widening participation in elections and narrowing of those with political power. In this, West Bengal demonstrates the same trend of a gradual concentration of power of decision-making—initially in the name of the party, but eventually in the hands of a single individual. Partha Chatterjee, in his essay on the peculiar disappearance of any discussion of caste from public discourse from West Bengal, says of the communist years: "One would have assumed that with the political mobilisation of the rural peasantry . . . there would have been many more leaders from the relatively better-off peasant caste in positions of state-level leadership." But instead, he concludes, there has been a "mysterious disappearance of caste" in West Bengal (Chatterjee 2016: 84). Again, Okho Dom is the perfect exemplar of such marginalization. Despite his charisma, his phenomenal intelligence, loyalty, and organizational abilities, he was never picked for a leadership role perhaps owing to his low-caste status.

Rising political participation and sustained victories in elections thus never translated into a wider democratization of access to leadership of parties in the Left Front. In fact, the opposite was true. Greater electoral success also brought greater authoritarianism and kindled the desire to win the next election by any means possible. These regimes continued undisturbed in between elections as long as the local comrades remained connected to the party chain of command, disbursed funds and political messages and cultivated their social capital skillfully to generate electorate dividends. The Left Front years could therefore not be characterized as "democratization" as such, creating as it did the possibility of despotic regimes across Bengal's countryside. There was certainly increased participation in elections but also a simultaneous erosion of respect for demo-cratic norms. It was easy, therefore, for the political parties that replaced the Left Front to cynically reproduce this grammar of politics, by replicating structures of authoritarian power and deep anti-democratic sentiments. The authoritarian baton seemed to have passed on from one party to another, and any new polit-ical party that attempted to win power was likely to adopt the same, if worse, grammar of politics.

So what of democratic culture? It would not do to leave the story of Indian democracy here. For we need to recall that the years of either having to work for or against the Comrade, and participating in every election as a voter, had also created some of the principles of an active citizen. Each election brought with it a reminder of the popular sovereignty of the voter, the equality of all cit-izens, and the political alternatives to the Left Front on the ballot paper. Each election—and there were more than twenty in the thirty-four years of their rule—reinforced the ideas of political democracy and forced an evaluation of different parties and their political culture. The Comrade's increasing intolerance toward dissent and competition and the downfall of basic civility in his reign of terror were undeniable, and thus each election forced a re-evaluation of his *modus operandi*. This emancipatory potential of participation in elections is pre-cisely what Ambedkar had articulated when, as early as in 1919, he "made the case that suffrage could itself serve an instructive role and that participation in political life would bring about consciousness among the lower castes" (quoted in Khosla 2020: 10). This experience came into play, as we observed in the first "event" of this book, when a seemingly intractable scandal was resolved by indi-viduals who mounted their first collective challenge to the seemingly invincible Comrade. By drawing on Max Gluckman's interpretation, we saw how gossip, far from being a mere "weapon of the weak," defined a moral community. It did this by creating a shared past among its members and by defining rules of en-gagement that emerged from moral evaluations of the scandal. In the process of resolving it, people honed their skills in doing politics—they learned the art of compromise required to build alliances, they learned to suppress individual self-interest to identify with a common cause with others, and they cultivated a ca-pacity to identify and broadly and positively with others that is the essence of the democratic character. The Scandal allowed them to identify that the Comrade's fixation on coercive power as an end itself was the very antithesis of a demo-cratic character. It is perhaps therefore important to be attentive to the ordinary citizens who are "bossed over" and who remain curiously invisible and passive recipients of violence and complicity in portrayals of India's criminalized politics such as this: "Pockets of mafia-owned democracies engage successfully in a cre-ative game of trust/distrust that allows bosses to rule over a particular sphere of interest by taking advantage of their local community support and caste agonistic relations or factions" (Michelutti et al 2018: 265). My attempt is to move away from such representations as democracy as a "thing" that can be owned by the mafia or someone else and instead to persuade the reader to think about democracy as a continual activity in which people are not merely "ruled over" but where they actively cultivate the resources to challenge such authoritarian figures.

Charles Taylor's writings reminds us that social imaginaries are not merely inherited ideas but are also shaped by contemporary practice, and if action shapes imagination, neo-Roman ideas of republicanism continue to remain crucial for twenty-first-century politics. As we have seen, the basis of ethical behavior in the spheres of kinship relations, labor and work, religious solidarity, and citizenship for the members of the village community were crucial ingredients in the cultivation of a political sensibility. These were the moments that incubated ideas about politics and citizenship that were able to transcend the transactional to generate the social imaginaries required for collective democratic life. The *virtù* and citizenship created thereby, acted as a bulwark against the confrontational and divisive "agonistic core of democracy" and forced participants to strive for a deliberative and consensual culture that made social life possible (Mouffe 2000). The silence inside the polling booth or the tense moment in which the harvested grain heap was divided or the pause just before an animal was sacrificed in a religious festival were moments in which the transactional was transcended. By studying such separate events of social life alongside each other, it is possible to assess their capacity for shaping social imagination. Only one of the four events—scandal, harvest, sacrifice, and election—was officially a "political" event, but together in the fullness of village life they produced and perpetuated a capacity of the demos and generated values that were critical for political life. An anthropological study of democracy is able to demonstrate that in order for a democratic republic to flourish, the work of non-political aspects of society require just as much careful study as the study of political institutions.

I conclude this book by noting that the cultivation of democracy is a continual civic activity. The metaphor of farming alerts us to ideas that are important to any process of democratization. Namely, it is impossible to merely plant ideas and expect them to flourish automatically. The plant needs a hospitable environment for its roots to spread, draw sustenance, and assimilate it into its body. "For what are constitutions and procedures once you have deformed the ground upon which their proper functioning depends?" (Rogers 2018). When established, the cultivator has to continue to nurture the new plant, support the new branches, nourish it with inputs, and ward off pests that threaten to devour it. The tree of democracy thus requires continual attention and activity. In this book, I have placed the ethnographic microscope on a single agrarian setting, to compare the analogical similarities between the cultivation of paddy and the cultivation of democracy by focusing on particular social events as potential resources of the values required for such a cultivation. Each iteration of such events, which by their nature are repetitive, helps recreate and sustain these values. The values created in each event also mutually reinforced each other and so the ideas of social equality in the egalitarian congregations of Eid prayers were reinforced through the orderly queues of polling stations. Eid prayers provided a model of egalitarianism for a low caste Hindu like Memdasi Dom, whose religion practiced untouchability, and such equality was in turn instantiated at the polling booth where she could exercise her constitutional right to political equality. The fleeting experience of each lingered long after these events, in what Veena Das calls the "evented everyday" and contributed to shaping the political subjectivity of Memdasi. Consequently, with each experience of this kind Memdasi was a little less willing to accept her inferior status and a bit more emboldened to demand a better deal from society. All of these events—Eid, elections, and others—were transcendental events in their own ways and brought into sharp relief the contours of values that were imperfectly articulated in everyday life but could be glimpsed as desirable during the event. These events in social life that brought people together in a collective activity made people aspire to be better versions of themselves and made up a bundle of values for their everyday lives *as well as* their official responsibilities as citizens who voted in elections. The scandal, harvest, sacrifice, and election discussed in this book were each such transcendental moments as they stood outside the flow of everyday life, created extraordinary social relations, and brought their participants into confrontation with truths that were both momentary and profound. In their own ways, they helped the participants to re-commit themselves to the ideas of common purpose, mutual responsibility, accommodation, and solidarity.

Ambedkar's call in 1950 for improving the anti-democratic soil of India can only be achieved by an active citizenship that remains committed to nourishing the ground for democratic culture to take root, being vigilant against contagion, and sharing the bounty of harvest while cultivating democracy.

*

Acknowledgments

This book is the culmination of research that began in the late 1990s, so I have accumulated debts over more than two decades. It is therefore a particular pleasure to be able to finally thank the many people who have been fellow travelers on this long journey. Some joined me for part of the way, providing good counsel and sustenance at critical periods, others were there at the very start to help me get going, and still others have stayed with me throughout. Writing a monograph is something of a pilgrimage—the destination justifies the journey, but it is the travel that brings sociality and knowledge.

Like Chaucer's pilgrims, my journey too began in spring, when I undertook a visit, funded by a Nuffield Early Careers Grant, to twenty different places in the Indian state of West Bengal to locate a suitable fieldsite. My sister, Krittika Banerjee, accompanied me on those life-changing few weeks as we discovered the part of India from where our family originated, whose language we spoke but where we had never lived. Since then, she has read my writings despite her own demanding work commitments, provided valuable feedback, attended my seminars, and shared her home and company in Mumbai as a reprieve in between my fieldwork visits. This work would not have been nearly as enjoyable without her and for that I am truly grateful.

For the initial interest in the subject of this book, my thanks go to the Lokniti team at the Centre for the Study of Developing Societies (CSDS)—for their National Election Studies surveys that generated findings that provoked my ethnographic research—in particular, my thanks go to Sanjay Kumar, Himanshu, Anthony Heath, Oliver Heath, Sandeep Shastri, K. C. Suri, and Banasmita Bora. CSDS provided a vibrant research base in India and I always came away enriched from even informal chats with the Lokniti team and the famous communal lunch with Ashis Nandy, Dhirubhai Sheth, and V. B. Singh, each of whom had their unique perspective on Indian politics.

My bridge to Lokniti was Yogendra Yadav, who had become part of our family in Delhi in 1994, and it was the depth and width of his formidable knowledge of Indian politics and society, combined with his mastery of political theory, that inspired my academic interest in Indian democracy. It was his observation that surveys revealed broad correlations but only ethnography could probe the deeper connections, that acted as a spur for this research. Since then he has remained an inspiration, interlocutor, occasional fieldwork companion, and, above all, my big brother. In this book I argue for the vital need for "active

citizenship" to make democratic politics possible, and Yogendra is the embodiment of such *virtù*.

My education in Indian politics has been greatly enriched by the writings of
some brilliant scholars, many of whom I am blessed to count as friends. Adam
Auerbach, Akeel Bilgrami, Anirudh Krishna, Ashutosh Varshney, Bhikhu
Parekh, Christophe Jaffrelot, David Gilmartin, Devesh Kapur, Dwaipayan
Bhattacharya, Faisal Devji, James Chiriyankandath, James Manor, Lisa
Bjorkman, Lisa Mitchell, Louise Tillin, Manisha Priyam, Neelanjan Sircar,
Patrick French, Partha Chatterjee, Peter D'Souza, Phil Oldenburg, Pradeep
Chibber, Pranab Bardhan, Pratap Bhanu Mehta, Ramchandra Guha, Rahul
Verma, Richard Eaton, Sanjay Ruparelia, Shalini Randheria, Shruti Kapila, Suhas
Palshikar, Sunil Khilnani, Tariq Thachil, Sarthak Bagchi, Steve Wilkinson, and
Sudpita Kaviraj have all been important influences through their research and
collegiality. I was lucky also to examine some outstanding doctoral theses by
Gilles Verniers, James Bradbury, Jeffrey Witsoe, Lipika Kamra, and Lipin Ram,
from whom I learned even more. Similarly, each of the volumes published in
my book series *Exploring the Political in South Asia* with Routledge, expertly
handled by Nilanjan Sarkar and then Shashank Sinha and Shoma Choudhury,
expanded my understanding of the scope of the political. I am thankful to the
authors in that series: Amélie Blom, Andrew Sanchez, Arild Ruud, Clarinda Still,
Geir Heierstad, Kenneth Bo Nielsen, Lucia Michelutti, Manuela Ciotti, Nicholas
Martin, Pamela Price, Stéphanie Tawa Lama-Rewal, and Uday Chandra, among
others.

Since March 1998, I have made innumerable visits to my research site,
funded by research grants by British Academy, Department for International
Development (DFID), European Research Council (ERC), Economic and Social
Research Council (ESRC), London School of Economics and Political Science
(LSE), and University College London (UCL). I am hugely indebted to Ben and
Kirat Rogaly for welcoming me into the warmth of their home in Shantiniketan
for a break during one of my very first fieldwork trips. There I also met some
brilliant people, many of whom have remained lifelong friends—Kumkum and
Ranjit Bhattacharya, Shibani and Samar Choudhury, and the late Sunil Sengupta
among them. As I continue to return every year, it is the prospect of their
warmth, wisdom, and excellent *adda* sessions when much knowledge is shared
that makes fieldwork trips so exciting. The very first field trip in West Bengal that
I undertook with my sister was made possible through the help and advice of
Manish Gupta, then Chief Secretary of the West Bengal government. After re-
tirement, his political career was launched by a phenomenal election victory in
2011 and latterly as Rajya Sabha MP. As his niece, following his career has made
studying politics in Bengal even more charged and exciting. In Kolkata, another
maternal uncle, M. K. Sen, provided a home and landing base for innumerable

visits. His eager reception, and those of his friends on early morning walks at the Dhakuria Lakes, gave my research findings an instant audience, and his newspaper clippings sent by post were invaluable for keeping up with news before newspapers went online. The dynamic Jawhar Sircar helped me first understand elections in West Bengal during his tenure as Chief Electoral Officer. His continuing friendship over the years as he rose to become one of the most senior civil servants in the country and his generous sharing of his vast historical knowledge of Bengal's religion and culture are cherished outcomes of this research.

In 2009, a grant by the UK Economic and Social Research Council allowed me to test one of my initial village-level ethnographic findings, that elections had a sort of sacrosanct status in Indian life, at an all-India level. This resulted in the volume *Why India Votes?* published in 2014, and I thank all twelve members of the team who contributed to that study. Dr S. Y. Quraishi was Election Commissioner in 2009 and has been a valued source of advice ever since.

I wish to thank all of the students who have studied Political Anthropology with me at Oxford University College London and London School of Economics and Political Science, for their questions and comments that have been so critical in clarifying my own thinking. Each of my PhD students has played a part in my intellectual journey, and to all of them I offer my thanks. In particular, I thank Fuad Musallam, Lexi Stadlen, and Rebecca Bowers who also provided research assistance. Mekhala Krishnamurthy was my doctoral student when she did her own brilliant work on agricultural markets, and I deeply value her extraordinary friendship and collaboration ever since.

In 2014, when I began to seriously focus on writing this book, Craig Calhoun kindly invited me to attend a meeting of the Centre for Transcultural Studies being held in Vienna. Thus began a series of conversations held in many different cities with an extraordinary group of scholars, each equally brilliant and generous, that continue until the present. These engagements gave the book a theoretical core and helped me find my own voice. It is a huge pleasure that *Degenerations of Democracy* by three of the Centre's key members, Craig Calhoun, Dilip Gaonkar, and Charles Taylor, will be published at the same time as this one. Craig Calhoun's contribution, in particular, has been enormous as he has always made time to provide intellectual excitement, encouragement, and inspiration despite his very busy schedule.

Ashutosh Varshney kindly invited me to publish the book in this series providing a much needed 'carrot' to look forward to. Charles Taylor, Deborah James, Frederick Schaffer, Laura Bear, and Sudipta Kaviraj all very kindly read various drafts of the whole manuscript, and their detailed feedback and suggestions helped strengthen the work immeasurably. Hilal Ahmed offered advice on some critical sections of the book, Maanik Nath and Tejas Parashar read the final manuscript in its entirety, and Dilip Menon and Nilanjan Sarkar provided feedback on the book proposal at the start of writing. The two anonymous reviewers for Oxford University Press provided tough but constructive comments on the first manuscript, and their approval of the final version was a hard earned win. The errors that remain are mine alone. The excellent David McBride and his team at OUP oversaw the production of the book. To each of the people named herein, I convey my unbounded gratitude for their generosity and noble acts of citizenship without which academic writing would not be what it is.

The ideas that have finally found their way to this book were variously born, challenged, discarded, and adopted at innumerable seminars. My thanks go to all of those who gave of their time and energy in the following universities: University of California Berkeley, University of Bern, Department of Anthropolofy and South Asia Institute, University of Cambridge, University of North Carolina, Chapel Hill, University of Chicago, South Asia Institute and World Project, Columbia University, University of Copenhagen, Delhi School of Economics Delhi University, Georgetown University at Doha, Duke University, Department of Anthropology University of Edinburgh, Graduate Institute University of Geneva, South Asia Institute University of Gottingen, Heidelberg University, Department of Sociology Jawaharlal Nehru University, Johannesburg, Centre for Social Sciences Kolkata, Kyoto University, International Institute of Asian Studies Leiden, Department of Anthropology, LSE, Department of Anthropology, University of Manchester, Melbourne School of Government, Infrastructure Development Finance Corporation Mumbai, University of Oslo, University of Oxford, Sciences Po Paris, Centre of Advanced Study University of Pennsylvania, School of Advanced Research Santa Fe, UCL, Yale University, and University of Zurich. In particular, I would like to thank K. Sivaramakrishnan and Jim Scott for inviting me to give a presentation at the Agrarian Studies Colloquium at Yale University, which inspired me to first consider cultivation both as practice and metaphor, and to John Dunn, whom I met there, for his subsequent interest in my work. My thanks also go to Bart Klem and others at the Melbourne School of Government whose invitation to deliver keynote lectures at their "Democracy in Transition" conference gave the anthropologist writing on democracy a much-needed boost. Special thanks also to all the colleagues gathered by Julia Paley at the Advanced Research Seminar at Santa Fe that led to the first ever volume of essays on the anthropology of democracy. And to Nic Cheeseman, Gabrielle Lynch, and Justin Willis for co-organizing a book workshop with me at LSE to discuss their excellent book, *The Moral Economy of Elections in Africa*, alongside mine.

My anthropological thinking about "the political" has been profoundly shaped throughout my career by some key scholars. I was very lucky to have been taught by the brilliant Jit Uberoi as a graduate student, and his own membership of the Manchester School and stories of Max Gluckman (right up until the final weeks of writing this book) were hugely formative to my own thinking. In the United Kingdom, Jonathan Spencer and his reimagination of political anthropology has been a critical inspiration. Friends and fellow anthropologists Amita Baviskar, Arjun Appadurai, Chris Fuller, David Gellner, Deepak Mehta, Douglas Johnson, Janet Carsten, the late John Davis, Lawrence Cohen, Marc Abélès, Mike Rowlands, Nandini Sundar, Ravinder Kaur, Rita Brara, Surinder Jodhka, Thomas Blom Hansen, Veena Das, and Wendy James have each inspired me in showing how profoundly insightful anthropological engagement can be. The inhabitants of Madanpur and Chishti, by allowing me to share their lives and knowledge with warmth and humour, made the practice of such engagement rewarding. These villages are my "research home" and continue to ground me as an Indian; for this I shall remain forever indebted.

The final and most intense phase of writing this book was during the "lockdown" enforced by the Covid-19 pandemic. The challenge was alleviated by Pandit Uday Bhawalkar's divine and meditative dhrupad music and the warm companionship of my cousins Amit and Sangeeta Banerjee and Kaushik and Ela Banerjee and friends Ananya Vajpeyi, Anjali Mody, Anu Dhillon, Ashish Bhatt, Basharat Peer, Chris Banfield, Christa Salamandra, David Wengrow, Gilles Verniers, Giti Chandra, Gopa Sabharwal, Graham Farrant (Ted), Jagriti Chadha, James Crabtree, Kathryn Earle, Manisha Priyam, Maitreesh Ghatak, Marie Pollet, Mekhala Krishnamurthy, Nandita and Ahona Pal Choudhury, Namita Gokhale, Nasser and Subur Munjee, Oroon Das, Partha Mukhopadhyay, Pragya Tiwari, Rakesh Sharma, Rathin Roy, R. P. Singh, Salil Tripathi, Sangeeta and Soumilya Datta, Sanam Arora, Sanjoy Roy, Seema Anand, Siddharth Varadarajan, Soumik Datta, Sujatha Venkatramanan, Sukanya and Ganesh Wignaraja, Susan Manly, Tanmay Misra, Vayu Naidu, Viniti Vaish, and Yamini Aiyar. Sincere thanks to Surina Narula who generously welcomed me to work in peace in her magical treehouse. Safina Uberoi and Lukas Ruecker have my sincere gratitude for being amazing godparents to my daughter and for their warm friendship.

My family in Bristol have been the in-laws any woman would wish for. Margaret and John Watts have been loving and encouraging parents, and Bethan has been a sister-in-arms in my adopted country. Their help with looking after our daughter also made fieldwork and writing possible, and for this I shall remain ever grateful. I never had a sabbatical to write this book, and writing it in the interstices of everything else was made possible by Prema Mudaliyar, who did the housework and also cared for my daughter.

My parents' home in New Delhi and their love and encouragement over the years was the bedrock on which this research grew. They would have been so proud to see the final product, my father would have dropped everything to sit down and read it while simultaneously ringing his friends to tell them of its publication. My mother delighted in my academic engagement with Bengali in adulthood, and I owe my competence in the language entirely to her own accomplished command and love of it. Also, for years her birthday present to me was an annual subscription to the journal *Economic and Political Weekly of India* that had to be purchased in person, and this was precious to me at so many levels. Her firm belief that women should always have their own pursuits independent of family and kinship and nurture the ability to think for themselves, has been the most valuable life lesson imparted by a mother. My father, despite being a busy surgeon, made time to read every word I published, and that in itself expressed his love more than any words could. His smile, when he learned that I had sent off the first draft of the book to the publishers despite my mother's recent passing, will forever remain imprinted in my memory. Since losing our parents, my sister, Madhulika Banerjee, has continued to provide the love and warmth of home during my visits to Delhi. Her career as a professor in Delhi University has also allowed me to remain connected to my academic roots, and her own inspiring work on the politics of knowledge has served as a constant reminder that the study of "politics" in India is much wider than the study of democracy and elections. Elliot Stechman has been the brother I never had growing up and has kept me grounded with his humor, bear hugs, tech competence, and mobile phone number, all of which made research in India a possibility and visits to Mumbai a joy. Madhulika and Yogendra's children Sufi and Sahaj, and Krittika and Elliot's daughter Mihi, have each in their own unique way made my life immeasurably richer with their presence and unconditional love.

My daughter, Aria Gitanjali, was born a third of the way through this research project and so had to endure it through her childhood. Her own growing passion for ethics, politics, and economics however reassures me that "collateral damage" is perhaps not always a bad thing. I shall forever remain indebted to her for never holding my absences against me and never denying me a back rub.

Finally, not a fraction of the research, travel, reading, thinking, and writing that has gone into this book would have been possible without my husband, Julian Watts. He has been an intellectual companion, patient listener, brutal editor, and my unwavering champion for over twenty-five years. He always encouraged me to "write the book I want," and so it is with gratitude and love that I dedicate it to him.

Mukulika Banerjee
London
July 2021

*

Notes

Preface

1. See Berggruen Institute report on "Renewing Democracy in the Digital Age" March 2020.
2. The names Madanpur and Chishti are fictional, as are the names of their inhabitants.

Chapter 1

1. Dipesh Chakravarty characterizes peasants as "relics of another time" (Chakravarty 2000: 249), as Anand Pandian reminds us (Pandian 2009: 249n5).
2. A small example illustrates this: None of my interlocutors ate at dusk, as I discovered by chance, having bought a bag of samosas to share once at the end of a long and tiring day. Everyone enthusiastically welcomed the rare treat, but rather than eat it each one politely held their samosa in their hand. Halfway through mine, I asked if they were not so hungry after all, but I was persuaded that they indeed were, while they continued to hold, rather than eat, the samosas. It was only my persistent questions that finally revealed that my friends did not ever eat at dusk because it was during that liminal time between day and night when they believed spirts went looking for food. "If we eat now, they will go hungry, so we will just wait for it to get dark," was how they put it. People clearly believed that spirts co-existed in the same environment with them and while this was not the subject of conversation often, it nevertheless shaped how people imagined their place in the world, the need to share resources even if it required them to show restraint in consumption when hungry. Such a simple explanation was not quite a "value" or "theory," but it was certainly a sort of shared understanding, a social imaginary that oriented everyday actions.
3. Another student on Max Gluckman was C. Parvathamma, who published *Politics and Religion: A Study of Historical Interaction between Socio-Political Relationships in a Mysore Village* (1971).
4. Here values are defined as "representations of the good or what people take to be, all things considered, desirable. That is to say, whether or not people at every moment desire the things that values represent, people do acknowledge in a second-order way that they are worth desiring. People know, to put it in terms that bear more centrally on issues of ethics, that it is good to desire them, even if this does not mean their desire for them is constant. Like roles and groups, then, people do not always immediately experience values in their fullest form in the ordinary course of things— sometimes during the flow of everyday life the ethical desire values are capable of

awakening is not to the fore—yet they can still, on reflection, appreciate their desirability. This is one sense in which we can say that values at times transcend ordinary experience" (Robbins 2016: 774).

5. Veena Das (along with Jit Uberoi) also incidentally introduced me to the ideas of the Manchester School when she taught me as a graduate student in Delhi many decades ago.

6. As Kaviraj notes, the distinction between the spheres of the economic, political, and social "were first conceived as intellectual suggestions and then written into the ontology of societies by the repetitive and daily practice of those ideas. This inaugurated an entirely novel way of deciding what was right or wrong conduct in a segmentary fashion, creating new boundaries for types of social acts within which people followed regional criteria of appropriateness that did not necessarily extend into other, adjacent spheres" (Kaviraj 2011: 4).

7. It also includes "planting labourers, as well as persons engaged in various farming related occupations such as sericulture, vermiculture, and agro-forestry, tribal families/persons engaged in shifting cultivation and in the collection, use and sale of minor and non-timber forest produce" (National Policy for Farmers, Ministry of Agriculture, Government of India 2007). A similarly wide definition has been used recently by the largest front of Farmers' organizations, AIKSCC, in its Manifesto of Indian Farmers (countercurrent.org).

8. I use the term *agrarian* interchangeably as an adjective and a noun.

9. See Sircar 2018 for an analysis of 2018 election results, differentiated by urban, rural, and agrarian voters.

10. I read Pandian's work having completed my own manuscript and was relieved to read a scholarly work that echoed my findings on the nature of agrarian civility. His work has been invaluable in refining my own ideas.

11. Jingcai Ying makes an interesting comparative case for how Confucianism provides a resource for the self-cultivation of democratic participation against political hierarchy in China and for going beyond merely casting ballots (Ying 2018).

12. Remarkably little has been written about "civility" in academic literature. I have found Edward Shils's discussion of civility to "suppress individual desire for the sake of a common good" an accurate definition for my argument (Shils 1997). See also Kloppenberg's (2016) who argues that the cultivation of a civic ethos is necessary for political democracy. (Thanks to Tejas Parashar for this reference.)

13. See the Preface for my remarks on how India's credibility in conducting free and fair elections stands compromised, particularly since 2014.

14. This last question has become arguably the most important question in contemporary India, and I comment on it in the Preface. Arguably, winning elections *at any cost* has come to define electoral democracy in India today. The means has become an end in itself.

15. I will return to a longer discussion of republicanism and democracy in the final chapter of the book.

16. My doctoral research was on the non-violent *Khudai Khidmatgar* movement of 1930–1947 by the Pashtuns in colonial India. See my book *The Pathan Unarmed* (2001).

17. This book also goes some way in confirming and providing texture to the results of large-scale surveys such as those conducted by Bardhan and Mookherjee on the reasons for the 2011 defeat of the Left Front.

18. West Bengal has the highest proportion of Muslims—27 percent of its population— among all states in India (except Jammu and Kashmir, which from 2019 is no longer a state) according to the 2011 census. They are poorest in West Bengal, Bihar, and Haryana.

Chapter 2

1. See a useful introduction to the collection *Village Society* (2012), edited by Surinder Jodhka. The anthropology of India has remained vibrant and theoretically innovative, and much of it has been either focused on the urban (Appadurai, Das, Hansen, Srivastava), indigenous populations (Baviskar, Sundar, Shah, Chandra, Sivaramakrishnan), the everyday state (Bear and Mathur, Fuller and Benei, Das), or the economy of markets and special economic zones (Krishnamurthy, Cross, Lieven, De Neeve). This has been in no mean measure because of India's rapid urbanization which is projected to reach 40 percent of the landmass by 2030. Despite this, during the same period, as part of the same policy decisions, assaults on the rights of indigenous societies and their resources have given rise to social movements and violent revolutions that have rightly been the focus of anthropological attention.

2. The collection *A Handbook of Rural India* (2018) is a handy compilation of some of this work, and there have been monographs on rural India published too— Govindarajan 2019 and Singh 2017 among them.

3. Caste endogamy has been so consistent that scientific evidence of the gene pool of the Indian population demonstrates remarkably little gene diversification, creating small islands of groups who share a genetic make-up (Joseph 2018).

4. I have discussed the issue of caste and political participation in Chapter 1 and I return to these themes in Chapter 7.

5. See Ruud 2003, pp. 122–130, for the stereotype, in some parts of rural Bengal, of Bagdis as "dangerous and destructive." In my fieldsite they were too few to be seen by others as being of consequence.

6. A fuller account of land reforms and agriculture can be found in Chapter 4.

7. Kamaal Baba's son was called Syed Pir, and his son was Bechu Mian, who had four sons. These four men, that is, the great-grandsons of Kamaal Baba, created the population in Tilaboni. One of the great-grandsons was called Syed Manuwar Ali, who had two sons, Amir Ali and Mohaib Ali, and Rabia was Amir Ali's granddaughter. Her brothers were Najabat Hussain and Hashem Ali, who were also grandsons of Amir Ali, and her two older sisters had been buried in Muhammadpur, Birbhum.

8. Kirman is located in the southeast of Iran and is best known for its luxurious blue-and-white pottery, a sort of faux porcelain, which flourished particularly during the Safavid period. It lay on the edge of the desert which stretches east to

modern-day Pakistan and, owing to its strategic location on an oasis, served as a stopping point on the trade route from the east. In the eighteenth century, it linked the overland route from India to the eastern ports of the Persian Gulf, and it is possible that Kamaal Baba may have heard about India from merchants and hitched a ride with them.

9. Amir Ali's wife, Shamma Bibi, was Mohit Ali's grandfather's sister Mohit Ali lived in Chishti during my research and will appear many times in the following pages. Amir Ali had one daughter, Qamrun Nisa, and four sons: Ali Muhammad, Baad Ahmed Hassan, Muhammed Hussain, and Abud Hussain. Ali Muhammad had eight daughters, but only one of them had children.

10. Arun Choudhury, a local intellectual and keen amateur historian with a well-stocked library on histories of Bengal, gave me some of this information.

11. The expression *Chaar Yaar* ("Four Friends") refers to the first four caliphs of Islam, who were also called Rashiduan or Khulafah Rashidun, meaning "rightly guided." They are: Abu Bakr (632–634 AD), Umar ibn al-Khattab (Umar I) (634–644 AD), Usman ibn Affan (644–656 AD), and Ali ibn Abi Talib (656–661 AD). Interestingly, they all were related to the Prophet Muhammad. Shia Islam, on the other hand, gives more importance to Caliph Ali and addresses him as *Ali-ul-waliullah*. This underlines the difference between Barelvi version of Islam of my respondents and Shias. While Barelvis don't always mark Muharram through processions as Shias do, in my fieldsite they may have done so because of the connection with Kamaal Baba and his origins in Iran where the influence of Shia Islam was strong. (My thanks to Hilal Ahmed for helping me understand these distinctions.)

12. There is considerable historical and anthropological literature around the differences among the Deobandis and Barelvis (Metcalf 1982; F. Robinson 1974; Sanyal 1996); what I present here are the explanations that my informants provided to me in response to my questions about their religion, why they had an *imambara*, and if they were different from other Muslim groups around them.

Chapter 3

1. We will meet Majhi again in the chapter six of this book, on "Elections," when we examine the key role he played in the eventual reversal of the Left Front's electoral fortunes.

2. Chapter 2 provides a detailed discussion of the political context.

3. I provide detailed discussion of the land reforms and paddy cultivation in Chapter 4, "Harvest."

4. I discuss the theme of dignity in greater detail in Chapter 4.

5. One acre = 3.03 bigha (in West Bengal).

6. See Ruud 2003, pp. 164–167, for a discussion of the institution of *bichar*.

7. This was characterized as the behavior of a "party state" by Bhattacharya (2016).

8. In 2006, the Master and his wife visited Ajmer Sharif, the well-known shrine in Rajasthan, and in 2009 they completed the Haj, a first for anyone from the village, which sealed their pre-eminent status as the most pious couple across both villages. Soon afterward, the Master's wife began to cover her hair completely with her sari, tucking it behind the ears to mimic a *niqab*, and talked about switching to wearing a proper hijab rather than the saris she now deemed revealing and un-Islamic. When I visited their house a year later, their green-eyed daughter-in-law was indeed wearing a hijab.

9. Hanif was also a classificatory uncle of Lulu and Mohit, as their father was Hanif's MBS.

10. See the previous chapter for a discussion of the extensive historical and kin links between Tilaboni and my fieldsite.

11. Mohit and Lulu were also related to Mustafa through their mother, and Mohit was a good friend of Amir (the father of the girl in the scandal).

12. Akhtar tacitly supported his brother but made his disdain of village politics plain in subtle and non-subtle ways. For instance, on the rare occasions I saw him, he was sitting on a chair (something very few villagers owned) at the entrance to his house on the main village lane, reading (as only he was able) the English daily *The Statesman* published from Kolkata. Ostensibly open to the village and its life, his broadsheet broadcast his superiority and kept casual conversations at bay. However, he was widely respected, as he could offer paid private tuitions in English in the village, and every family was grateful for this rare convenience. But he rarely spoke to adults and never to the other schoolteachers. We will meet him again at the start of Chapter 7.

13. The lower castes found that *madrasas* offered free schooling, boarding, and accommodation and so each family endeavored to send at least one son away for such an accommodation, mainly for social security but increasingly also for the prestige their sons now afforded.

14. Mansur did not invite Hanif either, which as the latter pointed out was ungrateful, given that he had once literally saved Mansur's life from a murderous debt collector.

15. A telling illustration of such a development is to be found in another village in West Bengal, and one that was at the heart of the high-profile Singur agitation in 2008 against the Left Front's decision to give away land to the building of a car factory. There, as Dayabati Roy's fine-grained work on two villages in Singur shows, even some landowning families who had in fact benefited from the sale of land nevertheless joined the agitation alongside the landless sharecroppers and agricultural workers, in solidarity. The mobilization of protest was therefore not only along class lines, but it was something that transcended them and created a wider solidarity of the rural. Roy herself characterizes this as "people responding more on community basis and for the community interest" and reflects an imagination of the social that was collective and solidary. "In Kadampur," she notes, "people responded to the landed acquisition move as a community . . . through collective solidarity, cutting across caste-class lines" (Roy 2019: 432).

Chapter 4

1. Discussed in Chapter 3, "Scandal."
2. People remembered over a hundred different varieties of paddy and could name thirty different types instantly that were grown up until the Green Revolution, but by the time of this study only two or three traditional varieties were being cultivated.
3. See D. N. Dhanagare, "Green Revolution and Social Inequalities in Rural India," pp. 134–145, in Jodhka 2018a.
4. Harriss explores what impact the agrarian reforms have had on power relations and measurable outcomes such as levels of living. Gazdar concludes from a WIDER project between 1987 and 1989 that there is a "lack of comprehensive benchmarks." Harriss offers an account of one village in Birbhum over a period between 1958 and 1991. A survey was conducted in 1982 which had been previously surveyed in the 1950s and 1960. He did another repeat survey in 1991. His conclusion is that the picture is not entirely gloomy but also that agrarian reform and redistribution alone offers no solution to the agrarian problem of West Bengal (Harriss 1983: 51, cited in Harriss 1993), the reason being that in his fieldsite, "by the time Operation Barga took place sharecropping was no longer a major issue, and its implementation cannot be seen as having constituted a major challenge to the agrarian power structure" (Harriss 1993: 1239). Instead, he attributes greater prosperity to "increased productivity of agriculture after the introduction of protective irrigation," from HYV "boro" paddy and the effects of organized action in increasing real wages. Harriss dismisses claims to the contrary as a "productionist perspective."
5. In an interview to Atul Kohli in 1987, cited in Harriss 1993: 1238.
6. We have seen the severe form this dependency could take at the village level, in the figure of the Comrade discussed in the previous chapter, whose writ ruled large over every aspect of people's lives. We examine the electoral implication of this relationship in Chapter 6, "Election."
7. Only the Comrade had access to electricity supply for his pumps.
8. HYV paddy had also introduced other problems, such as malaria since the pesticides used on the crop had driven mosquitoes into the village. The adoption of mosquito nets could be dated precisely to the introduction of HYV.
9. In just one generation, the cultivation of over fifty different varieties of paddy had dwindled to mainly two. Varieties such as *gobindobhog, shindurmukhi, khajur chorhi,* and *dokhin korma* are still grown in small quantities, as they are required for thatch.
10. See Govindarajan 2018 for a similar discussion of native versus Jersey cows.
11. 3.03 bigha = 1 acre; 6.32 bighas = 1 hectare; 20 katha = 1 bigha.
12. The landholdings of my research site were fairly representative of those in the state of West Bengal. As Bhattacharya records, "In 1982, there was a preponderance of small/medium tenants cultivating land belonging to small/medium landowners . . . and a whopping 81.6 per cent of West Bengal's agricultural households held less than 5 acres" (2016: 58–59).
13. Data from other places also confirms this linkage between ownership patterns and productivity. "Laffont and Matoussi use farm level data from Tunisia to show that a

shift from sharecropping to fixed-rent tenancy or owner cultivation raised output by 33 per cent and moving from a short-term tenancy contract to a longer-term contract increased output by 27.5 per cent" (Banerjee et al. 2002: 277).

14. For example, where a sharecropper and his wife would have been expected to plant paddy for a whole bigha, now four or five people were employed to do the same.

15. "The raw data as analysed by Rohini Nayar show that between 1960–61 and 1983–84 both money wages and real wages have always been higher in West Bengal that in a majority of other states" (Harriss 1993: 1238).

16. Under the new regime he could provide his own plow and oxen and take 75 percent of the profits, but if the landowner was in a position to do this himself, the sharecropper was not allowed to bring his own. Every bullock cost Rs. 7,000 to Rs. 10,000 to buy. Maintenance costs were Rs. 40 per day as fodder was not cheap if it had to be bought (1 kg of paddy husk cost Rs. 6, and 0.5 kg of paddy stalks cost Rs. 30). Please note, the average US Dollar to Indian Rupee exchange rate in 2000 was Rs 45 to 1 USD.

17. This observation is confirmed by scholars who report that "visible signs of destitution are disappearing from West Bengal's rural areas" (Bandhopadhyay 1997).

18. For a contrasting case of Indra Lohar from before Left Front reforms, see Bhattacharya 2016: 62–63. The certificate was then deposited in a bank against which Okho took out a loan for Rs. 12,000, a sum that took him eight years to pay back. Accounts of such forms of indebtedness were ubiquitous because of the lack of any other sources of credit available in the rural economy.

19. Bhattacharya reports that less than 9 percent of agricultural workers attended Krishak Sabha meetings even though they made up 75 percent of its primary membership (Bhattacharya 2016: 72).

20. Creating saplings (*bichon*) started with the dry grain being soaked for forty-eight hours in a large, flat vessel, then strained into a basket which was then briefly immersed in water just under boiling temperature to raise the temperature of the grain. (All the grains had to be lightly colored and roughly the same size and had to be replenished every few years). Then the grains were wrapped in dry sacking and put out in the sun as the seed needed to be at a constant temperature of 60°C to sprout. The combination of the heat from sunshine, the wind, and water from the damp seeds created the ideal conditions for the grains to sprout. This took about seventy-two hours, after which the little sprouts were spread out on a large, prepared field and immediately covered with ash to protect them from dew and further dampness. Once the first green shoots appeared, the field was covered in 0.5 to 1 inch of water, and once they had grown to about five inches in height, they were transplanted at a distance of about a meter apart.

21. This was quicker than for the HYV crop, which had to be sometimes threshed by hand as its stalks could be too long for the machines and so could take much longer.

22. By 2013, the daily wage had risen to Rs. 150 (about £1.50, or US$2.44).

23. The other sorts of labor arrangements within the village: *Keyote* (fishermen of the tanks) who kept half the profits from the sale of fish; the rest went to the owner who made the initial investment of eggs, nets and equipment, and maintenance. *Paloni* was another labor arrangement whereby the owner of a cow gave it away to a poorer family to look after it. They were paid Rs. 1,200 for the service and when the cow was

eventually sold, the Rs. 1,200 was recovered and the remaining difference was split between the owner and carer. See Ruud 2003: 58 for an account of similar arrangements in his fieldsite in neighboring Bardhaman.

24. Sizes of the landholdings were too small to require migrant labor—so it was really an instance of the village pulling together.

25. See Krishnamurthy 2018 for a recent account.

26. *Chasi tumi dakhal koro, dakhal korey chas koro*; Ruud 2003: 111–112.

27. *Bichon* was usually sold at Rs. 18 per kg (equivalent to 30 cents) when it was fresh and before the second harvest of the year, but if left too late the price could drop to Rs. 8 per kg. Hanif told me one year that he had about five tins of it, which was about 50–60 kg, but he had to wait until the first Wednesday or Thursday of the month of Poush had passed to sell it, because the Goddess Lakshmi was worshipped on those days and no commercial transactions took place. "Even the depots will be empty," he told me.

28. Vidya Venkat, "Why Can't the Government Provide a Higher Income for Farmers, Asks M.S. Swaminathan," *The Hindu*, August 16, 2017.

29. During this project, the wage for every 1,000 bricks went up from Rs. 90 to Rs. 120. During months with longer daylight hours, some workers made more than 1,000 bricks a day.

30. A major recommendation came from the agronomist M. S. Swaminathan in his report submitted in 2007, which recommended that the MSP should be set by adding 50 percent of the weighted cost of production to it. Successive governments failed to implement this, choosing instead short-term measures of loan waivers.

31. The dates for Ramzan were determined by the Islamic lunar calendar, so they varied from year to year.

32. See the epigraph to this book.

33. See Ruud 2003: 144–45 for an account of this relationship between inferiors and superiors of a "dominant, paradigmatic cultural idiom" exemplified in situations of request and supplication such as that between sharecropper and landowner. This required the former to be the supplicant but also placed a "moral obligation" to the latter to protect and care for all.

34. This was the infamous "two-cup" system ubiquitous all over India until recently, when even roadside tea stalls used two separate sets of crockery depending on the caste of the customer. I was at the receiving end of this discrimination myself inside the homes of even my closest friends in Madanpur and Chishti, as I was always served in the china cups reserved for non-Syeds, not being a Muslim myself. I was grateful for the experience because I learned firsthand what social discrimination feels like, which, as an educated upper caste Hindu Brahmin in India, I had never really experienced until then.

35. In large parts of India, however, it is customary for many Dalit and lower caste Hindus to eat beef, not least because it is the most affordable meat. But in the face of Syed elitism, this custom had been reversed in my research site. And in this, too, my Hindu identity came into play as I was not offered any part of the sacrificial meat which, they assumed, as an upper caste Hindu I would not consume. See Chapter 5, "Qurbani," for more on sacrifice and redistribution.

36. See also Bardhan, Ghatak, and Karaivanov (2007), in which it is demonstrated how lower land inequality can improve overall efficiency in collective action.

37. For the scheming Syeds, the *milads* also presented an opportunity for politicking under a culturally respectable veneer of piety and hospitality, which disabled the Comrade from unleashing extreme reprisals that more overt mobilization against him would have provoked. Therefore, they used them—through timing, guest lists, choice of orator, and the size of the audience—to play their own political games, as we saw in the previous chapter, "Scandal."

38. I have narrated the story in full in Banerjee 2011.

Chapter 5

1. I was advised that as a Hindu it could be a sin for me to watch cattle being sacrificed, so in deference to their concern, I put myself out of sight so as not to interfere in the solemnity of the occasion and stood instead inside a makeshift bamboo lean-to on the edge of the clearing and watched the proceedings through gaps in the cane.

2. I make this distinction by drawing on Maurice Bloch's work on the dual nature of sociality—the transactional and the transcendental.

3. West Bengal has the highest proportion of Muslims—27 percent—in its population, among all states in India according to the 2011 census. They are poorest in West Bengal, Bihar, and Haryana.

4. See Hilal Ahmed's discussion of performativity of Muslim practices in his recent book *Siyasi Muslims* (2019; especially pp. 32–41). He reports an interesting finding from an All India survey on Religious Attitude and Practices in 2015 that OBC (Other Backward Classes) Muslims appear to practice their religion more than Muslim upper-caste members do, which is clearly at variance from my own data.

5. The lunar calendar coincides slightly with the Bengali calendar, which is calculated differently from the Islamic one. Neither of these coincides with the solar Gregorian calendar that is used by the government of India (schools, post offices, banks, etc.) nor, of course, does it coincide with the agricultural cycle of cultivation. The average inhabitant of Madanpur and Chishti thus regulated their daily, monthly, and annual activities according to four different calendars.

6. Bengali, like other Indo-European languages, is written left to right, so it was striking to see the Bengali script being written from right to left in imitation of Arabic.

7. These are lands about 25 to 30 bighas that various people cultivate and pay the masjid half the share. This fund is the one that was being contested.

8. See Chapter 3.

9. Recall that Amir Ali was the father of Feroza, who was at the heart of the scandal discussed in Chapter 3.

10. A traditional monument to mark the martyrdom of Ali and his sons.

11. *Shinni* is a generic word for "offering."

12. A family of Shekhs had been making the tazia in Madanpur, and I saw it passed down three generations during the course of my study. Shekh Razak and his sons used to make the tazia and in 2013, when he passed away, his grandsons made the tazia for Muharram.

13. See Banerjee and Miller, *The Sari* (2003), especially pp. 238–240, for a fuller discussion.

14. These changes in the practices of Islam were by no means confined to Bengal, and identical changes have been reported from across South Asia. See, for instance, Kumar 2018 for an account of western Uttar Pradesh.

15. The Islamic months are: Muharram, Safar, Rabi' al-awwal, Rabi' al-thani, Jumada al-awwal, Jumada al-thani, Rajab, Sha'aban, Ramadan, Shawwal, Dhu al-Qi'dah, and Dhu al-Hijjah. Across South Asia, variations of these names are used. There is approximately two months' time between the two Eids.

16. In the days leading up to Qurbani, there was an air of tension as they were aware that sacrificing cattle could offend Hindu sentiments. The local administration laid on extra security with police jeeps patrolling the highways, and there was palpable tension. I personally did not, however, witness any clashes.

17. This is, of course, the same sacrifice as the Biblical narrative, in which Isaac is identified as the son and is offered for sacrifice.

18. See Chapter 3, "Scandal," for a more detailed account of the Comrade's politics.

19. Akbar's wife, Manohara, was my first host in the village and was the person with whom I had visited Tilaboni, described in Chapter 2.

20. Although on this occasion I wasn't at all sure that the money the Comrade put in his pocket would indeed find its way to the more pious Mehr.

21. Everyone assumed all day that as a Hindu Brahmin I would not eat beef, and it seemed too complicated to explain how I had gotten used to eating it during previous research in Pakistan and living in Britain. Thus, unlike everyone else, my largely vegetarian diet remained unbroken.

22. Reporting from France, Bowen observed that people found that the barriers to performing a proper Islamic sacrifice made the sacrifice meaningless and many preferred to send money to Palestine or elsewhere where people could make genuine sacrifices or where sacrifices could be offered in their name. They also cited another reason for doing so: In France, they consumed meat all the time, or their children did not like meat, o they preferred to send the money where people had less meat and were likely to only be able to consume it on this festival day. As one man put it, "I don't sacrifice. It's better to send money to Palestine or Chechen, where people have a greater need. Here we eat meat all the time, so it does not mean anything, but there they don't" (Bowen 1992: 100).

23. Fish was a luxury more easily acquired and available, given the hundreds of water tanks on the Bengal landscape, and though still beyond the budgets of most households, was consumed more often than meat.

24. Since 2014, after this study was concluded, and when the Hindu right-wing BJP took power at the central government, the consumption—or even a suspicion of consumption—of beef became the cause of lynching across the country, especially in states controlled by the Hindu right-wing BJP governments; see Kuroda 2018 and Govindarajan 2018 (Chapter 3) for an account.

25. If Hindus asked for *fitr* they were not refused, although *dan* given to them came from a different stock.

26. Werbner, in fact, identifies three different kinds of animal sacrifice in the context of Pakistani Muslims: *sadaqa* is an expiatory gift at the time of extreme danger of a life-threatening kind, in which the victim is given to the poor in its entirety; in *qurbani*, the Eid sacrifice, a portion is given to the poor and the rest is shared among kin and friends conceived of as equals; and in *zabah*, an animal is given as a tribute at a saint's lodge and is usually shared out as *langar* (Werbner 1998: 104).

27. See Jalais 2018 for a critique of Duara's category of "Asian" cosmologies and the distinction she draws between the Chinese and Indian actions toward tigers.

28. Even in a "non-hunting" milieu, it is worth noting that in the synthetic Shinto-Buddhist tradition of contemporary Japan, shrines are dedicated to the spirits of animals killed in medical research" (Lewis 2004: 936).

29. Owners of cattle could recover some of their costs through their sale.

30. Christianity challenged this very idea from the 1940s onward, and by the 1980s Hutchinson found that Nuer Christian communities believed that a "A sacrificed cow is a wasted cow."

31. A similar observation is made by Hutchinson in *Nuer Dilemmas* (1996).

Chapter 6

1. Plastic boxes were the best guarantee against termites, dust, and rainwater, and so precious items were routinely stored in them.

2. See Ruud 2016, particularly pp. 196–200, for an account of economic and social inequality in rural West Bengal before the introduction of Left Front–led reforms.

3. See Nancy Rosenblum (2008) on the importance of "partisanship" for democratic politics.

4. When diesel prices were Rs. 17 per liter, hiring rates were about Rs. 35 per hour.

5. Memdasi was also related to her sister-in-law (her husband's older brother's wife) through descent, as she was also Memdasi's father's sister's daughter. So the two cousins had married Tinkari and his brother.

6. See Chapter 4 in *Why India Votes?* (Banerjee 2014) for an extended discussion of election officials and the culture of the polling station.

7. Further accounts of Election Days can be found in Banerjee 2007, 2010, and 2014.

8. See Banerjee 1999 and 2004 for my analysis.

9. This was to describe Chattoraj's rather modest makeshift practice under the large banyan trees (called *bot*) outside the court buildings. Such advocates were known for providing bail payments and guarantees for criminals whom they then helped escape from the law.

10. Every little town and hamlet used to have a CPI(M) party office in West Bengal.

11. See Chapter 4 for the discussion of the rice pudding.

Chapter 7

1. The words *socialist* and *secular* were not there in the first version and were added in later years.
2. Mahatma Gandhi's birthday, October 2, being the other. Independence Day was a separate date and celebrated on August 15.
3. See Roy 2007 for a thought provoking analysis of a Republic Day Parade and nation-making.
4. See Parekh 2015 for a discussion of the adoption of *both* these terms.
5. See Chapter 2, "The Location of Power," pp. 72–109, in Madhav Khosla's *The Founding Moment* (2020) for a detailed discussion of this issue. I am indebted to his work for providing his scholarly and insightful analysis that is invaluable to my own argument on the importance of the agrarian.
6. Ambedkar's own views of a village were bleak, and his most frequently quoted statement on this subject is, "What is a village but a sink of localism, a den of ignorance, narrow-mindedness and communalism?" (Ambedkar, *Annihilation of Caste*, 1944, 1:48, quoted in Khosla 2020: 103). Ambedkar's early childhood was spent in a village, where he faced hideous discrimination on the basis of his caste. The rest of his life was spent mainly in the cities of Bombay, New York, London, and Delhi, and he never lived in a village again.
7. It was believed that "the lower one went in choosing the location of power, the more society would infiltrate the state" (Khosla 2020: 97). In a recent review of Madhav Khosla's book, Ashutosh Varshney points out that it was believed that this distance from the local was expected to create an emancipatory distance from caste, for the further one was from the local, the further one was from knowledge about the caste origins of the names and therefore the identities of candidates. This "anthropological reality of caste," he argues, is important to explain Ambedkar's refusal to institute structures of local (panchayat) government that were introduced only in the 1990s (Varshney 2020). As the following seventy years have demonstrated, Ambedkar's and Nehru's hopes were ill founded as caste continues to play an important role at all levels of politics, and is by no means exclusive to local village level politics.
8. Neeladri Bhattacharya's recent book *The Great Agrarian Conquest* shows, through the example of nineteenth century Punjab, how villages themselves were the product of colonial re-orderings and came to emerge as "the universal form of rural settlement" (N. Bhattacharya 2018: 12).
9. As we know from their biographers, neither Ambedkar nor Nehru had spent any of their adult lives living in a village or studying its social processes.
10. Such an argument is strengthened by Anand Pandian's work among the Kallars, where he argues there is a "*precolonial* tradition of civility in south India, one that derives much of its moral force from the exercise of virtue in agrarian milieus" (Pandian 2009: 34).

11. While there is some debate among political philosophers about the dating of this concept of active citizenship, there appears to be some agreement that Quentin Skinner's work has successfully shifted the paradigm by attributing the concept of "active citizenship" to a Roman rather than Greek vocabulary, as had been previously held (Skinner 2010). Marco Guena's 2010 essay on this debate was enormously helpful. The intellectual trajectory of this idea, therefore, runs from Cicero through to Machiavelli and right up to Arendt in the twentieth century (Baluch 2014).

12. Skinner attributes this idea of "neo-Roman" citizenship to Machiavelli in the sixteenth century, who, he argues, draws it from the Roman tradition of Cicero, Tacitus, and Justinian.

13. This, of course, draws attention to a tension "between Hobbes and political theories based on individual rights on the one hand, and republican theories based on *virtù* and public service on the other" (Geuna 2010: 69).

14. In this, Arendt's writings in the twentieth century are close to the republican tradition that Skinner identifies from Rome to Machiavelli to the Renaissance, for she advocates a politics as action and this action in public space as an action in world-making and self-making (Calhoun 1997).

15. The modern nation-state of India was formed out of the territories under the British colonial government alongside those territories held under hundreds of royal kingdoms called "princely states."

16. Chapter 4, "*Harvest*," provides a longer discussion of social and economic conditions of farmers and agricultural workers.

17. I thank Michael McQuarrie for drawing my attention to this study. The farmer's movement that started in November 2020 in India against three new laws introduced in the Indian Parliament that potentially strengthen corporate control of agriculture, is still going strong six months later at the time of writing It shares many features with the Alliance of Farmers and deserves an analytical comparison.

18. See Parasher (forthcoming) for a discussion of Ambedkar's use of Tawney's critique of Hayek's *The Road to Serfdom* to highlight the importance of state regulation for the "realization of liberal self-hood."

19. In America, too, the Populist Moment of 1890 was ultimately unsuccessful in fighting the might of the American corporate and banking system.

20. These places saw the incumbent Left Front government acquire agricultural land for a car factory in order to boost industrial growth in the state. Their utter disregard for the rights of the agricultural workers of that land, who were among their staunchest supporters, led to widespread protests. The main opposition leader, Mamata Banerjee, sensing an opportunity, led a series of sit-ins in which she was supported by thousands, and this paved the way for the rise of her party, Trinamool Congress, in the following elections. See Kenneth Bo Nielsen and others for an analysis of these events.

Bibliography

Ahmed, H. 2019. *Siyasi Muslims: A Story of Political Islams in India.* Penguin/Random House.

Ahmed, R. (ed.) 2001. *Understanding the Bengali Muslim.* New Delhi: Oxford University Press.

Appadurai, A. 1989. "Small-Scale Techniques and Large-Scale Objectives." In *Conversations between Economists and Anthropologists*, edited by P. Bardhan, 250–282. New Delhi: Oxford University Press.

Appadurai, A. 1996. *Modernity at Large: Cultural Dimensions of Globalization.* Vol. 1 of *Public Worlds*, edited by D. Gaonkar and B. Lee. Minneapolis: University of Minnesota Press.

Arendt, H. 1958. *The Human Condition.* Chicago: University of Chicago Press.

Asad, T. 1986. *The Idea of an Anthropology of Islam.* Washington, DC: Georgetown University, Center for Contemporary Arab Studies.

Bailey, F. G. 1969. *Stratagems and Spoils: A Social Anthropology of Politics.* New York: Routledge.

Baluch, F. 2014. "Arendt's Machiavellian Moment." *European Journal of Political Theory* 13, no. 2: 154–177.

Bandhopadhyay, D. 1997. "Not a Gramscian Pantomime." *Economic and Political Weekly* 32, no. 12 (March 22–28): 581–584.

Banerjee, M. 1999. "Mamata's Khomota." *Seminar*, August 1999, 30–35.

Banerjee, M. 2000. *The Pathan Unarmed: Opposition and Memory in the North West Frontier.* Oxford: James Currey.

Banerjee, M. 2004. "Populism or the Democratisation of Democracy." In *Regional Reflections*, edited by R. Jenkins. New Delhi: Oxford University Press.

Banerjee, M. 2007. "Democracy: Sacred and Everyday: An Ethnographic Case from India." In *Democracy: Anthropological Approaches*, edited by J. Paley, 63–92. Santa Fe, NM: SAR Press.

Banerjee, M. 2010. "Leadership and Political Work." In *Power and Influence in India*, edited by P. Price and A. E. Ruud, 20–43. New Delhi: Routledge.

Banerjee, M. 2011. "Elections as Communitas." *Social Research* 78, no. 1 (Spring): 75–98.

Banerjee, M. 2014. *Why India Votes?* New Delhi: Routledge.

Banerjee, M. (ed.) 2008. *Muslim Portraits.* New Delhi: Yoda Press and Bloomington: Indiana University Press.

Banerjee, M., and D. Miller. 2003. *The Sari.* London (Oxford): Bloomsbury (Berg Publishers).

Banerjee, M., and G. Verniers. 2020. "Unlike Colston or Columbus, Ambedkar Memorial Statues Deserve Their Place in Public Spaces." *The Print*, June 14, 2020.

Bengal *Journal of Political Economy*, Vol. 110, No. 2, April 2002.

Bardhan, P. 1989. *Conversations between Economists and Anthropologists: Methodological Issues in Measuring Economic Change in Rural India.* New York: Oxford University Press.

Bardhan, P., M. Ghatak, and A. Karaivanov. 2007. "Wealth Inequality and Collective Action." *Journal of Public Economics* 91, no. 9 (September): 1843–1874.

Bardhan, P., and D. Mookherjee. 2010. "Determinants of Redistributive Politics: An Empirical Analysis of Land Reforms in West Bengal, India." *American Economic Review* 100, no. 4 (September): 1572–1600.

Bardhan, P., D. Mookherjee, and N. Kumar. 2012. "State-Led or Market-Led Green Revolution? Role of Private Irrigation Investment Vis-à-Vis Local Government Programs in West Bengal's Farm Productivity Growth." *Journal of Development Economics* 99, no. 2: 222–235.

Bellah, R. 1991. *Beyond Belief: Essays on Religion in a Post-Traditional World.* Berkeley: University of California Press.

Béteille, A. 1979. "Homo Hierarchicus, Homo Equalis." *Modern Asian Studies,* 13, no. 4: 529–548.

Béteille, A. 2008. "Constitutional Morality." *Economic and Political Weekly of India* 43, no. 40: 35–42.

Bhattacharya, D. 2009. "Of Control and Factions: The Changing 'Party-Society' in Rural West Bengal." *Economic and Political Weekly* 44, no. 9: 59–69.

Bhattacharya, D. 2016. *Government as Practice: Democratic Left in a Transforming India.* Cambridge: Cambridge University Press.

Bhattacharya, N. 2018. *The Great Agrarian Conquest: The Colonial Reshaping of a Rural World.* Ranikhet: Permanent Black.

Bloch, M. 2008. "Why Religion Is Nothing Special but Is Central." *Philosophical Transactions of the Royal Society B* 363, no. 1499: 2055–2061.

Bowen, J. 1992. "On Scriptural Essentialism and Ritual Variation: Muslim Sacrifice in Sumatra and Morocco." *American Ethnologist* 19, no. 4: 656–671.

Breman, J. 1985. *Of Peasants, Migrants and Paupers.* Delhi: Oxford University Press.

Broomfield, J. H. 1968. *Elite Conflict in a Plural Society: Twentieth-Century Bengal.* Berkeley and Los Angeles: University of California Press.

Burawoy, M. 2014. "The Colour of Class Revisited: Four Decades of Postcolonialism in Zambia." *Journal of Southern African Studies* 40, no. 5: 961–979.

Calhoun, C. 2007. *Nations Matter: Culture, History and the Cosmopolitan Dream.* London: Routledge.

Calhoun, C. 2012. *The Roots of Radicalism: Tradition, the Public Sphere, and Early Nineteenth-Century Social Movements.* Chicago: University of Chicago Press.

Calhoun, C. 1997. "Plurality." In *Hannah Arendt and the Meaning of Politics.* Vol. 6 of *Contradictions of Modernity,* edited by Craig J. Calhoun and John McGowan. Minneapolis: University of Minnesota Press.

Calhoun, C., and M. McQuarrie. 2012. "The Reluctant Counterpublic." In *The Roots of Radicalism: Tradition, the Public Sphere, and Early Nineteenth-Century Social Movements,* edited by C. Calhoun, 152–181. Chicago: University of Chicago Press.

Calhoun, C., D. Gaonkar, and C. Taylor. 2021. *The Degenerations of Democracy.* Harvard: Harvard University Press.

Chakravarty, D. 2000. *Provincializing Europe: Postcolonial Thought and Historical Difference.* Princeton, NJ: Princeton University Press.

Chandra, U., Heierstad, G., and Nielsen, K. B. (eds.). 2016. *The Politics of Caste in West Bengal.* New Delhi: Routledge India.

Chatterjee, P. 1997. *The Present History of West Bengal.* New Delhi: Oxford University Press.

Chatterjee, P. 2008. "Democracy and Economic Transformation in India." *Economic and Political Weekly* 43, no. 16: 53–62.

Chatterjee, P. 2016. "Partition and the Mysterious Disappearance of Caste in Bengal." In *The Politics of Caste in West Bengal*, edited by U. Chandra, G. Heierstad, and K. B. Nielsen, 83–102. New Delhi: Routledge India.

Chatterji, R. 2015. "Conversations, Generations, Genres: Anthropological Knowing as a Form of Life." In *Wording the World: Veena Das and Scenes of Inheritance*, edited by R. Chatterji, 278–280. New York: Fordham University Press.

Cheeseman, N. 2015. *Democracy in Africa: Successes, Failures, and the Struggle for Political Reform*. Cambridge: Cambridge University Press.

Chibber, P., and Ahuja, A. 2012. "Why the Poor Vote in India: 'If I Don't Vote, I Am Dead to the State.'" *Studies in Comparative International Development* 47: 389–410.

Chopra, R. 2018. "Maps of Experience: Narratives of Migration in an Indian Village." In *A Handbook of Rural India*, edited by S. S. Jodhka, 360–376. Hyderabad: Orient Blackswan.

Cross, J. 2014. *Dream Zones: Capitalism and Development in India*. London: Pluto Press.

Dahlan-Taylor, M. 2016. "Beyond Barbarity and Concealment: Animal Sacrifice and Religious Slaughter in Islamic Responses to Postdomesticity." *Culture and Religion* 17, no. 3: 352–365.

Das, V. 1995. *Critical Events: An Anthropological Perspective on Contemporary India*. Delhi: Oxford University Press.

Das, V. 2010. "Engaging the Life of the Other: Love and Everyday Life." In *Ordinary Ethics: Anthropology, Language, and Action*, edited by M. Lambek, 377–399. New York: Fordham University Press.

Das, V. 2015. "Between Words and Lives. A Thought on the Coming Together of Margins, Violence, and Suffering: An Interview with Veena Das." In *Veena Das and Scenes of Inheritance*, edited by R. Chatterji, 400–412. New York: Fordham University Press.

Dewey, J. 1939. *Freedom and Culture*. New York: G. B. Putnam's Sons.

Donham, D. 1999. *History, Power, and Ideology: Central Issues in Marxism and Anthropology*. Berkeley: University of California Press.

Donham, D. 1985. "History at One Point in Time: 'Working Together'" In Maale (1975) *American Ethnologist 1985–05*, 12, no. 2: 262–284.

Dreze, J., and A. Sen (ed.) 1997. *Indian Development: Selected Regional Perspectives*. New York: Oxford University Press.

Duara, P. 2015. *The Crisis of Global Modernity: Asian Traditions and a Sustainable Future*. Cambridge: Cambridge University Press.

Eaton, R. 1993. *The Rise of Islam and the Bengal Frontier, 1204–1760*.

Eaton, R. 2001. "Who are the Bengal Muslims? Conversion and Islamization in Bengal." In *Understanding the Bengali Muslims: Interpretative Essays*, edited by R. Ahmed, 26–51. New Delhi: Oxford University Press.

Englund, H. 2018. "From the Extended-Case Method to Multi-Sited Ethnography (and Back)." In *Schools and Styles of Anthropological Theory*, edited by M. Candea, 121–133. London: Taylor and Francis.

Evans-Pritchard, E. E. 1956. *Nuer Religion*. New York: Oxford University Press.

Evens, T. M. S., and D. Handelman (eds.). 2006. "Introduction: The Ethnographic Praxis of the Theory of Practice." In *The Manchester School: Practice and Ethnographic Praxis in Anthropology*, 1–11. Oxford: Berghahn Books.

Evens, T. M. S., and J. L. Peacock. 1990. "Introduction." In *Transcendence in Society: Case Studies*, edited by T. M. S Evens and J. L. Peacock, 1–7. Comparative Social Research. Greenwich, CT: JAI Press.

Foltz, R. C. 2006. *Animals in Islamic Tradition and Muslim Cultures.* Oxford: Oneworld Publications.

Fuller, C. 1989. "Misconceiving the Grain Heap." In *Money and the Morality of Exchange*, edited by J. P. Parry and M. Bloc, 33–63. Cambridge: Cambridge University Press.

Sengupta, S., and H. Gazdar. 1997. "Agrarian Politics and Rural Development in West Bengal." In *Indian Development: Selected Regional Perspectives*, edited by J. Dreze and A. Sen. New York: Oxford University Press.

Gilmartin, D. 2015. "Rethinking the Public through the Lens of Sovereignty." *South Asia: Journal of South Asian Studies* 38, no. 3: 371–386.

Girard, R. 1977. *Violence and the Sacred.* Baltimore, MD: Johns Hopkins University Press.

Gluckman, M. 1963. "Gossip and Scandal." *Current Anthropology*, 4, no. 3: 307–316.

Gluckman, M, 2006. (in England)

Guena, M. 2010.

Goodwyn, L. 1978. *The Populist Moment: A Short History of the Agrarian Revolt in America.* New York: Oxford University Press.

Gooptu, N. 2007. "Economic Liberalisation, Work and Democracy: Industrial Decline and Urban Politics in Kolkata." *Economic and Political Weekly* 42, no. 21: 1922–1933.

Government of India. 2007. *National Policy for Farmers.* Ministry of Agriculture and Consumer Affairs Food and Public Distribution. New Delhi.

Govindarajan, R. 2015. "'The Goat that Died for Family'': Animal Sacrifice and Interspecies Kinship in India's Central Himalayas. *American Ethnologist* 42, no. 3: 504–519.

Govindarajan, R. 2018. *Animal Intimacies.* New Delhi: Penguin/Viking.

Guha, S. 2016. *Beyond Caste: Identity and Power in South Asia, Past and Present.* Leiden: Brill.

Gupta, A. 1998. *Postcolonial Developments: Agriculture and the Making of Modern India.* Durham, NC: Duke University Press.

Gupta, D. 2005. "Whither the Indian Village: Culture and Agriculture in 'Rural India.'" *Economic and Political Weekly* 40, no. 8: 751–758.

Hansen, T. 1999. *The Saffron Wave: Democracy and Hindu Nationalism in Modern India.* Princeton, NJ: Princeton University Press.

Harriss, J. 1993. "What Is Happening in Rural West Bengal? Agrarian Reform, Growth and Distribution." *Economic and Political Weekly* 28 (June 12): 1237–1247.

Harriss-White, B. 2005. "Commercialisation, Commodification and Gender Relations in Post-Harvest Systems for Rice in South Asia." *Economic and Political Weekly* 40, no. 25 (June 18): 2530–2542.

Harriss-White, B. 2008. *Rural Commercial Capital: Agricultural Markets in West Bengal.* New Delhi: Oxford University Press.

Hedley, D. 2011. "Sacrifice, Transcendence and 'Making Sacred.'" *Royal Institute of Philosophy Supplement* 68: 257–268.

Herring, R. J. 1983. *Land to the Tiller: The Political Economy of Agrarian Reform in South Asia.* New Haven, CT: Yale University Press.

Hubert, H., and M. Mauss. 1964. *Sacrifice.* Chicago: University of Chicago Press.

Hussain, S. W., and Khan, M. M. 2009. "Poverty Alleviation: The Redistribution Impact of Eid-ul-Azha Animals' Sacrifice on Rural Economy." *Journal of Managerial Sciences* 3: 249–260.

Hutchinson, S. 1996. *Nuer Dilemmas: Coping with Money, War, and the State.* Berkeley: University of California Press.

Jaffrelot, C. 2003. *India's Silent Revolution: The Rise of the Lower Castes in North India.* New York: Columbia University Press.

Jaffrelot, C., & G. Verniers. 2020. "A New Party System or a New Political System?" *Contemporary South Asia* 28, no. 2: 141–154.

Jalais, A. 2018. "Reworlding the Ancient Chinese Tiger in the Realm of the Asian Anthropocene." *International Communication of Chinese Culture* 5: 121–144.

James, W. 1988. *The Listening Ebony: Moral Knowledge, Religion, and Power among the Uduk of Sudan.* Oxford: Oxford University Press.

Jayal, N. 2013. *Citizenship and Its Discontents: An Indian History.* Cambridge, MA: Harvard University Press.

Jodhka, S. 2012. *Village Society: Essays from Economic and Political Weekly.* Hyderabad: Orient Blackswan.

Jodhka, S. S. 2018a. *A Handbook of Rural India.* Hyderabad: Orient Blackswan.

Jodhka, S. S. 2018b. "Rural Change in Times of 'Distress.'" *Economic and Political Weekly* 53, no. 26–27 (June 30, 2018).

Joseph, T. 2018. *Early Indians: The Story of Our Ancestors and Where We Came From.* New Delhi: Juggernaut.

Kapferer, B. 2010. "Introduction: In the Event—Toward an Anthropology of Generic Moments." *Social Analysis* 54, no. 3 (December):1–27.

Kaviraj, S. 2011. *The Enchantment of Democracy and India.* Ranikhet: Permanent Black.

Keane, W. 2010. "Minds, Surfaces, and Reasons in the Anthropology of Ethics." In *Ordinary Ethics: Anthropology, Language and Action*, edited by M. Lambek, 64–83. New York: Fordham University Press.

Khilnani, S. 1997. *The Idea of India.* New Delhi: Penguin Books.

Khosla, M. 2020. *India's Founding Moment.* Cambridge, MA: Harvard University Press.

Khosla, M. 2020a. "Constitution vs. Democracy." *Open Magazine*, January 17.

Kloppenberg, J. T. 2016. *Toward Democracy: The Struggle for Self-Rule in European and American Thought.* Oxford University Press.

Kohli, A. 1987. *The State and Poverty in India: The Politics of Reform.* Cambridge: Cambridge University Press.

Krishna, A. (ed.) 2008. *Poverty, Participation, and Democracy: A Global Perspective.* New York: Cambridge University Press.

Krishnamurthy, M. 2018. "Reconceiving the Grain Heap: Margins and Movements on the Market Floor." *Contributions to Indian Sociology* 52, no. 1: 28–52.

Kumar, S. 2018. "Agrarian Transformation and New Sociality in Western Uttar Pradesh." *Economic and Political Weekly* 53, no. 26–27 (June 30).

Kuroda, K. 2018. Visceral Politics of Food: The Bio-Moral Economy of Work-Lunch in Mumbai, India. Unpublished PhD thesis, London School of Economics and Political Science.

Laidlaw, J. 2014. *The Subject of Virtue: An Anthropology of Ethics and Freedom.* Cambridge: Cambridge University Press.

Lambek, M. 2010. *Ordinary Ethics: Anthropology, Language and Action.* New York: Fordham University Press.

Levien, M. 2018. *Dispossession with Development: Land Grabs in Neoliberal India.* Oxford: Oxford University Press.

Levitsky, S., and D. Ziblatt. 2018. *How Democracies Die.* New York: Broadway Books.

Lewis, I. M. 2004. Review of *Sacrifice in Religious Experience* by Albert I. Baumgarten The Journal of the Royal Anthropological Institute 10, no. 4 (December): 936.

Lieten, G. K. 1990. "Depeasantisation Discontinued: Land Reforms in West Bengal." *Economic and Political Weekly* 25, no. 40 (October 6): 2265–2271.

Linz, J., A. Stepan, and Y. Yadav. 2007. "'Nation State' or 'State Nation'? India in Comparative Perspective." In *Democracy and Diversity: India and the American Experience*, edited by S. K. Bajpai, 50–106. New Delhi: Oxford University Press.

Ludden, D. 1999. *An Agrarian History of South Asia*. Cambridge: Cambridge University Press.

Mallick, R. 1992. "Agrarian Reform in West Bengal: The End of an Illusion." *World Development* 20, no. 5: 735–750.

"Manifesto of Indian Farmers." 2018, December 9. countercurrent.org. https://countercurrents.org/2018/12/manifesto-of-indian-farmers/.

Marsden, M. 2009. *Living Islam: Muslim Religious Experience in Pakistan's North-West Frontier.* Cambridge: Cambridge University Press.

Mehta, P. B. 2003. *The Burden of Democracy.* New Delhi: Penguin.

Metcalf, B. D. 1982. *Islamic Revival in British India: Deoband, 1860–1900.* Princeton, NJ: Princeton University Press.

Michelutti, L. 2008. *The Vernacularisation of Democracy: Politics, Caste and Religion in India.* London: Routledge India.

Michelutti, L., A. Hoque, N. Martin, D. Picherit, P. Rollier, A. E. Ruud, and C. Still. 2018. *Mafia Raj: The Rule of Bosses in South Asia.* Stanford: Stanford University Press.

Mouffe, C. 2000. *The Democratic Paradox.* London: Verso Books.

Narain, S. "'Why I Don't Advocate Vegetarianism': Indian Environmentalist Sunita Narain Explains Her Position." Scroll.in, March 28, 2017. https://scroll.in/article/832980/why-i-dont-advocate-vegetarianism-indian-environmentalist-sunita-narain-explains-her-position.

National Sample Survey Office (NSSO). 2011. Annual Report. Government of India Ministry of Statistics and Programme Implementation. New Delhi.

Nielsen, K. B. 2016. "The Politics of Caste and Class in Singur's Anti-Land Acquisition Struggle." In *The Politics of Caste in West Bengal*, edited by U. Chandra, G. Heierstad, and K. B. Nielsen, 125–146. New Delhi: Routledge India.

Nielsen, K. B. 2018. *Land Dispossession and Everyday Politics in Rural Eastern India.* London: Anthem Press.

Nussbaum, M. 2013. *Political Emotions.* Cambridge, MA: Harvard University Press.

Oren, I. 2003. *Our Enemies and US: America's Rivalries and the Making of Political Science.* Ithaca, NY: Cornell University Press.

Otten, T., and Simpson, E. 2016. "F. G. Bailey's Bisipara Revisited." *Economic and Political Weekly* 51, no. 26–27: 25–32.

Palshikar, S., and S. Kumar. 2004. "Participatory Norm: How Broad-Based Is It?" *Economic and Political Weekly* 39, no. 51 (December 18): 5412–5417.

Pandian, A. 2009. *Crooked Stalks: Cultivating Virtue in South India.* Durham, NC: Duke University Press.

Pandian, A. 2015. "In the Event of an Anthropological Thought." In *Wording the World: Veena Das and Scenes of Inheritance*, edited by R. Chatterji, 258–272. New York: Fordham University Press.

Pandian, M. S. S. 2005. "Dilemmas of Public Reason: Secularism and Religious Violence in Contemporary India." *Economic and Political Weekly* 40, no. 22–23 (May 28–June 10): 2313–2320.

Parasher, T. forthcoming. "Ambedkar and the Welfare State." In *The Cambridge Companion to B.R. Ambedkar* Cambridge: Cambridge University Press.

Parasher, T. 2021. "Federalism, Representation, and Direct Democracy in 1920s India." *Modern Intellectual History*: 1–29.

Parekh, B. 2015. *Debating India: Essays on Indian Political Discourse*. New Delhi: Oxford University Press.

Parvathamma, C. 1971. *Politics and Religion: A Study of Historical Interaction between Socio-Political Relationships in a Mysore Village*. New Delhi: Sterling Publishers.

Piliavsky, A. 2014. *Patronage as Politics in South Asia*. Cambridge: Cambridge University Press.

Pocock, J. 2006. "Foundations and Moments." In *Rethinking the Foundations of Modern Political Thought*, edited by A. Brett, J. Tully, and H. Hamilton-Bleakley. Cambridge: Cambridge University Press.

Przeworski, A., M. Alvarez, J. Antonio Cheibub, and F. Limongi. 1996. "What Makes Democracies Endure?" *Journal of Democracy* 7, no. 1 (January): 39–55.

Robbins, J. 2016. *What Is the Matter with Transcendence? On the Place of Religion in the New Anthropology of Ethics*. Journal of the Royal Anthropological Institute 22, no. 4 (December 2016).

Roberts, N. 2015. "Setting Caste Back on Its Feet, [review of] Sumit Guha's *Beyond Caste*." *Anthropology of This Century* 13 (May). http://aotcpress.com/articles/setting-caste-feet/.

Robinson, F. 1974. *Francis: Separatism among Indian Muslims: The Politics of the United Provinces' Muslims 1860–1923*. Cambridge: Cambridge University Press.

Robinson, M. 1998. *Local Politics: The Law of the Fishes*. Oxford: Oxford University Press.

Rodrigues, V. 2011. "Justice as the Lens: Interrogating Rawls through Sen an Ambedkar." *Indian Journal of Human Development* 5 no. 1: 153–174.

Rodrigues, V. 2020. "Deriving Authority from 'We the People.'" *The Hindu*, January 26. Accessed July 22, 2020, at: https://www.thehindu.com/opinion/op-ed/deriving-authority-from-we-the-people/article30655212.ece.

Rogaly, B., and B. Harriss-White. 1995. "Sonar Bangla? Agricultural Growth and Agrarian Change in West Bengal and Bangladesh." *Economic and Political Weekly* 30, no. 29 (July 22): 1862–1868.

Rogers, M. 2018. "Democracy Is a Habit: Practice It." *Boston Review*, July 25.

Rosenblum, N. 2008. *On the Side of the Angels: An Appreciation of Parties and Partisanship*. Princeton, NJ: Princeton University Press.

Roy, D. 2019. "Politics at the Margin: A Tale of Two Villages." In *A Handbook of Rural India: Essays from Economic and Political Weekly*, edited by S. S. Jodhka, 424–435. Hyderabad: Orient Blackswan.

Roy, S. 2007. *Beyond Belief: India and the Politics of Postcolonial Nationalism*. Durham: Duke University Press.

2010. "Beyond Belief: India and the Politics of Postcolonial Nationalism." *The Journal of Asian Studies* 69, no. 2 (May): 639–641.

Ruud, A. 2003. *The Poetics of Village Politics: The Making of West Bengal's Rural Communism*. New Delhi: Oxford University Press.

Ruud, A. 2016. "From Client to Supporter: Economic Change and the Slow Change of Social Identity in Rural West Bengal." In *The Politics of Caste in West Bengal*, edited by U. Chandra, G. Heierstad, and K. B. Nielsen, 193–215. New Delhi: Routledge.

Sachar Committee Report. 2006. Ministry of Minority Affairs, Government of India. New Delhi.

Sanyal, U. 1996. *Devotional Islam and Politics in British India: Ahmed Reza Khan Barelwi and His Movement, 1870–1920.* New York: Oxford University Press.

Scott, J. 1985. *Weapons of the Weak: Everyday Forms of Peasant Resistance.* New Haven: Yale University Press.

Sen, D. 2016. "An Absent-Minded Casteism?" In *The Politics of Caste in West Bengal,* edited by U. Chandra, G. Heierstad, and K. B. Nielsen, 103–124. Routledge.

Shani, O. 2017. *How India Became Democratic: Citizenship and the Making of Universal Franchise.* New Delhi: Penguin/Viking.

Shils, E. 1997. *The Virtue of Civility: Selected Essays on Liberalism, Tradition, and Civil Society.* Indianapolis: Liberty Fund.

Singh, B. 2017. *Poverty and the Quest for Life.* New Delhi: Oxford University Press.

Singh, B. 2015a. "How Concepts Make the World Look Different: Affirmative and Negative Genealogies of Thought." In *The Ground Between: Anthropologists Engage Philosophy,* edited by V. Das, M. Jackson, A. Kleinman, and B. Singh, 159–186. Durham, NC: Duke University Press.

Singh, B. 2015b. *Poverty and the Quest for Life: Spiritual and Material Striving in Rural India.* Delhi: Oxford University Press.

Sircar, N. 2018. "BJP Should Be Worried after Assembly Poll Debacle in Hindi Heartland." *The Hindu.* Accessed at https://www.thehindu.com/news/cities/Delhi/bjp-should-be-worried-after-assembly-poll-debacle-in-hindi-heartland/article25729199.ece.

Sivaramakrishnan, K. 2015. "Ethics of Nature in Indian Environmental History." *Modern Asian Studies* 49, no. 4: 1261–1310.

Skinner, Q. 2006. "Surveying the Foundations: A Retrospect and Reassessment." In *Rethinking the Foundations of Modern Political Thought,* edited by A. Brett, J. Tully, and H. Hamilton-Bleakley, 236–261. Cambridge: Cambridge University Press.

Spencer, J. 2007. *Anthropology, Politics and the State.* Cambridge: Cambridge University Press.

Stadlen, A. 2018. *Weaving Lives from Violence: Possibility and Change for Muslim Women in Rural West Bengal.* PhD thesis, The London School of Economics and Political Science.

Stepan, A., J. Linz, and Y. Yadav. 2011. *Crafting State-Nations: India and Other Multinational Democracies.* Baltimore, MD: Johns Hopkins University Press.

Taylor, C. 1993. "To Follow a Rule." In *Bourdieu: Critical Perspectives,* edited by C. Calhoun, E. LiPuma, and M. Postone, 45–60. Cambridge: Polity Press.

Taylor, C. 2007. "Cultures of Democracy and Citizen Efficacy." *Public Culture* 19, no. 1: 117–150.

Tilly, C. 1995. "Democracy Is a Lake." In *The Social Construction of Democracy, 1870–1990,* edited by G. R. Andrews and H. Chapman, 365–387. New York: New York University Press.

Tsing, A. 2015. *The Mushroom at the End of the World: On the Possibility of Life in Capitalist Ruins.* Princeton, NJ: Princeton University Press.

Turner, V. 1957. *Schism and Continuity in an African Society: A Study of Ndembu Village Life* (Classic Reprint Series). Manchester: Manchester University Press.

Turner, V. 1966. *The Ritual Process: Structure and Anti-Structure.* Chicago: Aldine Transaction.

Turner, V. 1980. "Social Dramas and Stories about Them." *Critical Inquiry* 7, no. 1, On Narrative (Autumn, 1980): 141–168.

Van Gennep, A. *The Rites of Passage*. London: Routledge and Kegan Paul, 1960. (Original work published 1908)

Varshney, A. 2013. *Battles Half Won: India's Improbable Democracy*. Delhi: Viking Books.

Varshney, A. 2020. "'Democracy in India'": Review of Madhav Khosla's the Founding Moment. *Boston Review* (August), August 10. http://bostonreview.net/law-justice/ashutosh-varshney-what-we-can-learn-indias-improbable-democracy.

Venkat, V. 2017. "Why Can't the Government Provide a Higher Income for Farmers, asks M. S. Swaminathan." *The Hindu*, August 16. https://www.thehindu.com/opinion/interview/why-cant-the-government-provide-a-higher-income-for-farmers/article19498056.ece.

Verniers, G. 2018. "The Transformation of Backward Class Politics in Uttar Pradesh." *Economic and Political Weekly* 53, no. 33 (August 18).

Wade, R. 1998. *Village Republics: Economic Conditions for Collective Action in South India*. Cambridge: Cambridge University Press.

Weber, M. 1919. "Politics as a Vocation." (new translation) In Gerth and Mills (1946) (translated by) *From Max Weber: Essays in Sociology*. Oxford: Oxford University Press.

Wedeen, L. 2008. *Peripheral Visions: Publics, Power, and Performance in Yemen*. Chicago: Chicago University Press.

Werbner, P. 1998. "*Langar*: Pilgrimage, Sacred Exchange and Perpetual Sacrifice in a Sufi Saint's Lodge." In *Embodying Charisma Modernity, Locality, and Performance of Emotion in Sufi Cults*, edited by P. Werbner and H. Basu, 95–115. New York: Routledge.

Witsoe, J. 2013. *Democracy against Development: Lower-Caste Politics and Political Modernity in Postcolonial India*. Chicago: University of Chicago Press.

Yadav, Y. 1999. "Electoral Politics in the Time of Change: India's Third Electoral System, 1989–1999." *Economic and Political Weekly* XXXIV (34&35): 2393–2399.

Yadav, Y., and S. Palshikar. 2009. "Between Fortuna and Virtu: Explaining the Congress' Ambiguous Victory in 2009." *Economic and Political Weekly* 44, no. 39: 33–46.

Yadav, Y. 2020. *Making Sense of Indian Democracy*. Ranikhet: Permanent Black.

Yan, Y. 2011. "How Far Away Can We Move from Durkheim? Reflections on the New Anthropology of Morality." *Anthropology of This Century* 2 (October).

Ying, J. 2018. "Political Participation as Self-Cultivation: Towards a Participatory Theory of Confucian Democracy." *European Journal of Political Theory* 0 (0) 1–22.

Zigon, J. 2014. "An Ethics of Dwelling and a Politics of World-Building: A Critical Response to Ordinary Ethics." *Journal of the Royal Anthropological Institute* 20: 746–764.

Index

For the benefit of digital users, indexed terms that span two pages (e.g., 52–53) may, on occasion, appear on only one of those pages.